Praise for Janette Sadik-Kh

"[A] bicycle visionary."   —Fran

"Sadik-Khan manages to be equal parts Jane Jacobs and Robert Moses."   —*New York Magazine*

"If [Robert] Moses had owned a pink fingernail of [Sadik-Khan's] beguilement, he might have scored a bridge across the Atlantic."
—*Esquire*

"[Sadik-Khan is] an urban visionary who cuts through the gridlock."
—*Slate*

"Janette Sadik-Khan is like the child that Robert Moses and Jane Jacobs never had: an urban visionary determined to reshape the streets of New York, but with an abiding concern for the health of neighborhoods and the safety of their residents. If you care about the future of cities, read *Streetfight*."
—Michael Bloomberg, former New York City mayor

"This book is an urban epic as audacious as the changes Janette Sadik-Khan made to the map of New York City. She is a superhero for cities and an inspiration that streets built to human scale aren't impossible, but merely awaiting those who dare."
—Jan Gehl, urbanist, architect, author

"Cities are where innovation, creativity, and the unexpected happens, and Janette has helped make ours, New York City, safer, more livable, and more profitable all at once. I watched these exciting changes happen, but the really interesting part is how she managed to implement these changes quickly and cheaply. That's where other cities can use this as a manual for change on issues like health reform, education, and the arts. This, then, is not just a book about transportation."
—David Byrne, musician, artist

"To create safe and inclusive cities, being a visionary is not enough. You must also be an advocate, a communicator, a doer, and, perhaps most importantly, a street fighter. Janette is that person and this is a book that provides the proof of the possible for citizens and their elected leaders everywhere."   —Enrique Peñalosa, mayor of Bogotá

PENGUIN BOOKS

STREETFIGHT

Janette Sadik-Khan is one of the world's foremost authorities on transportation and urban transformation. She served as New York City's transportation commissioner from 2007 to 2013 under Mayor Michael Bloomberg, overseeing historic changes to New York City's streets—closing Broadway to cars in Times Square, building nearly four hundred miles of bike lanes, and creating more than sixty plazas citywide. A founding principal with Bloomberg Associates, she works with mayors around the world to reimagine and redesign their cities. She chairs the National Association of Transportation Officials, implementing new people-focused street design standards that have been adopted in forty-five cities across the continent. She lives in New York City.

Seth Solomonow is a manager with Bloomberg Associates. He was the chief media strategist for Janette Sadik-Khan and New York City's transportation department under Mayor Michael Bloomberg. A graduate of Columbia University Graduate School of Journalism, Solomonow has written for *The New York Times* and his hometown newspaper, *The Staten Island Advance*. He lives in Brooklyn, New York.

www.jsadikkhan.com
@jsadikkhan

Streetfight

Handbook for an Urban Revolution

JANETTE SADIK-KHAN

and Seth Solomonow

PENGUIN BOOKS

PENGUIN BOOKS
An imprint of Penguin Random House LLC
375 Hudson Street
New York, New York 10014
penguin.com

First published in the United States of America by Viking Penguin,
an imprint of Penguin Random House LLC, 2016
Published in Penguin Books 2017

Photograph and map illustration credits
Interior pages 50, 52–53, 56, 57, 58–59, 60 (top, bottom): From *Urban Street Design
Guide* by NACTO. Copyright © 2013 National Association of City Transportation Officials.
Reproduced by permission of Island Press, Washington, DC.
Interior pages 74, 76 (top), 81 (left, right), 82, 83, 86, 100, 101, 120–21, 131, 133, 137
(left), 140, 141, 156, 157, 160–61, 166, 167, 195, 216 (top, bottom), 217 (top, bottom),
219, 244–45, 246, 247, 259, 260; Insert 1, pages 1 (left, right), 2 (top, bottom) 3 (top
left, right), 4 (top, bottom), 5 (top), 6 (left, right), 8 (top, bottom), 9 (top, bottom),
10 (bottom), 11 (top, bottom), 12 (top, bottom), 13 (top, bottom), 14 (bottom),
15 (top, bottom), 16 (top, bottom); Insert 2, pages 1 (top), 8 (top, bottom), 9 (top,
bottom), 10 (top, bottom), 11 (top, bottom), 12 (top, bottom), 13 (bottom right),
16: Used with permission of the City of New York. © 2005–14. New York City
Department of Transportation. All rights reserved.
Other credits appear in the captions of the respective images.

ISBN 9780525429845 (hc.)
ISBN 9780143128977 (pbk.)

Printed in the United States of America
7 9 10 8

Set in Linotype Syntax Serif Com and Gotham
Designed by Amy Hill

*To the men and women
of the
New York City Department of Transportation*

Contents

CONTENTS

Preface

My six-year, seven-month, eighteen-day tenure as New York City transportation commissioner began with a meeting at City Hall, at the foot of the Brooklyn Bridge, in early spring 2007.

"Why do you want to be traffic commissioner?" the 108th mayor of New York City asked me.

It was my first time even in a room with Mayor Michael Bloomberg, the billionaire entrepreneur-turned-mayor, now flanked by six of his deputies, Knights of Camelot–style at an immense round table. Six years into his administration and two years into his second term, it wasn't clear to me that day who or what he was looking for in a commissioner. And here was his very first question.

His question wasn't a test. It's a common misconception that the commissioner's job is limited to managing traffic.

"I don't want to be the *traffic* commissioner," I responded. "I want to be *transportation* commissioner."

Bloomberg said nothing, and no one jumped in to break the tension.

Well, at least I got to meet the mayor, I consoled myself, confident that I had just blown the interview.

Nevertheless, I pushed ahead with my priorities, unsure how they'd be received. I wanted to make New York City's punch-line buses work better. I wanted to make bike riding a real, safe transportation option on New York's mean streets. I wanted to institute a toll for people driving into Manhattan during rush hour, creating the congestion that chokes the city, and use its revenue to make these new public transportation options possible.

These were far from mainstream transportation ideas, but I assumed that Team Camelot must have wanted to hear my pitch or they wouldn't have asked me to the table. Michael Bloomberg's reputation globally was for innovation and a by-the-numbers-please approach to governance. This was the mayor who created the 311 system that allows residents to dial one number to obtain virtually any city service. He had banned smoking in bars and trans fats from restaurants—trifles compared with his overseeing dramatic reductions in crime and wresting control over city schools from a notoriously ineffective Board of Education. But at the time I sat in front of him, there was no transportation leg to his legacy's table, no initiative, goal, or accomplishment on the scale of his other achievements that addressed the fundamental issues of congestion, danger, mobility, and economic stagnation on New York's streets.

So I was direct. I knew how the city worked and I wanted to change its transportation status quo. Fifteen years earlier I finished my tenure as transportation adviser to Mayor David Dinkins, after counseling him on local and regional transportation issues—subways, buses, bridges, transit hubs, airports, and highways—which included agencies and authorities and not just the transportation department he controlled. Since then I worked under President Bill Clinton at the Federal Transit Administration, helped run the transit practice at Parsons

Brinckerhoff, a major international transportation engineering firm, and was founding president of a subsidiary technology consulting company. Based on my audience with Bloomberg, I assumed that he and his team were not on the hunt for someone to ride out the rest of the term with little change or controversy. They wanted a commissioner who understood government architecture and the elements of transportation, but with a private-sector metabolism that thrived on ideas and innovative approaches to problems.

Glancing around the table as the interview continued, I did not sense much interest in these ideas. I was even more certain that my appointment would never happen.

I misjudged.

Bloomberg offered me the job after a second meeting, a breakfast of slightly burned toast and coffee at Viand, his favorite local diner on the Upper East Side. I discovered the reason there wasn't more palpable enthusiasm in the room when I first interviewed: The crux of this city-altering approach was already being codified into PlaNYC—a long-range sustainability plan guided by Dan Doctoroff, the visionary deputy mayor for economic development. PlaNYC had not yet been unveiled to the public, explaining why the mayor and his team didn't react to the various proposals that I had put forth during the interview.

PlaNYC was a detailed, 127-initiative blueprint for urban sustainability unlike anything New York or any big city had ever seen. It stated a goal of reducing carbon emissions by 30 percent while improving the efficiency and quality of life in New York City neighborhoods and business districts. It also took the unusual step of laying the groundwork needed to accommodate the one million more New Yorkers expected to live in the city by 2030, which would have a profound impact on the operation and allocation of resources of every city agency. And it was the first articulation of a vision that would require changing the basic design and use of city streets. For transportation it demanded new strategies, like developing networks of rapid buses and bike lanes, bringing open space into every neighborhood in New York City, and using less energy and more sustainable materials in the construction of streets. PlaNYC was a manual to rewrite the existing street code and overcome the myth that New York was an ungovernable city, a place where the status quo would always prevail.

This new vision came into focus as a growing advocacy movement hit critical mass, spurred by Transportation Alternatives, the Tri-State Transportation Campaign, the Straphangers Campaign, and political outsiders who often understood the goals of government more keenly than many people in office. With the release of PlaNYC, the advocates suddenly found an administration proposing traffic solutions beyond traffic signs and signals and dedicated to safety, efficiency, and transportation investment based on data.

Bloomberg introduced me to reporters and to the New York City public at a press conference on April 27, 2007, one week after PlaNYC was announced. "Don't fuck it up," he whispered to me after we finished our remarks. He was only half kidding. I didn't realize at the time that it was a piece of advice he gave all his appointees.

Back in New York City's Department of Transportation after a long hiatus, I knew that the agency influenced more than just traffic. New York City has 6,300 miles of streets, 12,000 miles of sidewalks, more than 1 million street signs, 12,700 intersections with traffic signals, 315,000 streetlights, 789 bridges, and the Staten Island Ferry, which moves 22 million people annually. Streets comprise 25 percent of the city's landmass, making the transportation commissioner the largest real estate developer in the city. The agency's chief mission is managing the hardware and responding to the daily emergencies that wreak havoc on it. New York City's Department of Transportation (DOT), with a head count hovering around 4,500 employees, is larger than the transportation departments for many American states. Instead of rural roads and highways, New York's portfolio contains some of the most valuable, dense, and contested real estate in the nation. Viewed through another lens, DOT had control over more than just concrete, asphalt, steel, and striping lanes. These are the fundamental materials that govern the entire public realm, and, if applied slightly differently, could have radical new impact.

New York desperately needed a new approach. City leaders, urban planners, traffic engineers, and the people who they serve have been hobbled by two opposite, increasingly unproductive tendencies. First, megaproject monomania, still embraced by mayors and pushed by engineers who want to build bridges, new highway flyovers, bypasses, interchanges, and stadiums to leave a mark and "do something" during their tenures. This tendency clashes with the second common practice: city residents who assert neighborhood-based preservation and resist not just neighborhood-destroying projects but also virtually any other change to the urban context. The future of our cities has fallen between these cracks, remaining stagnant as municipal governments plan big—sometimes too big—and urban communities routinely oppose changes in the status quo by thinking small—sometimes too small. What both parties lack, first, is a vision for how streets can support the life and vitality of both neighborhoods and the city as a whole, and, second, a shared vocabulary to identify and reach that vision amid mutual distrust.

For leaders, overcoming obsolete thinking demands the resolve, courage, and grit to withstand the slings and arrows that inevitably follow change. I discovered that it was more effective to use the language of choices and safety while working with local communities to put rapid-fire projects on the ground. We moved in real time, with materials we had on hand. Our projects then became instruments for the public to gain understanding, providing the support we needed to expand our approach. The fast implementation of projects proved to be far more effective than the traditional model of attempting to achieve near unanimity on projects even when you already have consensus that the status quo doesn't work. Efforts to reach an idealized consensus have resulted in years of indecision, inaction, and paralysis-by-analysis as leaders attempt to placate the opposition that accompanies any change to streets.

Every community has excuses for why changing the way they use their streets is impossible, impractical, or just insane. I learned firsthand that there is no end to the reasons for inaction. But inaction is inexcusable. As our cities grow, leaders and the people they serve cannot accept dysfunctional streets; they must fight to change them. The fight for these changes—well, that's just part of the job.

More than policy or ideas themselves, the most valuable lessons for any city involve the on-the-ground, practical experience of connecting vision to plans and then executing projects that produce positive change. Pinned above my desk during my six and a half years as commissioner was an adage from Harvard urban planning and design professor Jerold Kayden: "To plan is human, to implement, divine."

Based on real-world practice, not ivory-tower idealism, this book deconstructs, reassembles, and reinvents the street. We invite you to view something you experience every day in ways that you might never have imagined. We hope it inspires city officials, planners, and all other city residents to initiate changes in their cities around the world. The new operating code for streets we reveal in this book is already being translated into projects in global cities, from pocket parks and plazas in Mexico City and San Francisco to pedestrian- and transit-friendly road redesigns in Los Angeles and Buenos Aires, to parking-protected bike lanes in Chicago and Salt Lake City and reclaimed streets for pedestrians near the Colosseum in Rome. If it can happen in New York City, according to the Sinatra model of transportation theory, it can happen anywhere.

Streetfight

INTRODUCTION

A New Street Code

Every city street has an underlying operating code, and no matter how exotic the place, the streets from Melbourne to Mumbai to Manhattan are all failing our cities in exactly the same way. Signs and signals, lanes and markings, sidewalks and crossings, together these elements program the basic function of a street. The operating code is the underlying language that is given meaning when street design intersects with people. But it's the operation of the street—when we walk and when we don't, the way we stop and go, the intuitive way we understand the road as we drive, walk, and bike along it—that reveals the code's deeper meaning and its gaps.

Streets for the last century have been designed to keep traffic moving but not to support the life alongside it. Many streets offer city dwellers poor options for getting around, discouraging walking and stifling vibrancy and the spontaneous social gathering and spending that energize the world's greatest cities, dragging down economies that would otherwise thrive. Inefficient and poorly designed streets are the stage for chronic congestion and 1.24 million traffic deaths annually along 22 million miles of road worldwide. Until relatively recently, there has been no commonly shared vocabulary to name or describe these failures. People are unaware that streets can be a powerful force in urban life.

New York City embodies the strengths and contradictions of urban streets. A nineteenth-century street grid was imposed over Manhattan's pre-Colonial footpaths. Streets were then designed to maximize vehicle traffic under a twentieth-century city planning dogma, which grafted motor vehicles and an ideal of suburban progress onto a city where millions of people walk and ride subways and buses. Postwar New York was built for a future that forgot its dense and lively urban origins. Its new, car-focused infrastructure became an obstacle for the future that eventually arrived. The most visible outcroppings of this problem—clogged streets, traffic congestion, danger, inefficiency, and uninviting, overrun driving surfaces—have become immutable features of cities everywhere.

City streets, built in a different age, barely serve today's residents. Car-based urban areas have adjusted to increases in population only by adding to already obsolete infrastructure. Building new highways, widening streets, and endlessly sprawling the city's limits have merely multiplied the damage to city cores and smothered the very assets that make cities places where people want to live—their accessibility, convenience, diversity, culture, and immediacy. Interpreting streets as places only to move cars instead of people turns cities into uninviting places for people.

Cities have always been cradles of culture, technology, and commerce, where history's most luminous minds and civilizations converged. But little of this creativity is reflected on the streets of the world's growing megalopolises. Elected leaders, city planners, and citizens have few expectations for how city streets should perform, and without a clear understanding of the scope of the problem, few cities even have goals to make their streets safer and more walkable, reduce congestion, and discourage sprawl.

Streets are the social, political, and commercial arteries of cities. Such iconic addresses as Park Avenue, Champs-Élysées, Lombard Street, or Rodeo Drive identify social status. Streets mark political and cultural boundaries like 8 Mile Road in Detroit, Falls Road in Belfast, and the segregated roads of the West Bank. They play critical roles in democracies and in the transformative moments of history. Whether it's Tiananmen Square, Mexico City's Zócalo, the Bastille, Trafalgar Square, or Tahrir, Wenceslas, or Taksim squares, these are the spaces where life and history happen.

Every city resident is a pedestrian at some point in the day. A city whose streets invite people to walk, bike, and sit along them also inspires people to innovate, invest, and stay for good. Regardless of where you live or how you get around or how much you may detest a bike lane, bus lane, or plaza, streets matter. They are the mortar that holds most of the world's population together. They must be designed to encourage street life, economy, and culture.

City dwellers around the world are beginning to see the potential of their city streets and want to reclaim them. They are recognizing an unmet hunger for livable, inviting public space. Many cities have embarked on significant, headline-grabbing efforts to reclaim roads, bridges, tunnels, and rail rights-of-way and turn legacy hardware into the stuff of urban dreams—parks and greenways, city idylls that provide room to walk, bike, and play in the middle of a city where a highway once stood. Some cities are building bike lane networks and creating bike-share programs. Tactical urbanists reclaim parking spaces for a day and calm traffic with murals painted onto asphalt. Yet few of these strategies have been incorporated into the way that cities operate from the street up. Traffic planners and engineers still use outdated planning and engineering manuals that prescribe wide lanes, giving scant thought to how design can create walkable urban spaces. Even where the imagination exists and the political will is aligned, the effort to achieve these overdue transformations can quickly become a street-fight against the status quo.

During an intense, six-year period under Mayor Michael Bloomberg, New York City proved to itself, the nation, and the world that almost everything that was assumed about how urban streets operate was wrong. Real-world experience showed that reducing the number of lanes on carefully selected streets or closing them entirely not only pro-vided pedestrian space and breathed new life into neighborhoods, but also actually improved traffic. Simply painting part of a street to make it into a plaza, bike, or bus lane not only made the street safer, it also improved traffic and increased bike and pedestrian foot traffic and helped local businesses to prosper.

The revival of the city's transportation network was accomplished without bulldozing a single neighborhood or razing a single building. It was cheap—absurdly cheap—compared with the billions of dollars American cities have spent annually building new streetcar and light rail lines and rehabilitating or replacing aging roads and bridges. And it was fast, installed in days and weeks using almost do-it-yourself tactics: paint, planters, lights, signs, signals, and surplus stone. Overnight, cen-turies-old roads turned into pedestrian oases atop space that had been there all along, hidden in plain sight.

While this counterintuitive approach enjoyed widespread support and improbably high poll numbers, it also enraged a small but vocal army of opponents. They were a mix of people who disliked Mayor Bloomberg and were skeptical of any government action that was envi-ronmental, healthy, or "vaguely French." They denounced the changes and politicized the very data that should have transcended the passions surrounding these changes.

Street life improved by virtually every measure. But it was the push-back to this approach that got the biggest headlines. When you push the status quo, it pushes back, hard. Everyone likes to watch a good fight. And this most surely was a streetfight: a politically bloody and ripped-from-the-tabloids streetfight. I was—and still am—deeply embedded in that streetfight. Call me biased, call me crazy—many people have—but I am convinced that the fight to wrest back New York City's streets holds lessons for every urban area, and that the future of our cities depends on it.

1

The Fight

Along Prospect Park West on a cold, damp October morning in Brooklyn, the message of rage boiled down to a few signs, most seemingly written by the same hand on the same-quality poster board:

Bike Lane = Fewer Parking Spots

Prospect Park West Bike Lane Dangerous
to Seniors & Grandchildren

Changing Our Lanes Is Risking Our Lives

Don't Be Conned by Sadik-Khan

The rally of several dozen residents who lived near the street took up a small part of the sidewalk. Still, police were called, setting up barriers to keep order in the face of an arriving stream of about two hundred counterprotesters walking or riding bikes, a kind of street cavalry that overshadowed the original protest. It was the largest public confrontation of bike lane opponents and supporters in New York City's history, and, in 2010, it was likely one of the largest public demonstrations regarding a single transportation project since Jane Jacobs held the line against Robert Moses's Lower Manhattan Expressway half a century earlier. Led by Eric McClure and Paul Steely White, two leading voices for safer streets, the group of counterprotesters pedaled past, clutching their own signs with variations on the message: "We ♥ Our New Bike Lane."

The green paint marking the two-way, parking-protected bike path had long since dried four months earlier, and the lane quickly became one of the most heavily used bike routes in the city. Some residents claimed that the lane made the street more dangerous and that its design, with bright green paint, eroded the neighborhood's character. A lawsuit by a small group of residents alleged that the lane violated rules protecting historical districts and that the project didn't conform to environmental regulations. It also became, in the words of a local paper, struggling to keep up with the escalating rhetoric of the city's over-caffeinated tabloid newspapers, "the most controversial slab of cement outside of the Gaza Strip."

In many ways, the fight was distinctly urban, with posturing groups using the language of safety, community, and preservation in a fight against unwarranted city hall intrusion into their neighborhoods. It was difficult at the start of the New York City bike backlash in late 2010 and, even now, to appreciate the full cultural, political, and urban context of the project, coming fifty years after the very idea of the city seemed obsolete and as large segments of the populations of New York and dozens of American cities had already given up on city life.

The strife over Prospect Park West represented a perverse contemporary version of the historical battles between Jane Jacobs and Robert Moses. The Jacobs–Moses conflicts are part of the almost Shakespearean origins of modern New York. Moses today is remembered as a public works tyrant who answered to no authority but his own as he force engineered a car-based future onto New York. Jacobs, who gave voice to the alternative, envisioned a future built to a human scale instead of one designed to move as many cars as possible. Neither version of these caricatures captures the full extent of their impact, not just on New York but also on other cities. And as the myths about the Jacobs/Moses battles and competing visions for cities have deepened, they haven't always taught us the right lessons about how to make our streets and cities better.

A native of Scranton, Pennsylvania, Jane Jacobs moved to Depression-era New York City and emerged as an unlikely urban visionary in her adopted West Village neighborhood. Her signature work, *The Death and Life of Great American Cities* (1961), was an urban revelation, declaring in accessible language how a city's design can nourish or destroy its quality of human life. She blasted the urban planners of the first half of the twentieth century for "urban renewal" programs that destroyed old buildings—and the neighborhoods with them—in the name of progress and for building in their place cold, sterile high-rises set back on superblocks, sucking life away from the street.

As she wrote the manuscript for the book, Jacobs took her primary inspiration not from engineering manuals and texts on urbanism, but by following the people she saw on the street outside her second-story window—what she called "The Ballet of Hudson Street." Along the neighborhood's sidewalks, in the children, shopkeepers, bohemians, meatpackers, and longshoremen who plied the streets and visited its stores, pizza parlors, and local watering holes, she saw the story of the street.

To Jacobs, a well-functioning neighborhood city street has a little of everything: shops, cafés, schools, libraries, recreation, and destinations that encourage walking day and night. Buildings hold apartments but also neighborhood shops, doctors' offices, and office space. Having well-balanced street-level design activates the sidewalks and invites residents outside with their all-important "eyes on the street," keeping the street safe and neighborhoods engaged and connected.

"Lowly, unpurposeful and random as they appear," Jacobs wrote, "sidewalk contacts are the small change from which a city's wealth of public life may grow."

I can think of no better summation of street life, literally or metaphorically. While active street life generates neighborliness, which is a critical form of social "wealth," it is also quite literally good for business. Walkable, active streets generate their own public order, and their foot traffic fuels local shops. Walking is as much a factor in urban economics as it is in a city's safety and quality of life.

Jacobs's way of looking at streets still provides the most relevant organizing principle for modern cities. Instead of designing streets from afar and focusing on moving car traffic, planners need only look to the street and follow its use to find the solutions for its problems. "There is no logic that can be superimposed on the city," Jacobs wrote more than half a century ago; "people make it, and it is to them, not buildings, that we must fit our plans."

But instead of launching an urban renaissance, *Death and Life* was accompanied by years of urban decay and depopulation. White flight brought urban disinvestment as millions of city dwellers fled to suburbs, taking their taxes with them. Combined with the loss of industry and manufacturing within cities, the mass abandonment starved transportation infrastructure and slowed development within cities. Some cities fought back against highway projects as New York did and created new transit systems—and called on the federal government to take a bigger role in fostering public transportation. Cities have recovered some of their luster and remain some of the most attractive places to live in the nation.

More than a half century since Jacobs's *Death and Life*, city residents have long since lost the plot when it comes to the design of streets themselves. New York's Greenwich Village, Lower East Side, and SoHo neighborhoods are also some of New York's most desirable and expensive neighborhoods. But the streets that run between the narrow sidewalks—Canal Street, Sixth and Seventh avenues, Houston Street, Broome and Varick streets—have remained sewers for traffic, as broken and blighted today as they were when Jacobs left New York for a new life in Toronto in 1968. Until very recently, New York's streets reflected none of the inventive, bold spirit that New Yorkers display in everything else they do.

Despite Jacobs's laser focus on the complexity of city systems, generations of communities have remained focused exclusively on NIMBY ("Not in My Backyard!") fights over what they don't want city streets to be—highways, construction sites, residential or retail complexes. Her vision of dense, vibrant, inviting, and changeable public spaces remained unfulfilled, though there have never been more people trying to achieve her vision.

Jacobs described the New York street scene as a "ballet." As someone who has lived and worked in New York most of my life, and having watched decades of taxis, buses, pedestrians, trucks, bike riders, and double parkers duking it out, I'd describe city street life as more of a contact sport like rugby than ballet. But I understand Jacobs's meaning.

Like many New Yorkers I'm passionate about New York City streets. There's an exciting, thrilling sense to it all, an expansive energy and feeling that anything is possible. My urban education started early, exploring the streets of the city with my mom, Jane McCarthy. She has always been a passionate New Yorker with strong opinions about development, preservation, and the nuanced interplay between people on neighborhood streets. Hers weren't the skills of a dilettante; she was a reporter covering city hall for the *New York Post* and looked for facts as she also looked for the stories. We'd be caught up in a conversation and she'd constantly tell me to "Look up, look up!" at the buildings and people around us. If you paid attention you might notice things you'd never seen before. There's an old saying that real New Yorkers never look up.

But they also never really look down, at their streets. How many lanes are there? Why are odd-numbered streets westbound and even-numbered streets eastbound? Why are most north–south avenues one way? Why are some sidewalks wider than others? Why do some intersections have traffic signals and others signs? It was a great education and left a profound impact on how I viewed the city's operating system of streets and bridges and their importance for people. My backyard was Washington Square Park, just a few blocks from my mom's apartment, and our conversations often included Jane Jacobs and Robert Moses, whose names are forever entwined by the park.

I didn't grow up wanting to be a transportation commissioner. I wanted to be a lawyer and work on social justice issues—more Clarence Darrow than Jane Jacobs. I had been encouraged to go to law school by Marian Wright Edelman, the visionary leader of the Children's Defense Fund, during my first job out of college. After finishing law school I worked at a law firm, but it didn't take long to realize that wasn't where my passion lay. As soon as I was financially able, I left and was naturally drawn back to the political work that I was involved in before law school.

I joined the David Dinkins mayoral campaign in 1989, inspired by his progressive vision for the city. The conventional wisdom was that he couldn't win. Ed Koch was seeking a fourth term as mayor, and after twelve years most New Yorkers had forgotten what life was like without him. The Dinkins' campaign headquarters was located in Times Square at Broadway and 43rd Street, above a peep-show theater. We'd see women dressed in feathers and boas, sequins and crowns riding up in the elevators we shared with them. They definitely got off on a different floor. Around campaign headquarters I saw political luminaries like Bill Lynch, Harold Ickes, Ken Sunshine, and Don Hazen. Future mayor Bill de Blasio helped coordinate the volunteer division. It was a strong team of people working on a shoestring and committed to electing the city's first African American mayor. Dinkins's grace and quiet passion inspired us then and continues to inspire to this day.

Times Square circa 1989 was still in its raunchy era, with Ratso Rizzo hustlers hanging along sidewalks in front of tchotchke stores and adult theaters. Parents who walked through the square on the way to a Broadway show would place a protective hand over their child's eyes. It wasn't a place you'd choose to go if you could avoid it, and it was certainly not the cleaned-up Giuliani version that would come later, much less the pedestrianized Times Square we have today. For lunch we'd grab deli sandwiches and bring them back to the office. There was nowhere and no reason to sit outside. You would be careful walking on the side streets after dark.

After Dinkins won but before he was sworn in as mayor, I called my mom to talk about what city agency might be good to work for under the new administration. I told her that I wanted to do something that would have an impact and make a difference in people's lives every day. She waited a beat and said, "If you want to touch people's lives every day, you have two choices: sanitation or transportation." Maybe it was her background as a city hall reporter that gave her that insight, but she was right.

My career at DOT began as special counsel for state and federal affairs for Lou Riccio, whom Mayor Dinkins appointed transportation commissioner. Riccio was the creative genius behind curbside recycling and the idea of using recycled glass in asphalt—"glassphalt"—one of many innovations that marked his tenure. Shortly after, I was named director of the mayor's Office of Transportation, overseeing everything from strategies to improve the even-then-unloved Pennsylvania Station to improving access routes to the region's difficult-to-reach airports. Underground, the transit system had improved tremendously since the fiscal meltdown of the 1970s, when Gerald Ford famously told New York to "Drop Dead"—at least in the *Daily News*'s translation of the president's refusal to bail out the city. Aboveground, the city's bridge and road infrastructure was disintegrating. A previous first deputy transportation commissioner under Mayor Ed Koch, "Gridlock Sam" Schwartz, sounded the alarm about the dire disrepair of the four East River bridges, the backbone of New York's road system. The bill had come due after years of neglect, requiring billions of dollars and years of recovery projects solely to bring them into a state of good repair, a sad situation that most cities faced at the time.

New York's streets themselves were similarly decrepit in the early 1990s, but that wasn't enough to stop me from commuting to work downtown from our apartment in the West Village on the back of a bike steered by my husband, Mark Geistfeld. He was clerking for a federal judge near City Hall and every day we rode down Greenwich Street to my Worth Street office. I would sit on the seat as he pedaled, standing and maneuvering around pothole minefields and an obstacle course of yellow taxis. The bike was a one-speed silver cruiser we dubbed "The Tank." You didn't see a lot of bikes on the city streets at that time, and though there were a handful of bike lanes, there was nothing you'd call a network. Even ordinary street markings seemed hard to come by. It was always a joyful ride, coasting down the street, but it was dangerous. A total of 701 people died in traffic crashes in New York City in 1990, including one pedestrian every day. Twenty of them were cyclists.

Downtown Manhattan street life around this time amounted to sidewalk hot dog vendors and lunches eaten standing up. What public space there was could be found in front of courthouses and official buildings, grim and uninviting spaces likely to be occupied by homeless people and the city's less-savory elements. Traffic safety wasn't on the agenda. The quality of street life wasn't on the agenda. Plazas definitely weren't on the agenda. What made the agenda? Basic maintenance and repair and safety from crime. The waterfront road along the Hudson River, the site of the former West Side Highway near where I lived, was a jumble of dilapidated piers and parking lots, and the way there was littered with broken glass and crack vials. There was little attention given to the way the streets looked or felt. New Yorkers were desperately hanging on, trying to survive, not thinking about how these streets—the greatest asset in one of the world's most walkable cities—could be used. Even then I was certain New York's streets had more to offer.

I came to the job of commissioner twenty-six years after Robert Moses's death in a city that Moses might still have recognized. Moses saw in New York a city struggling to modernize and weighed down by its past. And more than anyone before or since, Moses had the means, the power, and the motivation to do something about it. Enabled by successions of mayors and governors and fueled by billions of federal dollars in Works Progress Administration and Interstate Highway funds, Moses amassed as many as twelve directorships and leadership positions over vital public works agencies, from the New York City Parkway Authority to the Triborough Bridge and Tunnel Authority to the state parks. The federal government created massive public works programs to build new urban roads and housing to replace the "slum" infrastructure of the nineteenth century. Moses was first in line to provide these "urban renewal" projects.

The almost incomprehensible list of projects that he moved from planning to implementation from 1918 to his departure from government in 1968 included seventeen parkways and fourteen expressways that ringed and connected the city, and aesthetic and engineering marvels like the Verrazano-Narrows, Bronx-Whitestone, and Triborough bridges. He more than doubled the acreage of city parks, built the United Nations and Lincoln Center, and brought innumerable playgrounds, public pools, and public beaches to millions of New Yorkers who couldn't afford summer homes or sleep-away camps to gain refuge from the hot summer days.

In his relentless push, Moses's projects also divided the city. Armies of workers bulldozed swaths of entire neighborhoods of Manhattan,

Brooklyn, and the Bronx, displacing hundreds of thousands of people in the process. Highway projects like the Cross Bronx Expressway disproportionately uprooted African-American and immigrant communities. Thousands of families were dispossessed in this way, often with the promise that they would be housed when reconstruction of new apartments was complete, but rarely with the results that Moses promised.

What occurred in New York City played out in all major cities in postwar America and was accelerated by the 1956 Interstate Highway Act, as the motor vehicle became the nation's de facto official mode of transportation. Signed by President Eisenhower, the Act authorized the creation of 41,000 miles of modern highways wide enough for the largest trucks and new roads, built right in the hearts of many American cities, destroying residential neighborhoods, dividing others, and hastening urban demographic shifts from city centers to the growing suburbs. Moses saw New York City as a traffic management challenge that could be solved—engineered, built, and erected into order. Engineered out of these street designs weren't just traffic conflicts but all of the complexities of the street—the messiness that Jane Jacobs saw as vital to the street's viability. No street-level stores, no strolling-friendly sidewalks where people could see others and be seen. People were meant to make use of whatever was left over on the street after space had been created for cars.

More than anyone else, traffic engineers like those who worked under Moses were the chief forces behind the building of new highways, depleting cities and nurturing the development of car-based suburbs and sprawl. They then claimed they were the only ones capable of solving the traffic problems they had helped to create, which they accomplished by building more and wider roads capable of processing even more traffic. The City of the Future—designed to be viewed from above, built for cars, a place where pedestrians were an afterthought—wasn't created by accident. It was by design.

The Futurama exhibition at the 1939 World's Fair in Flushing Meadows Park in Queens, New York, included a football-field-size model of the city of the future, where vehicles glided seamlessly along sweeping roads. Conspicuously missing were representations of the people or of any human activity that the street was presumably designed to encourage and support.   Alfred Eisenstaedt, *Life*

Although Moses destroyed much in his relentless path to modernity, it would be simplistic to dismiss him as a one-dimensional public works despot, and his was far from an original planning sin. Moses was shaped by the assumptions of his era, and it was an article of faith shared by planners in other American cities that the future would be driven by the motor vehicle. Moses today is largely seen as the archetypal destroyer of neighborhoods, whose arrogance was laid bare in Robert Caro's 1974 Pulitzer Prize–winning biography, *The Power Broker: Robert Moses and the Fall of New York*. While Caro and others have ascribed to Moses responsibility for the city's decline in the 1970s, New York turned around in the 1980s and, by the 1990s, grew to be a global economic leader and "capital of the world."

"Whatever the cause of the New York turnaround," historian Kenneth Jackson wrote, "it would not have been possible without Robert Moses." Moses left New York City far better equipped to grow and thrive than the Depression-era husk that he had inherited, and without his brazen and single-minded ability to complete projects, Jackson said, "Gotham would have lacked the wherewithal to adjust to the demands of the modern world."

As the Moses/Jacobs story has been told and retold over the last four decades, Jacobs's model of grassroots resistance has been co-opted into a perverse politics of rejecting new ideas—and celebrating each defeated project as a victory, even if that victory is the status quo. In recent years, pedestrian-, transit- and bike-friendly projects in dozens of cities, ranging from Adelaide and Sydney to London, Toronto, and New Orleans, have been regarded by residents with the same kind of fear and suspicion usually reserved for proposals to build Moses-like multilane highways. Speaking at public hearings, local residents and business owners invoke Jacobs-like language as a smokescreen to fight Jacobs-like projects. They oppose plans for walkable neighborhoods and bike lanes, claiming that they might congest traffic, make streets less safe, and pollute the environment or erode property values. By invoking Jane Jacobs, many NIMBYs today are effectively arguing that roads should be kept the way Robert Moses wanted them. It's one thing to turn back a proposed development—a new highway, a convention center, a too-tall building or out-of-scale, traffic-generating shopping mall. It's another thing to say yes to people-oriented streets based on fresh and innovative new ideas that affirmatively rewrite the street's operating code—its underlying geometry, essential function, and overarching meaning.

Jacobs understood that the neighborhoods and the streets of a city contain the seeds for renewal, and it is local residents who will ultimately lead the way. But after decades of lifelessness and danger, it's obvious that cities will not succeed in transforming themselves through market forces, consensus, or by waiting for infrastructure to crumble before taking action. Retrofitting our cities for the new urban age and achieving Jane Jacobs's vision today will require Moses-like vision and action for building the next generation of city roads, ones that will accommodate pedestrians, bikes, and buses safely and not just single-occupancy vehicles with their diminishing returns for our streets. Cities must adopt a more inclusive and humane approach to reshaping the urban realm and rebuilding it quickly to human scale, driven by a robust community process, but committed to delivering projects and not paralyzing them. Reversing the atrophy afflicting our city streets requires a change-based urbanism that creates short-term results—results that can create new expectations and demand for more projects.

In the last fifteen years, the forces arrayed to support streets oriented toward people instead of cars have won far more battles than they have lost. These forces—planners, elected officials, transportation leaders, and ordinary citizens—are redefining the battle itself with their strategies and focus on cities' economy, safety, and long-term sustainability goals instead of how many lanes and parking spaces can be crammed onto streets. Globally, new generations of transportation leaders and visionary mayors are rethinking the city and its relationship with its cars and the infrastructure that supports them. Cities on every continent are rebuilding their streets with bus rapid transit networks in months instead of years. Cities like San Francisco, Buenos Aires, and Mexico City are creating pocket parks atop former triangles of asphalt or reclaiming and activating forlorn spaces beneath highways, giving new life and creating the "small change" of street contacts from which public life can grow. Paris's Plages and the Promenade Plantée and New York City's High Line attract millions of visitors to former urban rail rights-of-way and roads turned into parks. These concepts have trickled down—and up—to tactical urban interventions that turn parking spaces into cafés or a mini park for a day. They are examples of urban alchemy, converting outmoded infrastructure into modern, public space that awakens cities and makes people want to move in and stay. These developments are particularly important for attracting younger populations back to urban centers, which are driving cities' rebirth.

These diverse urban transformations have inspiring applications that we are just beginning to understand. With them we can reignite our cities after a century of street stasis. But they are only the first step to an entirely new approach that must be built into the design of ordinary streets as much as commercial avenues or boulevards. By demanding and embracing smaller-scale interventions that can quickly and inexpensively reallocate space, we can begin to restore the balance of the street and replace the vestiges of last century's planning dogma, which ignored the human experience on that street.

This approach is based on a vision of planning the city that incorporates both Jacobs's view from the street and Moses's approach of cutting through development paralysis to implement change in real time. Because so much public space is paved today, we have an enormous amount of raw material. By using Moses's abundant roadbed as the stage for Jacobs's diversified, human network of streets, we have limitless opportunities for aggressive, change-based urbanism. Just because an avenue today has five lanes of busy traffic doesn't mean that tomorrow it can't be reprogrammed for another use that transforms the street's feel and function into that of a real neighborhood.

In July 2014, seven months after I stepped down as transportation commissioner when a new mayor came into office, a work team from New York City's Department of Transportation added a footnote to Manhattan's urban history: working with thermoplastic paint and concrete, the crew striped and heat-stenciled a parking-protected bike path directly in front of 555 Hudson Street in Greenwich Village, the former home of Jane Jacobs.

Jane's Lane, a protected bike path in front of Jane Jacobs's former home at 555 Hudson Street, Manhattan, arrived fifty-three years after the publication of *The Death and Life of Great American Cities*. Seth Solomonow

The design of the bike path, now running alongside the curb, protected by the line of parked cars on the other side, wasn't new to Manhattan's streets. The lane connected Hudson Street with an existing bike path built six years earlier just north of Jane's three-story, red-brick home. When it first appeared in 2007, a protected bike path was a foreign concept on American streets, one that seemed to upset the balance of the street and was viewed as an enemy to traffic, graphically illustrated by the fight in 2010 over the bike lane on Prospect Park West. By 2014, it was just another part of the streetscape.

2

Density Is Destiny

I often tell people that if they want to save the planet, they should move to New York City. But it could be any big city. And it's not just a matter of bright lights, landmarks, great restaurants, entertainment, museums, and cultural institutions. Cities' geographic compactness, population density, and orientation toward walking and public transportation make them the most efficient places to live in the world. Large cities like New York or Mexico City offer the best odds for sustainable growth as global populations increase rapidly. The collective energy of millions of people concentrated into high-rise buildings instead of being spread out over hundreds of rural and suburban miles is itself a reason why so many people are attracted—culturally, professionally, politically, and practically—to cities like New York. But there is also an economic sustainability-in-numbers case for dense city living.

New Yorkers have a carbon footprint 71 percent lower than that of the average American, a function of driving less, living vertically, and the economies of scale that come with centrally located goods and services. Fifty-nine percent of people who work in Manhattan get there by public transportation, nearly twelve times the national rate. More than 10 percent walk. The city has lower per capita energy use than anywhere else in the entire nation, largely due to people living more compactly in smaller, more efficient homes that are easier to heat and cool and that are connected to common water and sewer networks. Two thirds of the American population now lives in the nation's one hundred largest metro areas, occupying just 12 percent of the nation's land area yet generating three quarters of the nation's economic output.

But what can cure us can also kill us. Urban population is expected to grow—by 1 million people in New York City alone from 2007 to 2030, and by nearly 100 million more people nationwide by 2050. Adding a population nearly the equivalent of the nation's four largest states to cities and their suburbs could easily exhaust their ability to house and move people or provide them with basic services and utilities, bringing their economies to a halt and pushing development even farther outside of urban areas. Concentrating as much of that nationwide growth efficiently in cities will thus be one of the most important strategies for nations to embrace during this century. Living in cities isn't a random demographic result. It's a choice. In order to attract, retain, and accommodate rising populations, our leaders must rapidly implement strategies that make cities more attractive places to live while making their infrastructure function more efficiently to meet the growing demand.

Making cities a choice preferable to the suburb cuts against a long-standing antiurban bias in the United States based on a view that cities are dangerous, crowded, and havens for crime. The suburbs provide open space and quiet where people can raise families in safe, leafy communities, away from city grit. In fact, as we have learned over the last fifty years, living in suburbs has hidden costs that make New York City look like a cozy Swiss hamlet. A hidden but far greater environmental price tag is borne through the driving, emissions, and maintaining and building of new roads. Suburbs and exurbs not only force long-distance commuting in cars, but also require cars to be used for *every* trip, no matter how banal. Zoning requirements in many suburbs restrict commercial development and office parks to segregated areas, guaranteeing that residential communities will be far outside of walking distance for any activity. Unlike in Jane Jacobs's compact neighborhood, a trip to the suburban store for a half gallon of milk may be a five-mile drive. Visiting the doctor, going out to dinner, and getting the kids to and from school require thousands of car trips annually—trips that could be made on foot and by transit en route to and from work in a city.

After years of rhapsodizing about the virtues of pristine forests, modern environmentalists have changed their tune on the city. Instead of fighting to preserve the spotted owl in the forest, they are taking the fight to cities, advocating smart or compact urban growth as part of an antisprawl strategy. It's better for the planet to build one fifty-story residential tower in the heart of Manhattan than to force developers to build hundreds of residential units across former greenbelt farmlands. Denser, better-functioning cities mean fewer people fleeing to the country along with their cars and the roads, parking lots, strip malls, and the low-efficiency HVAC and sewer systems needed to support them.

Seen this way, many of New York City's neighborhoods aren't nearly dense *enough*, particularly if they want to retain even some of the varied architecture and small-scale streets that make cities great. The urban economist Edward Glaeser wrote that simply rejecting denser, taller development creates more problems if the overall number of available homes doesn't keep pace with population growth. "When the demand for a city rises, prices will rise unless more homes are built. When cities restrict new construction, they become more expensive." Expensive like San Francisco, where antidevelopment policies have greatly limited new market-rate home building in the hope of preserving affordability. Stunting new residential construction is one of the reasons why housing in San Francisco has become so scarce and thus less affordable to the very people the policy was intended to help. And by limiting denser urban development within city limits, more people are forced to sprawl even farther around the Bay Area, eroding the greenbelt—a recreational oasis that makes San Francisco such an attractive city in the first place.

People don't move to cities because they're efficient places. They move where the quality of life, convenience, and price lead them. Despite the natural advantages of cities, political leaders haven't fully capitalized on them. Cities don't come with owners' manuals. Within city transportation departments, most street design practices were standardized by traffic engineers long ago, with no tradition of innovation or experimentation. Transportation-as-usual in most of the world's cities means building, expanding, repairing, or replacing as many roads as possible and brushing aside anything not tested or explicitly authorized. In this way, cities have tended to operate in much the same way that their cities have sprawled: by doing things the way they've always been done, by relying on out-of-date engineering manuals and deviating only when forced.

The inertia of outdated street design isn't merely dangerous, it reflects outmoded assumptions about how people want to use their streets. Americans today are driving fewer miles on average than a decade ago, the first sustained drop since the oil crisis of the 1970s. Fewer young Americans are even bothering to get driver's licenses. In 1983, 87 percent of nineteen-year-olds had driver's licenses; by 2010, that number was below 70 percent. And more are opting for rented or shared cars and riding bikes instead of buying a car, as automobile sales to Americans under thirty-five dropped 30 percent from 2007 to 2012. On the transit side of the ledger, ridership in 2014 reached its highest level since the start of the car boom in 1956. The federal government has missed these dramatic shifts, forecasting consistent, high growth in driving even as average miles traveled has flattened out or decreased over the last decade.

Federal policy incentivizes people to live in sprawling suburbs. The federal gas tax, designed as a mechanism for drivers to pay for the upkeep of the roads they use, hasn't been adjusted in two decades, asphyxiating the Highway Trust Fund and transportation infrastructure reinvestment with it. This is no small sum: it's been stuck at 18.4 cents since 1993. Simply not adjusting the tax for inflation for two decades has reduced the tax's value to just 11 cents, not counting the flatline in driving.

The misreading of what is occurring in America isn't confined to driving. While spending money to build roads is seen as a public investment, critics characterize public transportation as a wasteful welfare subsidy. The pervasive myth that public transportation riders are subsidized and that people who drive pay the full cost of their trips has never been less true than it is today. Many drivers indignantly believe that by filling their tanks with gas and paying for registration and insurance, they've paid more than their fair share. But recent data show that drivers don't pay the full cost of the roads they drive on, and they've never paid less. A 2015 study by U.S. Public Interest Research Group (PIRG) found that from 1947 to 2012, American taxpayers as a whole paid $1 trillion more to sustain the road network than people who drive paid in gasoline taxes, tolls, and other user fees. In 2012, $69 billion in highway spending came from general tax revenues. Driver taxes and tolls pay for only about half of the cost to build and maintain the physical infrastructure needed to drive. The remainder is paid for with general tax revenues, including 10 percent from municipal bonds issued to pay for new road projects.

Roads are expensive to build in the first place, but they require ongoing maintenance, monitoring, repair, and rehabilitation during their lifetimes. So who pays for roads? Everybody does, no matter how much they drive. U.S. PIRG estimated that accounting for these costs, every American household pays more than $1,100 in addition to whatever they pay in direct transportation costs to drive—even if they don't drive at all. And that money subsidizes an inequitable use of roads. Governments spend more general tax revenue on highways than on transit, walking, and biking *combined*. So people who walk, bike, or take public transit are effectively subsidizing the least efficient transportation mode at the expense of their own way of getting around.

And this subsidy has other costly effects. A 2015 study by Todd Litman and the Victoria Transport Policy Institute and the London School of Economics confirmed the long-standing reality that car-based suburbs require expensive infrastructure investments and personal vehicle and fuel costs, while causing pollution and the environmental and health problems brought by physical inactivity. Sprawling distances also mean long travel times, traffic congestion, and slowed deliveries. These issues aren't merely inconveniences; the study found they affect the entire economic and developmental metabolism of urban America, a $1 trillion a year drag on the American economy, or 13 percent of the nation's economic output, slowing growth.

The Interstate Highway System was the greatest transportation idea to come from our federal government to connect cities, but there hasn't been any organizing principle *within* cities themselves, much less a unified policy that takes the view from the street. And for decades, no one has expected much from their cities' transportation leaders, least of all on the fundamental principle of urban traffic safety. This neglect has forced cities into thinking for themselves and developing strategies that don't require federal vision or largesse. The human cost of inaction is inefficient and even deadly, but the political stakes for people who design and build city streets couldn't be lower. The public has generally had lit-

tle interest in change and limited expectations beyond reducing congestion, filling potholes, and a general concept of improving traffic. As long
as planners and the engineers whose job is increasing cities' automotive
capacities hear that the public has no appetite for change and no interest
in safety, the message reinforces official behavior to do nothing.

And the consequences of these low expectations couldn't be higher.
Transportation is one of the few professions where nearly 33,000 people
can lose their lives in one year and no one in a position of responsibility
is in danger of losing his or her job. People are rewarded for completing
multibillion-dollar megaprojects that do little to nothing to improve
congestion, safety, or mobility. Those who do transportation-as-usual
by focusing on the smoothness of city roads and futile road expansions
tend to have jobs for life, even as traffic problems stagnate or worsen. In
this job, those who fight against obsolete transportation ideas and work
to create new choices, improve safety, and reduce congestion are the
ones whose jobs are on the chopping block. They must be willing to get
the shit kicked out of them, then get up and continue the job.

A big obstacle to implementing new strategies is embedded within
the very design manuals that govern city streets. In the United States,
the federal *Manual on Uniform Traffic Control Devices* (MUTCD) and *A
Policy on Geometric Design of Highways and Streets*, known as the
Green Book, published by the American Association of State Highway
and Transportation Officials (AASHTO), provide the blueprint for the
design of the nation's 2.6 million miles of paved roads. These decades-
old standards contain remnants from the era of Moses yet are still
found in binders on the desk of every engineer—and are part of the
reason why our streets have been frozen in time ever since.

First published in 1935, the MUTCD has had a lasting impact on
American city streets. The massive document sets guidelines for how
many cars over how long a period shall result in a stop sign, traffic signal, or turn lane. It provides standards on roadway width and lane size,

gradations of shoulders and specifications for length, color, and characteristics of striping and signs. These are bare-minimum baselines for the installation of streets, markings, and signs, which, in practice, help city streets to operate more like highways and less like neighborhoods. In the MUTCD's more than eight hundred pages of diagrams, human beings are conspicuously absent from any representations of the street.

These standardized manuals are as instructive in building safe, lively, and economically vibrant streets as a car manual is in teaching people how to drive. Traffic engineers say these documents tie their hands and they're afraid to attempt new street designs that are safe but not specifically authorized. The guidelines also smother innovation with their silence on modern pedestrian- and bike-friendly treatments, reflecting none of the experimentation and experience from American streets. The typology for protected bike paths is nowhere to be found in the MUTCD, even as two hundred of these new treatments have been installed nationwide in Chicago, Washington, D.C., Indianapolis, San Francisco, and Portland, Oregon—more than fifty cities in total in nearly half of all fifty states. New York City's forty miles of protected paths installed by 2014 led to dramatic decreases in traffic injuries by all street users, not just bike riders.

In the absence of guidance, some cities have found new inspiration in *Designing Walkable Urban Thoroughfares: A Context Sensitive Approach*, produced in 2010 by the Congress for the New Urbanism and the Institute of Transportation Engineers. The guide was a huge step forward simply by including real-world examples of street design principles that cities have implemented and by representing people in the guide's designs and their perspective of the street.

And as more cities have experimented with innovative and bold street treatments, the heads of their transportation agencies have for the first time created their own playbook, incorporating designs that are now being perfected in cities across the continent. *The Urban Street*

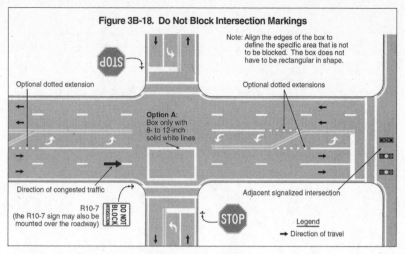

Figure 3B-18. Do Not Block Intersection Markings

Note: Align the edges of the box to define the specific area that is not to be blocked. The box does not have to be rectangular in shape.

STOP

Optional dotted extension

Optional dotted extensions

Option A:
Box only with 8- to 12-inch solid white lines

Direction of congested traffic

R10-7
(the R10-7 sign may also be mounted over the roadway)

DO NOT BLOCK INTERSECTION

STOP

Adjacent signalized intersection

Legend
→ Direction of travel

Like Moses's Futurama exhibit, the federal manual used for street design features no people. MUTCD

Design Guide, an urban how-to guide produced by the National Association of City Transportation Officials (NACTO), a group that I ran while transportation commissioner and which I now chair, provides a compendium of real-world street innovations that are tailored to the dimensions of city streets, not interstate highways. The guide details a broad range of protected bike path designs, detail on curb extensions that shorten crossing distances for pedestrians, and bus lane and other lane treatments that can reduce the speed of passing cars and make people who walk, bike, take transit, or just linger feel more at home.

As of this writing, nine states and forty-five cities have endorsed the NACTO *Urban Street Design Guide*, and the federal government endorsed it thanks to the leadership of former U.S. transportation secretary Ray LaHood.

This guide gives cities a "permission slip" to try new designs and are bold statements of imagination on what streets could be like in our increasingly dense urban areas. They may ultimately be the new "Green Book" for the twenty-first century. How do we get from design to implementation? It takes vision and it takes a plan.

31

3

Setting the Agenda

As a rule, 95,000-word documents about urban health and long-term sustainability aren't headline news, much less the stuff of dinner-table conversation. The news on Earth Day 2007 was different. Mayor Bloomberg unveiled PlaNYC (pronounced "Plan-Y-C") at the American Museum of Natural History, beneath its famous 94-foot-long, 21,000-pound fiberglass blue whale, underscoring the urgency of the message. The unusually direct language the mayor used at the event was as rare as the animals that filled the museum halls, and it made news.

The document that Mayor Bloomberg and Team Camelot under Deputy Mayor Dan Doctoroff produced (PlaNYC) was the first real inventory of the city's collective resources, assets, and deficiencies. It systematically reverse-engineered the city to accommodate expected population growth, amortizing the costs of investments over decades instead of election cycles, and looked at the impact of growth on health, the environment, and quality of life. From 2000 to 2005 alone, New York City's population grew by 200,000 people.

Doctoroff recalled that the plan didn't start with trying to solve the ultimate challenge of New York's long-term growth, but with trying to solve a single problem then facing the city: where to house the vast stockpiles of chemical salt needed for city plows when it snowed. The municipal land needed for the salt storage set in motion an inventory of city properties, which in turn forced officials to think about the properties needed for the equipment that carries and disperses the salt. The process quickly led to inquiries about lots for vehicles, for refueling them, and for transfer stations to carry out the waste—the banal stuff of municipal real estate.

As the exercise unfolded, Doctoroff recognized they were contemplating essential questions of the city's long-term health, not just addressing today's problems. "We realized that planning for the future was more than an exercise in creating space for government operations," he told me. "By 2030, there will be nine million people in New York City," Doctoroff says, a net increase of nearly a million people, or the equivalent of adding the current populations of Miami and Boston into the five boroughs.

To address the increased demands on the city, PlaNYC returned to a central theme: density is New York's destiny, and city planning must leverage that strength to enhance mobility and the quality of city life and avoid sprawl. Successful urban density isn't simply a matter of tall buildings stacked next to one another. City residents require both space and privacy, green space and open sky, breathing room and room to run. How cities deliver their services must be organized in ways that can be maintained over decades without depleting their coffers or making neighborhoods and the environment inhospitable.

Determining how these pieces fit together is a problem of public space design, and it's inextricable from the underlying city goals and policies. The plan's 127 proposals would increase the city's housing stock by 265,000 units, expand wetlands and plant a million trees, build more efficient buildings and install street lighting that uses less energy. To reduce greenhouse gases, PlaNYC also sought to lower emissions by having fewer vehicles on the roads and enabling all New Yorkers to live within a ten-minute walk of open space. By investing more in ten years on sustainable infrastructure, the city could have a greener, more attractive city and realize savings from those investments fifteen, twenty, and thirty-five years later.

In 2007, the idea of planning beyond the length of a term in office was still a political fantasy. Sustainability plans for entire cities were still a rarity in the first decade of the new millennium. Similar plans had been drafted in Seattle and San Francisco. London in 2004 released the London Plan, one year after implementing its first congestion fee for cars entering the city center. But these plans lacked unifying sustainability themes across all city agencies to reach beyond urban planning and into the essential issues of land use, energy, waste management, air quality, and climate change.

Such strategies recognize and emphasize that ideas can outlast the people who drafted them. "Cities without plans tend to be politically disenfranchised with fragmented governments," says Transport for London's commissioner, Sir Peter Hendy, knighted in part for his success managing the city's transportation plan during the 2012 Summer Olympics. "As a result, they don't have any long-term purpose, don't have any long-term plan, and haven't done much. Whereas [in London] we have this massive population and economic growth, and it's fueled by all sorts of policies being executed alongside congestion charging—cycling, renewal of the subway—which then make the plan work. I think that is an incredible lesson here and for the rest of the world."

One of the first urban planning frameworks in the United States was established in Oregon more than forty years ago, and it has served as a great model and impressive success story. Inspired by urban development models from early-twentieth-century England and led by visionary governor Tom McCall, the state legislature in 1973 required Oregon cities to establish urban boundaries outside of which commercial and residential development is prohibited. Every five years cities can assess their land use needs for the next twenty years, and if they believe there is a compelling need, they must make their case before the legislature to open new tracts of green space for housing or business. Some opponents object that by concentrating new growth within city boundaries, the boundaries artificially inflate real estate prices that should have been left to the free market. But something else has happened. Portland has become a model for transit and human-powered transportation. Its bike commuting rate of around 6 percent, while laughably small by European standards—and even considering that commuting trips represent only a fraction of overall bike trips—is the closest thing to Copenhagen among American cities of more than half a million people. Bike commuting tripled there from 2000 to 2012, and streetcars ply the car-free streets of downtown. One generation's planning helped dictate the next generation's infrastructure investment. In 2015, Portland officials opened the Tilikum Crossing, a 1,720-foot bridge that was the first span over the Willamette River in forty years. The bridge, known as the Bridge of the People, was designed to carry trains for Portland's light rail MAX system, streetcars, buses, bikes, pedestrians, ambulances, and fire trucks, but no private cars.

In other American cities, by contrast, urban planning is often absent from agendas. Houston, Texas, is renowned for having no long-term plan or even a unified zoning code that spells out what kinds of buildings can be built where. The result, predictably, is that Houston's population of 2.2 million is sprawled over more than 625 square miles, or about one tenth of the people in Mexico City spread throughout a slightly smaller area.

Comprehensive urban planning is a productive exercise in itself. PlaNYC reframed the idea of the city and repudiated the idea that cities (not just New York) are environmental, social, and economic lost causes. "We went from cities being a problem to density being the solution," said Rit Aggarwala, the sustainability guru Doctoroff brought in to manage the development of the report. The result was a document that was written in clear and accessible language and its positive tone reflected the belief that cities are sources of national strength.

While PlaNYC had high-level goals for congestion pricing, bike lanes, and bus rapid transit, it didn't spell out what that infrastructure should look like or the strategies to implement it. That was my job as the newly appointed commissioner of DOT. I immediately started by translating these goals into a strategic action plan for the 4,500-person agency, and, most important, building a team that could execute it. The first play was to identify the talent already within the agency, which would let us get to work fast.

As my right hand, I appointed Lori Ardito, a smart, seasoned DOT professional to oversee operations—paving and fixing roads, installing signs and signals, and keeping the Staten Island Ferry running on time. Her appointment also reassured the DOT establishment that I valued their skills and input. It also made it easier when I brought in a cadre of people from outside the agency—some who were former critics of DOT or who brought decades of experience from inventive private sector practices. They would help expand the capabilities of the entire team and push the bureaucracy to act with a nimbleness it had never seen. We set out to achieve big goals and change the very nature of the business and how we got things done. On my team were people who shared my brand of strategic thought and impatience with government dithering, like Jon Orcutt, a creative and pragmatic transportation advocate and leader to run our policy shop and major initiatives.

My friend Margaret Newman, an architect with a razor-sharp design eye, became my chief of staff and elevated our aesthetic and lighting standards. Andy Wiley-Schwartz came from the Project for Public Spaces to head DOT's fledgling new office for public space. Another key player was Bruce Schaller, a data guru with years at the transit, parks, and taxi departments, to lead the agency's new Planning and Sustainability Division and help manage the plan to inaugurate five new bus rapid transit lines and meet the biggest goal of all: congestion pricing. Starting on our new course with this new team, we had no choice but to work fast—there were only thirty-two months before the mayor's second term would expire.

We started by developing an action plan for implementing PlaNYC's transportation agenda. The agency's deputy commissioners led a top-to-bottom audit of the department to plan our path forward instead of lurching from emergency to emergency. Within the first year we produced the agency's first-ever strategic plan, Sustainable Streets, a conversion of PlaNYC at the transportation level, with goals and benchmarks for a better city. It set forth goals to cut traffic fatalities by half and to bring dedicated bus lanes, enhance public space, and bike infrastructure across the city. DOT's sustainable future meant more recycled asphalt, more bridge investment, more cleaner-burning fuels in our operations, more efficient lights on our streets, and, critically, a new neighborhood communications strategy.

Another big part of the agenda was overhauling the public outreach process. For years DOT had communicated with communities through a curt exchange of form letters. A resident or civic group would request a stop sign or traffic signal and, after a study of traffic volumes and the number of pedestrians crossing the street, the department usually responded in a letter saying "No." No, the intersection did not have enough traffic to meet federal guidelines for installing a traffic signal. No, not enough pedestrians crossed the intersection to warrant a stop sign. In the view of the citizens, by saying no, the government had failed in a basic responsibility to do something and solve an obvious problem. What they didn't know is that the underlying problem that they were concerned about might have had more effective solutions. The 12,700 intersections in New York City with traffic signals are no less prone to dangerous speeding and adding new ones may create new problems. Signals can spend more than half their time green, leaving plenty of time to speed. And many drivers who see a green light at a distant intersection often feel induced to hit the gas to increase their chance of beating the eventual red light. This is why transportation departments install traffic signals primarily to control the right-of-way, not to regulate speed.

Instead of mailing letters that simply denied traffic signal requests, we posed a new question to these communities: What problem were they trying to solve? Were there other strategies that were not considered because they were not specifically requested? If the problem was speeding, we could look at the possibility of narrower lanes, speed bumps, and parking restrictions near the corner so stopped cars wouldn't block the visibility of crossing pedestrians. Creative street design, not stop signs, could change safety on a street. To better define the problems and showcase new solutions, we developed workshops called DOT Academy, where agency staff made presentations to elected officials, community board leaders, and their staffs so they would know what we did and what to ask for—instead of stop signs and traffic signals.

At typical public meetings, city officials lecture community members for twenty minutes, then take questions. This format works against general public participation and in favor of the few who feel passionate enough to declare an opinion before a room of people—often the most extreme opinions, which frequently result in a polarized room. People with moderate opinions remain silent and stay out of the conflict, which means decision makers don't hear a full range of views. To encourage participation and also provide a better gauge of public wishes and sentiment in programs like our rapid bus projects, we arranged planning meetings that would seat participants at individual tables in groups of ten or even fewer, each one moderated by transportation staffers who jotted down ideas and provided details of proposed projects. Each individual—a resident, a business owner, a representative from a local institution—now had the chance to have his say, civilly, and resolve differences among themselves.

Of course the general public is not the only one engaged in the street business. The departments of design and construction, parks, buildings, planning, environmental protection, and others all developed projects that touched the streets. To put all these agencies on the same street design page, we pulled together eleven agencies and started working to create New York City's first ever street design guide. It includes the latest in designs piloted in New York or used in other cities—like bioswales that channel flooding rainwater from streets into landscaped tree pits, curb extensions that decreased crossing distances for pedestrians, and new techniques in street marking.

The collective impact of these plans, processes, and policies was a wholesale government rebranding. We were changing the language and the expectations of what the department was capable of and responsible for, and how it should use the resources under its control. In so doing, we helped expand and transform people's expectations of the city itself. We didn't eliminate tensions and opposition, but created a goal-based approach to government that resulted in better projects and outcomes, which, while they would not please each of New York's 8.4 million traffic engineers, would better serve more of them than ever before.

But nobody was served well by the traffic that had existed since Moses's time. The very first item on the transportation agenda at City Hall was a plan to deal with congestion and the chronic underfunding of our transportation network. This wasn't the first time I tried to tackle the problem. As Mayor Dinkins's transportation adviser, I oversaw a report on the feasibility of tolling the East River bridges to fund the capital and operating needs of New York City's bridges and streets.

Swarming traffic persists as an inescapable part of daily life in Gotham and most major cities. Manhattan's population of 1.6 million doubles every weekday as commuters descend upon the borough's clusters of entertainment, finance, fashion, publishing, academia, dining, and media. As vivid as traffic is in Manhattan lore, a relatively small number of people are in vehicles. Only 6.6 percent of the 1.6 million people who travel to work in Manhattan daily drive alone, compared with a national average of 76.4 percent. Instead, public transportation is the choice for 59 percent of commuters who arrive at their Manhattan desks—riding aboard subways, buses, ferries, and commuter trains that connect the city and its suburban counties. That makes New York a public transportation nirvana compared with the national average of just 5 percent of commuters taking transit.

Even a small percentage of people driving alone is a huge absolute number in a metropolitan area of 20 million people. Cumulatively, within the five boroughs including Manhattan, drivers make 7.7 million daily car trips and rack up 30 million miles daily. These large numbers of vehicles require an immense amount of room while they are moving and while they are parked, which is why most New York City street space has been devoted to them. This disequilibrium is itself a daily streetfight, with taxis, pedestrians, bikes, buses, pedicabs, deliverymen, trucks, and street vendors in an uneasy dance for space, pace, and safety. Cars and trucks double-park to make deliveries, blocking lanes and forcing dangerous and traffic-inducing merges. Millions of hours of people's lives are collectively spent stuck in traffic annually, getting nowhere while emitting fumes into local neighborhoods. The Partnership for New York City estimated in 2006 that congestion cost the region $13 billion each year in economic and health matters.

Our goal was to rebalance these streets, bringing greater equity to the transportation network and reducing the impact of congestion. The price of entering the city by car—free at many bridges—was the linchpin. There is no active congestion pricing system in the United States, yet paying tolls to use bridges and roads is a rich, if loathed, American driving tradition. I remember years ago fumbling for change to throw into a toll basket on the New Jersey Turnpike or Interstate 95 in Connecticut, a step up from handing over a crumpled bill and coins to a toll collector at one of the city's tunnels or bridges. By the late 1980s, electronic toll collection like E-ZPass started to snap up tolls without your having to hit the brakes. Despite this tradition, people who drive tend not to see a correlation between the price they pay to use the road and the poor quality of and congestion on that road. The idea of paying a toll to enter an area, as opposed to using a bridge or road, still remains as foreign a concept today as the idea of paying for driving at all.

"I was a skeptic myself," admitted Mayor Bloomberg when he publicly discussed congestion pricing for the first time. "But I looked at the facts, and that's what I'm asking New Yorkers to do. And the fact is in cities like London and Singapore, fees succeeded in reducing congestion and improving air quality."

Singapore introduced the first congestion pricing and taxing system in 1975, which officials married to new transit investments and strict rules on owning cars, decreasing traffic volume and leading to a long-term increase in the use of transit. In the early 2000s European planners started to pick up on the quiet, pocketbook power of charging people to drive. To reduce congestion and vehicle emissions, London officials in 2003 introduced a fee for drivers coming into the city center on weekdays. By 2006 the plan reduced congestion within the zone by an estimated 30 percent and decreased greenhouse gases by 16 percent. Meanwhile, Londoners walked and took buses in increasing numbers. Stockholm, Sweden, introduced a pilot congestion charge program, one that it made permanent in 2006, within months of PlaNYC's launch. Again, traffic decreased. From my first day in office I was thrust into this, the most controversial issue in the city. Joined frequently by Bruce Schaller and Rit Aggarwala, I became one of the public faces of the battle at public hearings and testimony in front of the Metropolitan Transportation Authority, the city council, and other public meetings required before a policy can take effect.

We thought that charging people who drive into downtown Manhattan might succeed in ways that pleading, cajoling, and engineering never could. Congestion, danger, lack of parking, and aggravation hadn't dissuaded many New Yorkers from driving, and having one of the world's best transit networks wasn't enough. Maybe the price would tip the balance.

The original proposal in PlaNYC was a charge of $8 for vehicles to enter Manhattan anywhere south of 86th Street weekday mornings through early evenings. Faced with a new toll, a driver who wouldn't have thought twice about commuting before might do some quick math and ask herself "Is this trip really necessary?" Beyond reducing congestion itself, the goal of the charge was to raise a projected $380 million a year to improve transit options, reduce crowding on subways and buses, and upgrade the heavily used but aging transit network. This piece was critical. It's not enough to use tolls to get people to change how they get around. Cities need to provide new and more reliable transit options. The congestion charge would give cities the means to do it.

Despite New York City's manifest traffic problems, New York drivers would not be so easily convinced that anything could be done—or even needed to be done—about it. Part of the problem wasn't the policy or the goals but the branding. Congestion pricing was unfortunately named, with two problems, traffic and payment, united in one pithy phrase. It was also awkwardly abstract, rooted more in the basic concept of supply and demand. Inconsistent tolls at New York City bridges and tunnels, which are run by different agencies and authorities, tempt millions of annual drivers to "bridge shop" for the least expensive trip. Instead of taking a direct route across tolled bridges, people drive, some in large trucks, miles out of their way to reach the four toll-free East River bridges to Manhattan: the Brooklyn Bridge, the Manhattan Bridge, and the Williamsburg and Queensboro/Ed Koch bridges. Drivers then course along local streets to reach the Port Authority's Holland Tunnel and Lincoln Tunnel and their free one-way trips to New Jersey. An alternative, more direct trip to New Jersey might really be through Staten Island, where a cash toll at the MTA's Verrazano-Narrows Bridge starts at $16 round trip and can run $124 for a seven-axle truck (and no, that's not a typo as of 2015!). The network incentivizes people to drive through Manhattan for free. Charging vehicles to enter Manhattan would change that message.

Opponents framed the debate not in terms of traffic—Would it or wouldn't it succeed in reducing congestion or improve public transportation?—but as an attack on poorer New Yorkers. Elected officials railed that poorer residents live farther from subway stations and bus stops and had no choice but to drive. Paying a daily congestion pricing fee to drive to work in Manhattan could add up to $2,000 in tolls a year that hit those who can least afford to pay it. Wealthier New Yorkers, the argument continued, wouldn't flinch at the toll and would continue to drive. It should come as no surprise that the chief spokesman making that argument was a state legislator from Westchester County, one of the five wealthiest counties in the state by median income that is heavily populated by commuters.

Residents from Queens, Staten Island, the Bronx, and Brooklyn—the populations congestion pricing was targeted to help—also inveighed that it would be unfair that their tolls would be used to fund a public transit system they did not use. Yet in the example of one borough, Brooklyn, census data showed that 57 percent of households don't even own a car. The households that did own cars enjoyed a median household income a full 100 percent higher than those without cars. And while we may think of Manhattan as the sole business hub in town, about two thirds of Brooklyn workers don't work in Manhattan, commuting instead to work within Brooklyn, in another borough, or in a neighboring county. Those who commute regularly to Manhattan overwhelmingly take public transit. By the time the math of congestion pricing was wrestled to this level, the data showed that 97.5 percent of Brooklyn residents wouldn't have to pay a congestion charge to get to work.

Despite passionate arguments against congestion pricing, New Yorkers backed the proposal 67 percent to 27 percent in a poll, provided that the proceeds would be used to improve transit service. Even the typically raucous editorial boards at New York City's newspapers supported the plan or at least hedged. After an intense national competition for federal funds under the Urban Partnership Program, U.S. transportation secretary Mary Peters offered New York City $354 million to implement a congestion pricing program, conditioned on the state legislature's approval of the plan by spring 2008.

The political battle developed into a six-month full-court press, a blur of meetings, charts, and statistics. A subsequent New York City Council vote to authorize congestion pricing wasn't really close, but the atmosphere in the chambers was no less dramatic, yielding a 30–20 yes vote on March 31, 2008. But elation at the city council vote turned to dejection in Albany. The final decision on congestion pricing wasn't the mayor's or even the city council's alone. New York State prohibits New York City from a range of revenue collection practices without authorization from the legendarily ineffectual state legislature. State legislators in April 2008 smothered the plan without even taking a vote, typical of the institution, led by Sheldon Silver, who stepped down from the assembly speakership in disgrace in 2015, following his arrest and subsequent conviction on charges of corruption. Silver claimed that the assembly would have defeated the proposal had it been brought to the floor for a vote. But by not taking a vote, the assembly deprived New Yorkers of the opportunity to know where their elected leaders stood on the issue and why—and had no way to hold them accountable for the decision.

The news seemed almost unreal, the cowardice particularly galling because the legislature had forced us through so many procedural hurdles and dozens of public meetings, hearings, and media battles, only to do nothing. "What we are witnessing today is one of the biggest cop-outs in New York's history," Mayor Bloomberg spokesman John Gallagher said as the plan foundered.

We had lost this particular battle but had changed the conversation about how New Yorkers get around and who pays for it. The congestion pricing debate has made New Yorkers more receptive to projects like rapid bus systems. And congestion pricing remains on the table. The latest iteration of the tolling proposal is called Move NY, promoted by former transportation first deputy commissioner Sam Schwartz. The new plan, being discussed today at editorial boards, community boards, and political meetings, takes a five-borough view by lowering tolls at crossings where drivers lack good transit alternatives while instituting tolls at others so that motorists pay more or less the same toll wherever they cross—and whenever they enter Manhattan below Sixtieth Street. It may not be this plan, but I remain convinced that it's not a matter of *if* some kind of tolling plan will be introduced in New York; it's a matter of *when*.

4

How to Read the Street

A century-old, fundamental traffic principle, ignored by a century of transportation planners, is that you get what you build for. Building more lanes only creates more traffic. Although decades of evidence confirm this principle, state transportation departments are still staffed with people whose primary mission is to build and maintain more roads. As long as planners widen roads and build new ones; as long as drivers have poor transportation options and remain insulated from the full cost of their trips; and as long as government policies encourage people to live in far-flung suburbs, we will have an even more sprawling urban future.

"This looks like Carvana!"

It was May 2014, and an exuberant Los Angeles mayor Eric Garcetti stood with state transportation officials on a balcony overlooking the Sepulveda Pass and a four-and-a-half-year project to build a ten-mile carpool lane on the northbound 405 freeway. Following an extended construction nightmare, opening a year late and $100 million over budget, just finishing the $1.1 billion job was as close as you could get to car-based nirvana in this town.

If there's any city that's a punch line for car-based planning and traffic, it's Los Angeles, and the 405 (Southern Californians always use the definite article) holds a special stature as one of the worst-of-the-worst roads in the hemisphere. It's a transportation facility where peace of mind dies faster than you can say, "Have a nice day." An average of three hundred thousand vehicles daily cruise that stretch of the Sepulveda Pass at speeds that dip well below twenty miles per hour. Transportation officials wanted to chip away at that delay. By dedicating a northbound lane for carpool vehicles only from which people driving alone are strictly banned, the project filled the final gap in a seventy-mile continuous lane for vehicles carrying multiple occupants. At best, the five-mile extension was expected to cut peak travel times on the Sepulveda section of the 405 by ten minutes. While that may not seem like a lot of time in a commute, every minute saved from the frustration of stop-and-go traffic is a welcome reprieve for Angelenos. It's also evidence that planners are "doing something" about traffic. The carpool lane might encourage more people to share rides, in turn removing a few cars from general traffic lanes, reducing congestion and helping the environment. Those optimistic expectations turned out to be grossly misplaced.

Six months after the lane's opening, a study by a private transportation data-analysis firm found that travel times on the 405 had barely changed or had actually gotten slightly worse. During the peak drive time from four to seven p.m., travel on the northbound 405 from the 10 to the 101 freeways took thirty-five minutes—one minute longer than the same trip in the previous year. With an added lane, everyone expected traffic to improve at least proportionally faster. Yet traffic remained just as bad. So what happened? Did an engineer miscalculate?

To understand how roads like these work, and how to fix them, we need to start at the core of the core, on a city street through the heart of downtown. We need to learn how to read the street.

Like highways, the city streets and sidewalks where much of the world's population now lives are largely bleak, utilitarian corridors, their design invisible to city dwellers. Despite this invisibility, the streets' operating code connects cities and their inhabitants physically, commercially, and psychologically. Virtually all city denizens spend at least part of the day on, along, or crossing the street. Schoolchildren and deliverymen. Commuters heading to work. Residents and visitors ambling around to shopping districts. Tourists threading through the city to local attractions. They walk, they jog, they bike and travel in cars, minivans, buses, and box trucks. And they typically move along a grid-based matrix designed by engineers and decorated with standard-issue traffic controls and markings: zebra-striped crosswalks, hash-marked lanes, red stop signs, and bright yellow school crossing signs—and the functional, often-ignored traffic signals and streetlights. This is effectively urban design for most of the world's population.

On our busy urban avenue it's almost impossible for people to see past the buses, the taxis, ambulances, other pedestrians, delivery trucks, parked and double-parked cars. We don't notice the street un-less it changes. But beyond the moving parts, the street's underlying design is hidden in plain sight. It's a kind of engineering archaeology, as what we see is not just the street as it is today, but also what planners thought the street should be when they designed it fifty years ago or longer.

Many people would glance at the illustration on the next page and say, "It looks like a street." But let's take this model street apart and read between the lanes. This example is a one-way street with four twelve-foot lanes. It's similar, give or take a lane or a foot or two, to thousands of miles of streets that city dwellers live, walk, or work on. It's Spring

A model street: One-way, four twelve-foot lanes, countless road design possibilities.   NACTO/Courtesy of Island Press

Street in Los Angeles, Pitt Street in Sydney, or Camden High Street in London. Two parking lanes flank the road, one on each side along the curb. The two center lanes are dedicated for moving vehicles. Where our model street meets an intersection, pairs of parallel lines perpendicular to the flow of traffic mark the crosswalk where people on foot can cross the forty-eight-foot street with the pedestrian signal.

Let's look more closely at these twelve-foot lanes. Twelve feet isn't a random number. It's a standard width on many highway lanes, as laid out in the federal guideline meant to create highway lanes able to accommodate the widest semis safely. So what's good for the highway must also be good for city streets, right? Not so much. A 2015 Toyota Camry is only about six feet wide, and the vast majority of trucks and commercial vehicles are less than eight and a half feet across. When you multiply the up to six feet of excess lateral space built into every traffic lane, you can begin to see how this street is grossly overbuilt. This model street alone may contain more than twenty feet of excess road space not actually needed to move or park vehicles. Multiply that by hundreds of thousands of miles of lanes in thousands of urban areas around the world and you'll find millions of miles of sidewalks, bus and bike lanes, and public spaces—entire cities—trapped within our streets.

Why are streets and their lanes so wide in the first place? The theory, if someone would explain it, might go like this: wider streets mean more room to move more cars, and wider lanes give cars a buffer so they don't hit one another. So in reality, all this excess space is hidden within thousands of streets simply to give cars breathing room twenty-four hours a day, year-round. With such a generous buffer, streets should be the safest places on earth. Yet they are congested and dangerous. Highway hypnosis makes planners treat city streets like highways, divvying them up into lanes like turnpikes under the theory that bigger is better. Once the street is laid out, the space between sidewalks is presumed to be the domain of the motor vehicle. Each of these assumptions only compounds the wrongheadedness of the one that preceded it.

By reading the street accurately you can reallocate the space already there—no expensive reconstruction required. Two of the four lanes on our model street are reserved for parking and the remaining two for moving traffic. No room for bikes and pedestrians, right? Look again: without eliminating traffic lanes, there is more than enough room to add a bike lane and to shorten the distance that pedestrians must cross by two full lanes. A lane can be dedicated for buses without banning parking or ripping out sidewalks. As if by magic, ample space is available for many uses. How is this possible?

First, we can expand the use of a street by narrowing its lanes. Reducing the width of the two parking lanes that flank the street from twelve to just nine feet leaves more than enough room to park even an oversize vehicle. These dimensions can be reinforced by painting a line on the street marking where the parking lane ends. This simple change can yield six full feet of space that can now be reprogrammed for other uses.

Same street, different way: The same number of traffic lanes but with added room for a protected bike path, bus lane curb extensions for pedestrians that reduce crossing distances from four lanes to two, connecting with a landscaped safety island. NACTO/Courtesy of Island Press

Six feet is more than enough room for a bike lane, and we haven't even touched the moving traffic lanes yet. Now, where will this new bike lane go—between the lane of parked cars in the left part of the picture and a lane of moving traffic? Let's try something different. Look at the parking lane on the far right. You might be accustomed to seeing only parked cars along virtually every curb in every city, but there's no law—legal,

moral, or otherwise—that requires it to be there. It's a convention, a choice. If we place the bike lane where the parking lane was, the parking lane becomes a "floating" lane, parallel to but not alongside the curb. By placing the bike lane on the side of the road opposite the bus stop, bus and bike traffic won't cross paths.

So now we have a bike lane at the curb and a parking lane next to it. If we narrow the two moving lanes from twelve to ten feet each, there is enough room for moving traffic and an additional four feet of roadbed.

This reclaimed space can be added as a buffer between the bike lane and the parking lane so the car doors of people getting out of their vehicles don't swing into the bike lane and "door" a passing bike rider. The remaining two ten-foot traffic lanes are better organized and, by their very narrowness, safer. Clearer markings reinforce these changes and telegraph to motorists that they shouldn't speed or change lanes unnecessarily.

Now, what's going on at the intersection? For the cost of concrete, we can easily extend the sidewalk out into the curbside lane adjacent to the crosswalk. Known as a curb extension, "bulb-out," or "neck-down," this particular extension can create space for passengers to board and exit without the bus having to pull to the curb. By extending the curb into the roadbed on one side and building a pedestrian refuge island on the other, we've reduced two full lanes that pedestrians must cross, cutting nearly in half the territory where people on foot and those in cars are in one another's paths.

The surprising reality about the remaining ten-foot travel lanes is that they are safer than the twelve-footers. Highway-size lanes induce highway speeds and lane-changing tendencies that go with them. Wide-open lanes provide more room for the driver of one car to wind up in another's blind spot. The biggest consideration in how fast people drive isn't the posted speed limit or how traffic signals are timed, but the street's design speed—the vehicle speed that the street was designed to accommodate safely. Traffic engineers assume that people will drive fast on a particular road, so they build wide lanes hoping that they will keep these fast-moving cars farther from one another and thus safer. But the wider lanes don't just accommodate the posted speed limit—they can actually induce higher speeds. When the road removes obstacles to speeding, it cancels out any safety benefits that the extra room would have given.

"In cities," the urban designer Jeff Speck told me, "we set our speed based upon how safe we feel; the speed is a function of our feeling comfortable, which is a function of friction—are there cars coming at me, are there parallel parked cars, how wide are their lines, are there bikes, what are the sight lines?"

Changing the street's geometry by reducing the width of individual lanes, and therefore bringing vehicles closer together, would seem to create the conditions for more collisions and jostling of cars. But a funny thing happens when people driving cars suddenly find themselves in closer quarters on the road: they tend to exercise more caution and drive more slowly, and lower speed is more effective than wider lanes in averting and reducing the frequency and severity of crashes on city streets. Narrow lanes and design changes can provide cues for motorists to slow down and stay in the lane. The driver sees a slimmer, tighter, and more clearly defined lane, hence the nicknames for this kind of intervention: "road diet" or "traffic calming."

Extending the curb at the crosswalk also corrects one of the most basic design flaws in city streets: the rounded, right-angled corner. The very wideness of the crosswalk itself provides no prompt for drivers to slow down, inviting them to make the turn at high speed, and it offers no protection for pedestrians against turning trucks and buses. The grid makes sense to the human sense of order, but this intersection design encourages drivers to "cut" the corner when they turn. On a vast number of city streets, the first step for someone walking is a parking lane, not even a lane necessary to keep vehicles moving. This is the part of the street where people are most likely to walk and it is also the spot where it's hardest for drivers to see. Their sight lines are often blocked by parked vehicles and other obstructions, and by pedestrians losing six inches of height by stepping from the sidewalk into the road. This design needlessly increases the risk of being struck and serves little traffic engineering purpose. Future streets should be built to a different standard.

The missing links in the conventional design are curb extensions. Curb extensions on both sides of a street can give pedestrians nearly twenty fewer feet of moving vehicle space that they have to cross. The extended sidewalk enhances pedestrians' profiles on the street, making them more visible to drivers as they enter the crosswalk. Narrowing the crosswalk may not physically narrow the traffic lanes, but the double-sided extension sends a powerful message to drivers to ease up on the gas.

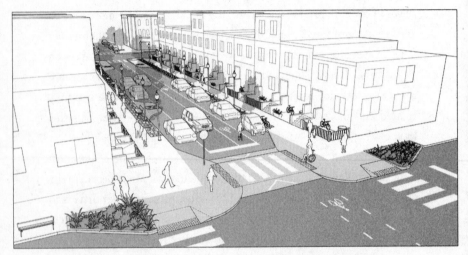

Curb extensions, shaded in this image, decrease crossing distances for pedestrians, reclaiming crosswalk space not needed to move traffic, establishing the presence of people crossing the street and cueing drivers to slow down.   NACTO/Courtesy of Island Press

Two-way streets offer similar challenges and opportunities. The two-way street in the figure on the opposite page has three moving lanes in each direction and parking lanes on both sides. For wide, multilane streets like these, many cities are discovering a design principle that has wide-spread applications: when it comes to lanes, less is more. Fewer but more efficient lanes can move traffic better than more, poorly designed lanes.

Without dedicated lanes for turning vehicles, a three-lane street with traffic in each direction may be little better than a street with only one traffic lane for both directions. For example, a car moving in one direction may be stopped in the leftmost of the three lanes, waiting for a break in traffic moving in the opposite direction before making a left turn. That single, stopped car may block an entire line of cars behind it for a whole light cycle, forcing those drivers to inch their way into the middle lane and slowing that lane as well. The same thing may happen

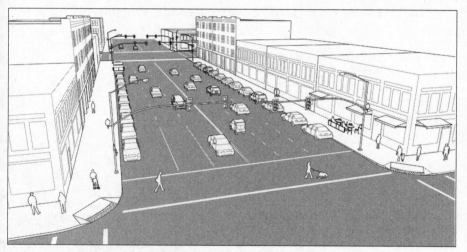

A common two-way, eight-lane street: More than meets the eye.
NACTO/Courtesy of Island Press

at the same time in the far right lane, with a vehicle waiting for a break in pedestrians to cross before turning right. When you add the real possibility that a vehicle may already be double-parked or stopped somewhere in that right lane, you have that much more traffic trying to get around these stopped vehicles via the middle lane. We are asking each lane to do too many things—turns, through traffic, parking—and none is functioning efficiently. The street fails.

Reducing three lanes to two doesn't reduce the amount of traffic that the street can process; it can sustain or even increase traffic capacity. At the intersection, dedicated turn lanes can segregate turning cars from traffic in the main two lanes, letting them proceed straight through the intersection smoothly. The two lanes removed from through traffic can be reassigned for protected bike paths on either side, plus a median in the middle of the road can be allocated to make the street more attractive. Pedestrian islands provide safe stations during the long walk across the street, and one can be designed to accommodate passengers getting on

Less is more: Two efficient lanes plus turn lanes at intersections can be better for everyone than three free-for-all lanes.　NACTO/Courtesy of Island Press

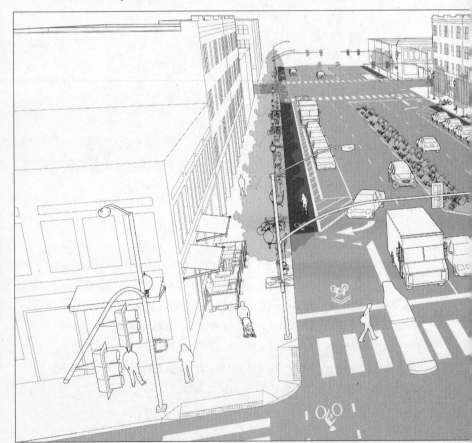

and off the bus. We installed a similar design on Fourth Avenue in Brooklyn, a busy road that carries overflow from the Gowanus Expressway. Travel times and traffic volumes on the street remained little changed while the number of pedestrians injured fell by 30 to 60 percent.

In old cities in the Northeast and even on the West Coast, not all streets are designed on a perfect grid. They can still offer opportunities in their angles, where a street crosses a grid on an angle or where multiple streets meet and create complex crossings. In the next picture, three roads converge, one of them just short of an intersection, leaving

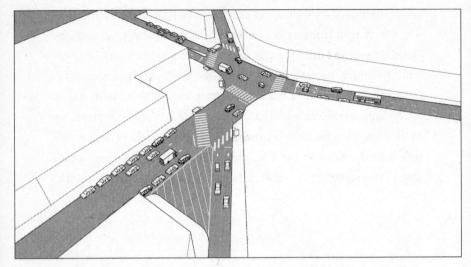

Beyond the grid: Where three roads meet, irregular angles make for abundant unused road. NACTO/Courtesy of Island Press

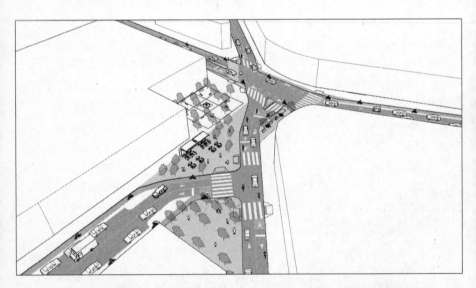

Reconfiguring complex intersections can activate un- or underused road space, as with the plaza in the lower part of the image; or create new space, as with the plaza higher in the image; all while organizing traffic better and providing room for pedestrians and bike riders. NACTO/Courtesy of Island Press

a large triangle of empty space not needed to move cars. This effectively creates a three-way intersection, which is difficult to organize and creates confusion and unsafe conditions.

There are infinite ways to redesign this kind of intersection, but the basic principle is to simplify the street and make it easier to use. In the top image, we can merge the two lower legs of the intersection in order to make clear two-way crossings. This simplified design creates pedestrian space at two different corners. In the bottom image, the space expands the available sidewalk area where there is already open space adjacent to a building, activating that space and providing room for food vendors, tables and chairs, and foot traffic. Bulb-outs, sidewalk extensions, and neck-downs that narrow the street complete the design at all corners of the intersection.

These are just a few of the limitless possibilities hidden within city streets around the world today. There are thousands of ways to tailor the design to the specific geometry and needs of the road, turning what today appear to be traffic liabilities into components of a healthier street tomorrow. The most important factors are observing how a street is being used and building that use into the street itself.

Knowing how to change the street is only one part of the challenge. Understanding what the problem even is in the first place can be more confounding. For most city dwellers, a traffic problem means traffic congestion. It's one of the most vexing issues affecting urban quality of life. Busy streets and highways are ugly, noisy, and inconvenient. Nobody wants to be stuck in traffic and no one wants to live too close to them, yet many cities make it hard to live or get around without depending on these unloved roads. Roads are built for cars, and this combination stifles vital human behaviors like social interaction, physical activity, and spontaneity. And as these roads extend the distance we travel between home, work, and play, they turn our cities' in-between neighborhoods into drive-through corridors.

Ask anyone stuck in traffic what should be done to "fix" it and you probably will get the clear answer: more and wider roads! Compared with most controversial public issues, traffic is seen by every city's self-appointed traffic engineers as the simplest problem to address. When in the driver's seat, people see traffic congestion as evidence that infrastructure hasn't kept up with traffic demand. Too many cars and the road isn't big enough. Just build another lane to accommodate the excess cars and I'll get to work on time. Problem solved, right?

Remember what happened with the 405 at the beginning of this chapter? As we've seen, traffic congestion isn't a matter of too little *supply*—roads—it's a product of overabundant *demand*—too many people driving without credible transportation alternatives. Increasing the supply of road space doesn't alleviate traffic; it almost always allows more people to drive more. If building roads actually resulted in less traffic, then surely after sixty years of interstate highway construction we would all be cruising at highway speed.

Instead, thousands of road-building and -widening projects have resulted in more lanes, more roads, but no less traffic. Evidence has mounted showing that spending billions of dollars on road projects is no more effective at stemming congestion than building *nothing*. That's right: cities that built no new highways had no more (or less) congestion than cities that spent billions on expansions like the 405. A 2009 study by Gilles Duranton and Matthew Turner, two economics researchers at the University of Toronto, compared driving data from cities that invested in new roads from 1980 to 2000 with cities that didn't. The data "suggest a 'fundamental law of road congestion' where the extension of most major roads is met with a proportional increase in traffic." Not just a close correlation, but for every one mile of road built, vehicle miles traveled increased by one mile.

The term of art for this lockstep growth in traffic is "induced" or "latent" demand. It's a tedious topic for those who have seen city after city around the world ignore this fundamental principle and the devastating effect it has on our cities. When modeling the impacts of a project that will increase capacity, traffic planners assume that roughly the same number of people driving on a street today will use the street after the new road or lane is built. Urban designer Jeff Speck, who has seen this assumption play out on the streets of hundreds of cities and towns, says it's the mark of "the fundamental intellectual bankruptcy of traffic engineering as a profession and its unwillingness to acknowledge that environment influences behavior."

"And that plays out both in terms of traffic and in terms of safety," he told me. "In traffic it's induced demand, the idea that you add a lane to absorb traffic without acknowledging that that lane will cause traffic."

After building an eight-lane highway in a major urban area, a city almost invariably finds itself with eight lanes of slow-moving traffic soon thereafter. When, in an effort to ease that traffic, the eight-lane road is expanded by 25 percent to ten lanes, the city will eventually have ten lanes of traffic and nearly 25 percent more traffic, not 25 percent less. What's most dismaying about this planning principle is that it has been almost universally ignored over the last half century. Writing in 1955, at the dawn of the interstate age and the Moses era, urbanist Lewis Mumford observed that trying to address congestion by building more traffic lanes is like trying to prevent obesity by loosening one's belt.

As we have seen, the road tells you how it wants to be used, and conventional traffic studies don't factor in what invariably happens when motorists—who are people, not mathematical constants—are greeted by a wider road: they drive more. Once motorists see that a road has been widened, more people will be inclined to drive more frequently, slightly more confident they won't hit traffic. When combined with natural growth in local population, more people will drive on that road. Maybe they are people who would have lived closer to their job, but once the road opens, the range they are willing to drive increases. The number of miles traveled by car goes up, hitting capacity soon after the road is opened. By building more and wider highways, cities are not building their way out of congestion. They are building how many lanes of congestion they will have.

So if the *capacity* of road isn't the underlying problem behind congestion, what can we do about the *volume*—the supply? Managing people in cars isn't a matter of adjusting streams as you would taps of water. Traffic volumes result from people's transportation choices, and many cities have few, poor, or no alternatives provided by their public transportation networks. Cities today are designed for private vehicles not because it is the most efficient mode, but because most other transportation options were rendered impossible following planning decisions made decades ago. Instead of building new roads, urban planners need to start with building new transportation choices. If cities truly want a future where more people choose to take buses or trains, to bike or walk, then cities must invest in trains and buses, bikes and better streets. Yet, as the New York experience has shown, this seemingly obvious concept is counterintuitive in practice. It is in fact a transportation Copernican revolution. And as in the Renaissance, the battle is not just with the science or locked in a debate among traffic engineers; it's within the culture and the idea of whom streets serve.

Urban engineers have a century of case work that has been inculcated in the autocentric view that transportation *is* a car, and pedestrians, bike riders, and public transit passengers—all street life—are natural enemies of this order. It wasn't always this way but the result of a concerted effort, writes historian Peter Norton. Frightened by the arrival of fast-moving automobiles on city streets and the casualties and congestion they caused in the early twentieth century, residents, schools, and civic associations reacted with horror and sought to limit car speed. The automobile industry offered an alternate version of events: pedestrians

were to blame for their own casualties. Defenders of the private automobile invented the concept of "jaywalking" and created safety campaigns and educational materials for schools that reinforced an idea that
streets are for cars—and that pedestrians should take responsibility for
their own safety by fearing and avoiding the street. Drivers learned that
the street was theirs and to stop for red lights instead of for people, a
principle for the operation of streets that exists to this day.

What if no new roads were built? Would cars eventually pile up in
the middle of the street like so many dirty socks in a laundry hamper?
Another way of looking at it: If California transportation officials hadn't
built the new lane on the 405, would the cars not have come? If cities
tore down old roads instead of repairing or replacing them, what would
happen to the traffic? San Francisco's Embarcadero today is a grand
boulevard lined with palm trees, active waterfront properties and a
port, a streetcar and high-visibility bike lanes. There's no sign today of
the hundred thousand cars that formerly used the Embarcadero Freeway as it ran by the Ferry Building before it was damaged in the 1989
Loma Prieta earthquake. The Embarcadero was one of numerous Bay
Area roadways damaged beyond repair. Mother Nature made real something that San Francisco residents had contemplated but were too afraid
to actually try: tear down the elevated eyesore and improve access to
their famous and picturesque waterfront.

While it may have taken an act of God to change the transportation
network twenty-five years ago, more cities today are choosing new approaches to their elevated roads instead of spending billions to rebuild
what has failed or become obsolete. Madrid tore down a freeway and
created in its place an underground complex of highways, converting
six miles of space into parkland called Madrid Río (Madrid River). Officials in Seoul razed an elevated highway to reveal the humble Cheong-
gyecheon Creek hidden beneath that is now the centerpiece for a park,
programmed with art installations and public events. What was once

shrouded in darkness is now an attraction where thousands of people snap selfies.

Some cities have buried highways as opposed to removing them, a costly task that can have the effect of sweeping traffic problems under the rug. Even as cities accelerate sustainable strategies, the opposite tendency remains as more cities invest billions in traffic-moving projects that can reinforce or expand the city's footprint. After more than a decade of political battles, Seattle in 2011 started to tear down State Route 99, the Alaskan Way Viaduct, which carries about 110,000 cars daily. The viaduct was built in the early 1950s, when many American cities were on highway-building binges. Similar to the Embarcadero Freeway in San Francisco, the viaduct was damaged in a 2001 earthquake. Just as San Francisco replaced its highway with a street-level, pedestrian-friendly boulevard, Seattle opted to build a street-level waterfront park in the footprint of the former viaduct. So far, so good. But they also chose to build a replacement highway tunneled beneath downtown Seattle. Total cost estimate: $3.1 billion.

The boring machine used to dig out the tunnel was so massive—57.5 feet in diameter and weighing 14 million pounds—that Seattleites gave it a big name: Bertha (actually the first name of Seattle's first female mayor). Big Bertha had only started drilling when the drill was damaged and work came to a halt in December 2013, about 1,000 feet into its 9,270-foot path. Because of the drilling technology, the tunnel created behind Bertha was narrower than the drill itself, so it was impossible to retract the drill and fix it. Instead, workers had to dig a massive 120-foot rescue shaft to hoist out the drill head's 2,000-ton mass. Two years elapsed before Bertha was back on track.

While there is seemingly no end to how far suburban Los Angeles is capable of sprawling, or how much Seattleites are willing to spend to keep the same amount of vehicle traffic moving, other cities have taken a different approach with their highways. One of the most frequently

invoked examples of smart development is Vancouver, British Columbia, where city officials in the beautiful West Coast port city made the
explicit decision in the 1960s not to build downtown highways. This
approach complemented progressive zoning rules that encouraged
dense, mixed-use development, increased transit, and initiated a long-
term policy to increase space on the street for pedestrians and cyclists.
Vancouver's downtown today sprouts sleek residential towers built
atop shorter town houses and street-level retail, set back from the street
to let sunlight reach the street. Thousands of bikes cruise Dunsmuir
Street, the city's bike superhighway, and plans are under way to remove
vestiges of the city's driving past, such as the century-old Georgia and
Dunsmuir viaducts.

"Our city has a great reputation but it's tended to be evolutionary
rather than revolutionary," said Brent Toderian, a former Vancouver
city planner and one of the city's foremost public realm thinkers.

This evolution has made the city an example for the rest of the world,
but has not managed to elevate transportation beyond political, passionate, and counterproductive fights when it comes to deciding how to
pay for a city's transportation needs. As a rule, city residents can be
counted upon to express a hatred for their public transportation system
usually reserved for visiting sports teams. And if you ask people to pay
more in fares or taxes to support a service they feel maybe doesn't work
so well, the answer often comes back: *Hell no.*

Vancouver's leaders in spring 2015 put the question to voters in a
referendum on whether to levy a 0.5 percent tax to fund $7.5 billion of
investments over a decade; to revitalize the subway and commuter rail
network; bring new buses to the city; expand ferry service; and build a
new bridge. If officials saw in the vote the political cover they would
need to pass a tax increase, they miscalculated. Critics claimed that
Vancouver's transit system, TransLink, was poorly managed and provided middling service, so voters should deny new funds until it first

resolved its problems, such as the salary of the system's chief executive officer.

"It's become a referendum on just about everything except transit infrastructure," Toderian told me in the weeks before voting was completed. The debate over more funding for transit is "more likely about whether you're mad at the mayor or you think the CEO of TransLink makes too much. . . . And what we got is a polarized campaign instead of an intelligent conversation."

Vancouver voters defeated the plan in 2015 after a withering, five-month campaign. Opponents effectively portrayed Vancouver's transportation network and the people who ran it as inefficient and incompetent, and, in so doing, cut off new sources of funding to guarantee that the agency couldn't do its job efficiently or competently.

"Welcome to our existential crisis," says Gordon Price, an urban planner and former Vancouver city council member. Price says that the referendum wasn't just a defeat of a funding stream, it was a calculated discrediting of government policies in the public interest, and a blow to Vancouver's status as a "green dragon"—a mighty example of an environmentally balanced city.

"If you can get Vancouverites to vote against transit—if you can kill the green dragon in its own den—every politician across the country and across the States and in Australia will look at what happened in Vancouver and be in despair."

Hundreds of cities and municipalities are moving through these same processes, passionately debating whether public transit is worth the investment while attempting futilely to build their way out of congestion with increasingly expensive roads. The result so far has been the worst of both worlds, with congestion and starved transit.

In Los Angeles, the future urban streetscape could be less like the 405 and more like Broadway in that city's downtown. Mayor Garcetti's transportation department, under the leadership of Seleta Reynolds, is revitalizing downtown L.A. with expanded pedestrian space along its own Broadway, and with bike lanes and city-backed curbside patio seating in former parking spaces along Spring Street. A bike master plan is taking shape alongside a Great Streets program to redesign corridors in fifteen neighborhoods and create safer, more walkable communities within the nation's car capital. Metro, its transportation agency, has launched rapid bus networks and gone from zero miles in 1990 to 87 miles of subways and light rail by 2015. The Obama administration proposed $330 million to fund Metro's Purple Line subway extension and create a downtown regional connector system, and the city is working on a $2 billion, 8.5-mile light rail to Los Angeles International Airport. Los Angeles today is the capital of urban transit investment. Still, residents of Beverly Hills protested the planned Westside subway expansion beneath Beverly Hills High School, saying the tunnel was close to an earthquake fault and would create a possible explosion hazard. A judge threw out the case in 2014.

Downtown Los Angeles is also first in line for the city's bike-share program, and the district's progress could easily be a model for pedestrian-friendly and place-making projects in Hollywood, seven miles away. In 2012, then-council member Eric Garcetti worked with his predecessor, Mayor Antonio Villaraigosa, to alter zoning regulations in Hollywood that would allow high-rise residential and commercial buildings. Higher-density buildings would provide needed housing and take advantage of the city's subway system, decreasing dependence on single-occupant vehicles for every trip.

Despite these virtuous-sounding aims, neighborhood residents opposed the plan with an intensity largely absent from the decision to build the traffic-inducing 405: "More is not better, bigger is not better," a president of the local homeowners' association said at a public hearing. "Hollywood needs limits, protections and preservations, not destruction and high density. Please save Hollywood. Once it's lost it will be gone forever."

The up-zoning succeeded. Hollywood is still there. Los Angeles may yet have a chance to develop more like a city and less as an ever-sprawling suburb, but this change won't be without controversy and people fighting it fiercely, on dubious grounds, to maintain streets exactly as they are—even if they are broken, dangerous, congested, and underperforming.

Seattle mayor Ed Murray gets this and isn't betting his city's future on Bertha or the tunnel to replace the Alaskan Way Viaduct. In 2015 he campaigned for a transportation referendum that included a package of street, transit, and state-of-good-repair improvements. While Vancouver voted down a transit referendum just a few months earlier, Seattleites ultimately agreed to $930 million in property tax increases over nine years to fund new rapid bus systems, bike lanes, and radical street and sidewalk redesigns. "Seattle will get moving again," Murry said on election night as it became clear the ballot would win, despite heated opposition. "If current trends continue, while the rest of the nation says no, Seattle says yes—we can be a livable city and an affordable city. Seattle can move forward."

More and more cities are moving forward with plans to expand pedestrian, transit, and biking zones. Dublin, Ireland, in 2015 announced a €150 million ($164 million) plan to improve downtown streets for people who walk, ride bikes, or take transit. London mayor Boris Johnson has embarked on a bike superhighway building spree through the heart of the city, with expenditures on bike lanes tripling to £913 million ($1.4 billion) over ten years.

Paris mayor Anne Hidalgo has led the way with a plan to sharply reduce private vehicles in central Paris by 2020, launching its own €150 million plan to double the city's network of bike lanes and triple ridership to 15 percent of trips. These efforts follow Seville, Spain, which has rapidly developed into the bike capital of southern Europe, with cycling rates growing eleven times over the last decade and with seventy-five miles of protected bike paths built in the city. These sums, while significant, are a fraction of the $3.1 billion being spent in Seattle for the highway tunnel, and far less risky. As of this writing, and as I bury my face in my hands, California's state transportation department is mulling a $5.6 billion tunnel to extend the 710 freeway in Los Angeles, a process that could take six years of Carmageddon construction.

By designing infrastructure and developing real estate to support people who walk, ride bikes, or take public transit, cities aren't merely meeting existing demand, they are creating demand for the kind of growth the city wants to see and needs to survive. If planning past is prelude, cities that invest in sustainable streets will get what they build for.

5

Follow the Footsteps

Before there was a New York City, there was a Broadway. Originally *breede weg* in pre-Colonial Dutch Nieuw Amsterdam, Broadway was one of the island's first roads at a time when there was an actual wall built at Wall Street to keep out native incursions and Five Points was a pond within a swamp. New Amsterdam was built atop, over, and through existing footpaths. The resulting settlement was akin to a medieval European town, with short buildings and narrow, curved streets. Roads emanated in every direction, with activity concentrated around miniature villages through the eighteenth century. What is today Broadway followed the outline of the Wickquasgeck Path, formed by the feet of the Native American inhabitants who made Manhattan an original walking city.

There were likely practical reasons why Broadway took the path it did; it may have been the shortest distance between pre-Colonial settlements in Manhattan, avoiding hills, rivers, and swamps. In a sense, Broadway was New York City's earliest desire line. Desire lines are naturally occurring

A worn grass path created by thousands of footsteps illustrates where a sidewalk, bus stop, and crosswalk should be on Mosholu Parkway in the Bronx. NYC DOT

travel patterns that reflect where people naturally want to travel. In modern urban planning, desire lines are the natural, spontaneous way that people use public spaces, often contradicting the way the space was designed. These signatures are usually direct, practical, and leave physical evidence, like a footpath worn into a park lawn where pedestrians cut a corner to get from one sidewalk to another. They may also become visible over time and reveal themselves deductively, such as when people ride bikes through a park for one block to reach a bridge entrance instead of taking a three-block route along one-way streets.

Desire lines are the native operating code for a new approach to urban design. Instead of asking why people aren't following the rules and design of the road, we need to ask ourselves why the rules and design of the road aren't following the people. If a street tells people on foot to cross at marked crosswalks hundreds of feet distant, they may instead opt to cross, illegally and dangerously, midblock to reach their destination. Desire lines are a road map of opportunity, and they represent a challenge to the view of streets as places to move cars and the dogma that isolating people from the streets is the only way to protect them.

Viewing sidewalks as valuable space and understanding how people want to use them is critical to activating the entire street and the cities defined by them. Sidewalks aren't raised concrete streets for pedestrians. They are the front yards for city dwellers, as important as any suburban lawn. Whether neighborhood sidewalks or commercial corridors like Fordham Road in the Bronx, Nostrand Avenue in Brooklyn, Victory Boulevard on Staten Island, Flatbush Avenue in Brooklyn, or the warren of narrow streets in Manhattan's Chinatown and Little Italy—these in-between places are a stage for New Yorkers, the urban filament where people sense and connect to the city's energy.

In walkable cities, sidewalk design can encourage walking by creating opportunities for things to do and see along the way. This could be shopping, eating, or clustering services in a particular area, which can enhance connectivity and eliminate the need for cars to run multiple errands. And sidewalk life isn't just about movement. In a kind of urban koan on New York City's streets, people sitting on fire hydrants and leaning on light poles, buildings, and railings daily make a silent but profound statement: there is no place on our streets and sidewalks to stop and do nothing. Yet doing nothing is paradoxically one of the animating forces in a city.

Walking is a complicated language. Unlike cars on a street, people on sidewalks are free to walk in both directions or in jagged lines. But among the billions of trips people make on foot every day, there are relatively few collisions and people are generally able to walk at different speeds, stop, and turn around without needing marked lanes or causing traffic jams or lethal pileups. People know how to read the sidewalk, and there are unspoken, unmarked lanes that people intuitively understand.

Closest to the building, on the left in our image on page 77, is an

A desire line on 51st Street between Sixth and Seventh avenues in Midtown Manhattan, where hundreds of pedestrians daily cross midblock to reach the entrance of a pedestrian arcade (at left) instead of walking hundreds of feet to the corner crosswalks.   NYC DOT

Desires fulfilled. By following where people crossed the street, we revealed a new crossing between Sixth and Seventh avenues. We called it 6½ Avenue, in a nod to Harry Potter, hinting at the simple magic that paint and planters can provide for pedestrians.

area where people can stop to finish a conversation when leaving or entering the building, or wait for a date or a ride. Next is the walking lane in the center, ideally five to seven feet wide in residential areas and eight to twelve feet wide in downtown or commercial areas. Next to the pedestrian zone on the right of the image is the street furniture or curb area, which may be lined with parking meters, utility poles, mailboxes, or streetlights and thus an ideal zone to place other street furniture. We don't usually think of benches or planters as "furniture," in the

Sidewalks are the front yards for city residents and the front door for local businesses. Designs that enhance the pedestrian experience at the street level will add to the quality of life in neighborhoods and support local commercial districts.   NACTO/Courtesy of Island Press

same sense as a La-Z-Boy or a potted ficus we add to our living rooms. But there are increasing numbers of amenities that can line this area, including bike racks or bike-share stations, newspaper racks, and, if you're lucky, pits for shade-giving trees.

We've plotted out an ideal sidewalk, but most city sidewalks don't look this good. So how do we get to there from here? By identifying the desire lines. In the case of most cities, we are not designing a new street as much as we are revealing what is already there. Working in New York City with the Danish architect and urban designer Jan Gehl (whom I hired after seeing his work in Copenhagen), we undertook a detailed study to understand *how* New Yorkers actually use their streets. Instead of laying rubber tubes across a street connected to a counting machine to count only passing cars, Gehl's team of dozens of trained public life surveyors fanned out across the city to look closely at how people on foot use city spaces. How many people were stopping? How long did they linger? How long were streets so crowded that they impeded business and transportation? How many building fronts were closed, dilapidated, or uninviting?

To quantify the quality and not the mere physicality of the public space, they counted pedestrians in the study area every ten minutes, timed how long people stayed in a space, and observed whether they sat and ate lunch or read a newspaper. The team also assessed how crowded a sidewalk was; twelve people per minute per yard of sidewalk width is the rule-of-thumb cutoff before people on foot start looking for alternate routes or walk in the street. They looked at how many obstacles blocked the sidewalk. This was a radically different approach, requiring observation and qualitative measurements from trained observers sent out to focus on the qualities of the interactions that people had with the public realm.

The study focused on Broadway and some of New York's busiest streets. On Main Street in Flushing, Queens, pedestrians outnumber all vehicle passengers by two to one, yet they have less than one third of the street space. Exacerbating the crowded sidewalks are newsstands, vendors, and other obstructions that cut walkable space in half and invite "pedlock"—gridlock for pedestrians. The narrow sidewalk forces pedestrians to spill into the street, where they block cars and drag down transit. This was most telling in the lack of children and older people counted on the street—they were only 10 percent of the pedestrian population even though they comprise 30 percent of the city's population, a sign that they were avoiding the street out of fear for their safety.

The study opened the door to the many imbalances and opportunities with the street. The challenge was figuring out how to restore the balance and elevate the importance of pedestrians and other vulnerable people on the street. By following the footsteps and tracing an outline of the way people use the street today, we could uncover the design of the city we will want to live in tomorrow. These streets of tomorrow can be outlined today in paint.

Yes, paint.

Transforming a car-clogged street into inviting shared space doesn't always require heavy machinery, complicated reconstruction, or millions of dollars. Planners can reorder a street without destroying a single building, double-decking a street, or building a streetcar, light rail system, or highway interchange. It can be accomplished quickly by using the basic materials that every city has access to—in New York City's case more than six thousand miles of streets—and the basic stock that all city transportation agencies already have in their supply depots or available through existing contracts.

Yes, I mean paint. Hundreds of thousands of gallons of it. Whether it's off-the-shelf industrial paints, thermoplastic (a polymer cooked directly onto pavement), or epoxy-modified acrylic coatings, paint has an amazing ability to telegraph a road's rules of order through color, texture, and geometry. Combined with the other basic transportation tools, such as concrete lane dividers and plastic stanchions and reflectors, these simple materials are the building blocks of innovative new public space.

The mind-set required for such an approach is something I learned from my father, Orhan Sadik-Khan. A Tatar who grew up in wartime Europe and was educated at the American University of Cairo, he emigrated to the United States as a young man to attend Stanford Business School. He was the biggest influence on my life—funny, smart, imaginative, wildly successful, and never afraid to embark on a new mission. He spoke five languages but was fluent in the most important one—understanding people. He brought a direct approach to challenges, not surprising given his adventure-laden childhood, and gave me one of the most useful pieces of advice that I have ever heard: throw mud balls at the wall and see what sticks. I understood this to mean that not everything you try works out. What's important is to see what works, and keep trying.

Our first attempt to refashion a street was in the picturesque DUMBO (Down Under the Manhattan Bridge Overpass) neighborhood of Brooklyn, where our team met with representatives of businesses to repurpose the roadbed beneath the Manhattan Bridge. At the base of one of the bridge's arches, a frontage street runs on an angle against the grid, creating triangles of unused space, not unlike what we saw at the complicated intersections in chapter 4. More than a dozen cars parked on one such triangle of underused space at Pearl Street, putting this scrap of cobblestone on the short list for the World's Most Picturesque Parking Lots. The mere fact that city transportation representatives were reimagining anything was itself a sea change. The department was then viewed largely as a signs-and-signals bureau, typically making headlines only for traffic management, such as turn restrictions for vehicles on Midtown's crosstown streets to help unclog rush hour traffic.

Working with community representatives in the summer of 2007, we developed a plan to reprogram the parking spaces as a pocket plaza, cordoning the area with space-defining thermoplastic that sends the message for cars to keep out. Throwing paint (as my mud balls), we used a vibrant green epoxy acrylic coating to mimic an open "green space," giving a cue to pedestrians that the triangle was intended for them, then we furnished it with patio tables and chairs to remove any doubt. Large soil-filled pots planted with saplings were added on the periphery, along with surplus granite blocks from bridge projects. These multipurpose amenities offered shade in the summer and made the rough asphalt seem more humane. It provided protected seating in a beautiful neighborhood that lacked space for people to stop and relax. The topper was that the local business improvement district agreed to fund the maintenance of the plaza—cleaning and sweeping the space and taking in the seats and tables every evening.

The space transformed from a place where people wanted to park

Pearl Street plaza in DUMBO, one of New York City Department of Transportation's first place-changing projects, in 2007. It required only the basic tools already in every transportation department's arsenal: paint and the street space already there. Even years later, people still believe that these before and after pictures are a designer's renderings, too vivid and appealing to be real-life images. NYC DOT—Ryan Russo

into a place where people wanted to be. Workers in nearby buildings brought lunches to the tables sheltered beneath the plaza's umbrellas with coffees and snacks purchased at local cafés and food trucks. The transformation was fast—a couple of weeks—and easily integrated into the neighborhood. The mud ball stuck. Unfortunately, my father died just days before we cut the ribbon on that first plaza. I think of him every time I walk through one.

These interventions worked in a traffic enclave like DUMBO where there is little through traffic. The bigger question was whether they would work in other settings, like a free-for-all Manhattan intersection. In Manhattan, we quickly proved that this intervention was no fluke by replicating our results at Ninth Avenue and 14th Street. The complex

Ninth Avenue and 14th Street, on the border of Chelsea and the Meatpacking District. Former lanes for uptown traffic on the left were reversed, allowing downtown lanes to be converted into an asphalt triangle big enough for a community-maintained plaza. This project

and traffic-choked street was left over from the mid-twentieth century when the area was filled with meatpackers and old-world industry. By 2007, the neighborhood was alive with new office space, the Chelsea Market retail complex, and nightlife. Preparations were under way for the High Line, near Ninth Avenue, guided by the leadership of New York's planning commissioner, Amanda Burden, and it was becoming clear that the area would soon resemble the nearby upscale Greenwich Village, abandoning its bleak past as an after-hours drug-scoring, cruising strip. We reversed two uptown lanes on Ninth Avenue between 14th and 16th streets to downtown only. By doing so, we no longer needed three downtown lanes in the center of the street near 14th, so we cordoned off the triangle of suddenly in-demand new space with

solidified the rapid plaza design palette and showed how smart traffic management could reprogram street space without causing traffic congestion. Soon after, an Apple store opened at the location and Google moved in just up the street. NYC DOT—Ryan Russo

thermoplastic paint and texturized gravel. What happened to the traffic that used those two uptown lanes? The grid happened. The relatively small volume of uptown traffic on Ninth Avenue was easily accommodated on side streets, and delivery trucks could reach businesses by changing their routes slightly.

The opening of the plaza was reported in a relatively new transportation and urbanism news platform, *Streetsblog*, which covers the quotidian news of street design and would become the most attentive and enlightened chroniclers of the urban revolution unfolding on New York City's streets. They wrote the stories that readers would never find in newspapers and hyperlocal blogs obsessed with conflict, detailing lane widths and the minutiae of signal timing and turn lanes, and they treated safety with grave seriousness. They were partisan at times, calling out elected officials for obstructing changes to the street, critiquing arguments by reporters and columnists they felt were lacking, or amplifying arguments that didn't get ink anywhere else.

"If DOT's new plazas on Willoughby and Pearl Streets in Brooklyn are any indication," *Streetsblog* wrote in these early days, "the demand for this type of public space is huge and it's going to be a hit with lunchtime and evening crowds regardless of the proximity to busy traffic." These words were among the first of hundreds of posts on our projects to appear on the site, which has since expanded to cities across the nation.

The support of neighborhood groups and the absence of traffic complications at Ninth Avenue and 14th Street helped establish an immediate public acceptance of the changes. Once you changed a space, its new configuration became obvious and unassailable, and people immediately abandoned whatever attachments they had to the way it used to be. The transformation of the street itself was the best example and catalyst for its approval. This understanding—remarkably simple but also remarkably powerful—helped solidify the strategy of trying out change instead of endlessly waiting for change to come out of a drawn-out process designed to avoid disagreement at all cost. The strategy, process, and tools used in DUMBO and at Ninth Avenue and 14th Street provided the street-design and community-outreach template for hundreds of projects to come, setting us up for the greatest transformation yet: Broadway.

The problem with modern Broadway started in 1811 when New York's planners laid out the city's grid system but retained diagonal Broadway. Following the road's original footpaths, Broadway cuts across the grid, carving three-way intersections wherever it intersects both an avenue and a cross street. In the process it creates the iconic traffic gorges that today we call Times Square, Herald Square, Madison Square, and Union Square. Less beloved than the squares are the triangular firing squads of traffic where these three streams of traffic meet, creating a compound transportation/engineering problem of time and space that could dumbfound astrophysicists.

While city traffic signals can be on a sixty-second cycle, providing, say, thirty seconds of green light time to one direction of traffic at a time, what happens when you must assign green light time for a third stream of traffic? One option, giving only twenty seconds of green light time to each of the three directions, may not be enough time for a group of vehicles to make it through the intersection on one green signal, or long enough for a pedestrian to cross the street. Another option is to add green time to the third direction of traffic, say thirty seconds. This in turn will add to the time that drivers in the other two streams will have to remain stopped. Instead of waiting thirty seconds at a red light for a green light, drivers will have to wait for the two thirty-second green signals of the two other streams of traffic, doubling their wait time to one minute. Meanwhile, even more traffic backs up at the red light, reducing the possibility that they can all get through the intersection on a single green light. The result? Traffic congestion.

Another "problem" for traffic: people. People's desire lines often don't correspond to traffic signs, signals, and crosswalks supposedly designed for everyone's safety. This was one of the problems we had in mind while looking at Madison Square, where Broadway meets Fifth Avenue and 23rd Street, in the shadow of the landmark Flatiron Building. Traffic on 23rd Street at Fifth Avenue was heavy enough that cars often had trouble making it through the intersection on a single light cycle. Factoring in Broadway traffic made it only more toxic.

From the pedestrians' view on 23rd Street, crossing the combined streams of traffic from Fifth Avenue and Broadway was a harrowing 170-foot, seven-lane journey. In reality, a configuration this large tells pedestrians to fend for themselves, crossing against the light and looking

Madison Square: Follow that man! His life may be in peril but in his steps are the outlines of what's needed at this 170-foot-wide expanse of asphalt.   NYC DOT

for breaks in traffic—and often getting stranded on safety islands in the middle of the road when the light turns red. The confusion and long wait times for a Walk signal frustrated hundreds of pedestrians daily into abandoning the crosswalk and cutting across the street midblock. In these dangerous desire lines, we saw the outline of a safer street design. The solution was elegant and started not at the intersection itself but one block upstream, just north of 24th Street where Broadway and Fifth Avenue first intersected: a redesigned intersection that fit in better with the grid, consolidating Broadway vehicle traffic onto southbound Fifth Avenue or Broadway. This alteration didn't fundamentally change the traffic pattern but merely simplified it. The better-regulated merge upstream meant we no longer needed as many southbound traffic lanes at 23rd Street. This let us reclaim two full lanes of Broadway roadbed just above 23rd and three lanes of Broadway just below it, east of the Flatiron Building. In the immense wedge of former traffic lanes above 23rd Street we outlined a plaza in thermoplastic and filled in the remaining space with a texturized gravel treatment adhered to the asphalt, evoking the compacted gravel of pedestrian paths in Paris's Jardin du Luxembourg or nearby Bryant Park, but at a fraction of the cost and time.

A stretch of asphalt empty of cars was an invitation for human-scale street life to emerge. Minutes after workers set out the first construction barrels to detour traffic and start work on the plaza, a group of art students materialized, sat on the blacktop, and started to sketch nearby buildings. This was one of the most moving examples of urban place making and it illustrates just how hungry people are for public space. By looking at where people placed their feet and posteriors, we saw the outline of the city we needed to build. The people took care of the rest.

By September 2008, within less than three months, the plazas at Madison Square were ready—light speed by municipal standards. Mayor Bloomberg and representatives of local business associations cut

Madison Square in progress: Following the footsteps of pedestrians, we created sixty-five thousand square feet of pedestrian space in former roadbed at Madison Square, which was instantly occupied by New Yorkers from the first moment that construction barrels were placed on the street. The square returned to Madison Square: Bonded gravel, tables, chairs, and umbrellas create an urban oasis where cars once roared.   Top: Courtesy of the Flatiron/23rd Street Partnership. Bottom: Seth Solomonow

the ribbon on what totaled sixty-five thousand square feet of pedestrian space at the square and along Broadway, an urban expanse larger than a football field in the middle of the city, and the most significant change to Broadway in decades. People immediately occupied the space as if it were always there. Less noticed was that the project also removed one of Broadway's three moving traffic lanes south of 42nd Street all the way to 25th Street, placing both a bike lane at the curbside and pedestrian plazas in former parking spaces. Traffic moved as well as before but more safely, with better organization.

An unexpected surprise from the Madison Square plaza was how it emerged immediately as a popular gathering place despite its location adjacent to one of Manhattan's great parks. Why would so many people choose the plaza over the park? "For the same reason that people at a dinner party gather in the kitchen instead of the living or dining room," says Andy Wiley-Schwartz, who helped design the spaces and got community leaders to step up and take care of them. From the plazas, New Yorkers and visitors alike can watch the parade of people walking and take in views uptown of the Empire State Building and the Flatiron Building downtown, unobstructed by scaffolds, utility poles—or park trees. "People want to be where the energy and the activity are, and that's where they naturally gravitate," Wiley-Schwartz says.

Some New Yorkers who had been accustomed to the street's previous alignment stopped in their tracks in disbelief, unable to figure out exactly what had happened and where exactly all the new space had come from. Others, true to their New York natures, barely noticed and kept walking. Each step in this evolution seemed monumental in itself, yet New Yorkers took to the changes instantly, giving us the confidence to take the strategy to its natural next step at one of the most famous patches of real estate in the world: Times Square.

6

Battle for a New Times Square

In Times Square today, a wide-angle camera lens captures thousands of pedestrians spread across two-and-a-half-acre ribbons of pedestrian space with a right angle of traffic cutting through. It's difficult to recall that just a few years ago, this balance was completely reversed and Times Square was a Gordian knot of traffic. When I first walked through Times Square with the eye of a commissioner, 89 percent of the 183,000 square feet of space between buildings from 43rd to 47th streets belonged to cars, even though 82 percent of the people passing through—356,000 a day—did so on foot, spilling off the sidewalk into the street, with traffic whizzing by. Times Square by that point had already outgrown most of its legendary seediness and shed the peep-show theaters that were the backdrop for *Midnight Cowboy* (and the offices where I worked for David Dinkins's 1989 mayoral campaign). By 2008 the business profile of the square had changed into a mix of tchotchke shops and modern retailers alongside the established hotels and theaters, and the streets were swarmed day and night and serenaded by an infamous guitar-playing cowboy, clad only in white underwear.

But beneath the showbiz glare of Times Square lay a fundamental transportation problem: 137 percent more pedestrians were struck by cars in Times Square than on adjacent avenues, a tragic product of the masses of people walking in the road. The streets themselves were old and warped, pooling with water after every heavy rain. The existing roadbed was basically composed of layers of street strata, with streetcar rails and other remnants of bygone transportation eras paved over the decades. It was a classic transportation problem hidden in plain sight. And that problem, once again, was Broadway, which meets Seventh Avenue at Times Square and Sixth Avenue at Herald Square, creating wide, irregular intersections. Instead of trying to force Broadway to work with the grid, we looked at how to make the grid work better without Broadway.

In late 2008, we initiated a plan to correct this anachronism and its dangerous consequences, resulting in one of the most transformative and rapid redesigns of a public space in modern urban history. By closing diagonal Broadway to cars at Times and Herald squares, we restored the right angles of the traffic grid. Along Seventh Avenue in Times Square, the street was reconfigured with a fourth driving lane. The traffic signals were retimed to give motorists more "green time"—the length of the green light. Clearer signaling and simplified intersections created safer crosswalks. Pedestrians had fewer lanes to cross and wouldn't have to guess where the next car was coming from.

Farther downtown at Herald Square, instead of slicing green light time three ways where Broadway, 34th Street, and Sixth Avenue collide, simply taking Broadway out of the grid would leave the two remaining traffic streams with 50 percent more green light time for drivers—or walkers or bikers. On Sixth Avenue the length of the green light increased from thirty-two seconds to fifty-three seconds; on Seventh

Avenue the duration of a green light increased from forty-five to fifty-four seconds. In both cases, the simplified timing also meant shorter waits at red lights for everybody. We estimated that travel times would improve by 37 percent through Herald Square and by 17 percent through Times Square.

In the process of fixing the grid for better traffic management, removing vehicles from Broadway created vast tracts of new pedestrian space for the 82 percent of people in Times Square who walked. Pedestrians could safely stop, snap pictures, and take in the city without creating pedlock.

"I remember when she came and told me about it, and I signed on," Bloomberg later told a reporter about my pitch to close Times Square. "Well, first I thought it was the stupidest idea I'd ever heard. Ten minutes later she had convinced me," he said.

That didn't mean Bloomberg had accepted the proposal at face value. It just started the process. The original plan slimmed Broadway by one lane and added plazas at every square from 59th Street all the way down to Union Square at 17th Street. Bloomberg wanted to see if the plan would work before extending it south of 23rd Street, leaving Union Square out of the initial project. This still left the hardest parts, Times Square and Herald Square, where the Macy's Thanksgiving Day Parade concludes next to its flagship store. Bloomberg was right in that if the project worked at Times and Herald squares, it would be easy to extend it to Union Square. And he also insisted on a dedicated right-turn lane at 45th Street, letting vehicles reach side street theaters.

The mayor was also reassured by the fact that the project would begin as a pilot and then be reassessed after six months to ensure that it did what we said it would do. Experimentation is embedded in Mike Bloomberg's DNA. Having created his own financial data and information empire, Bloomberg had little patience for people who argued against even trying something new.

The decision to redesign Times and Herald squares came just as the 2009 political season was gearing up. Bloomberg and the city council had simultaneously enraged opponents and elated supporters with a controversial and successful effort to reverse term limits, allowing the city's elected officials to run for a third term, citing the urgency posed by the economic crisis of 2008. It was a heated campaign. At the final meeting on the project, most of Bloomberg's advisers objected to implementing the Broadway plan within six months of Election Day, which would court political risk and traffic disaster as New Yorkers decided whom to vote for. Bloomberg bristled at aides who recommended that he postpone the project until after the election: "I don't ask my commissioners to do the right thing according to the political calendar," he told them. "I ask my commissioners to do the right thing, period." The remark still gives me goose bumps.

Reviewing the Times Square plan, Mayor Bloomberg's communications director, Jim Anderson, knew that Times Square would be deeply scrutinized, more intensely than the intervention at Madison Square. He focused on the green time that the plan would give to drivers in Midtown and built a public relations strategy around it: this wasn't merely a plaza that would give people a nice place to walk; this was a solution to Midtown congestion. This messaging was a masterstroke that would help convince New Yorkers that the plan was at least worth trying. We sat around a table in an alcove at City Hall, brainstorming what to call this project. Anderson's deputy, Farrell Sklerov, blurted out what would become the project's name: "Green Light for Midtown."

As we worked with the neighborhood's hospitality, entertainment, and commercial industries, led by Tim Tompkins, president of the Times Square Alliance, and with business leaders on Thirty-fourth Street, including Macy's, the final design took shape. The plan created more green light time for people driving cars, and pedestrians would have an additional two and a half acres of public space. At a project cost of $1.5 million—

a tiny fraction of what it would cost to reconstruct a little-used street in Brooklyn for cars—and using only paint, markings, signs, and planters, this was the public space deal of the century. It worked out to less than $14 per square foot of real estate at the Crossroads of the World. This was a bargain that might not have been matched in the city since the Dutch purchase of Manhattan four centuries before, adjusting for inflation.

On a cold morning, February 26, 2009, in a hotel dining room overlooking a Times Square pulsing with high-wattage LED screens, the mayor unveiled the plan for reporters. "This midtown traffic mess is one of those problems that everyone always talks about, and you always say there's nothing you can do about traffic," he said. "Well we're not going to just sit back, we're going to try to do something about it."

This was a bold declaration in front of the New York City media, which, while having lain relatively low over much of the previous two years, now suddenly was paying close attention. The plan was obvious fodder for the tabloids: the mayor and his transportation commissioner think they can close one of the city's major arteries through the heart of its densest and most chaotic locations—a virtual black hole of traffic. *How can closing one of the busiest streets in the world make traffic better?* The idea seemed insane to many observers.

In the three months between announcement and implementation, the plan for Times Square became as much a public relations campaign as a transportation engineering or construction challenge. The race was on to present the details to everyday New Yorkers, particularly those who lived and worked in the neighborhood, before they could be preemptively spooked by daily headlines. On one track, we conducted a packed calendar of public meetings, most of them positive and constructive, as we presented the plan to community boards and theater and property owners, holding their hands and explaining how traffic would still be able to find its way to, through, and around Times Square. The project could not have proceeded without their support.

A public space revolution at the Crossroads of the World:
Broadway at Times Square was a river of traffic dating
back centuries. NYC DOT

Closing the roadway to vehicles in 2009 created an instant river of people on Broadway and quickly made the square one of the world's biggest pedestrian and retail destinations. The project also restored the grid and pushed Seventh Avenue through Times Square at a right angle, simplifying traffic.   NYC DOT

On the other track, media began to predict the End of Times Square. "Dead End Streets" and "The Wrong Crusade" screamed the headlines in just one of the tabloids, where one writer forecast that "the 'experimental' scheme will create a broad loitering zone along the Broadway side of the bowtie, where we can avail ourselves of such dubious pleasures as noshing alfresco on benches. Never mind that New York's climate is suitable for that less than half the year. Never mind that sidewalks are meant for walking, not idling." New York's cabbies predicted a gridlock end-of-times with drivers unable to stop for fares or move once they found one. Other papers and editorial boards were skeptical but hedged. In classic New York fashion, they wanted to reserve the right to gloat if the plan went horribly awry or say it was no big deal if it succeeded: let's give Bloomberg and Sadik-Khan enough rope to hang themselves. "If it all works," a tabloid editorialized, "Sadik-Khan will be a small hero. If it fails, she'll be a goat."

The time had finally come to just do it. At about seven p.m. on Memorial Day eve, surrounded by DOT road crews and curious onlookers, we looked at one another as if to say, "How hard can this be?" We held our collective breath and rolled, dragged, slid, and shifted blaze-orange traffic construction barrels into place. With just a few pieces of these inexpensively produced, factory-fabricated plastic containers, the traffic-choked legend of Broadway was officially closed to cars through Times Square.

In a moment of panic hours before the closure, we thought about those art students who immediately sat down on the street in Madison Square. Where are the 356,000 people who walk through Times Square daily going to sit down once we open Broadway for pedestrians? We had café chairs and tables on order, but the wheels of municipal procurement didn't move as fast as our traffic barrels, and it would be weeks before they arrived. The moment called for creativity and a bit of dumb luck. Tim Tompkins of the Times Square Alliance made feverish phone calls to find cheap seats, locating 376 beach chairs in lollipop colors at $10.74 each from Brooklyn's Pintchik hardware store. The result was an immediate Broadway sensation. Within minutes of the closure there wasn't a free beach seat in the house. Families plopped down with their shopping bags, sharing a laugh, reminiscing about seeing a show, and many just gazed up at the lights as if the chairs had always been there. People could do something as simple as stop and take a picture without fear of being run over or mowed down by a taxi or a surly New York driver. Tap dancers strutted and musicians performed as crowds gathered to watch. Hot dog vendors handed out free franks. Some visitors brought baseball gloves and played catch in the suddenly open space.

Faced with the dramatic reinvention, the media debated not the merits of the change, but whether the beach chairs were too kitschy. "I've had people say to me both that it's a stroke of genius and that I'm the king of trailer trash," Tim Tompkins told *The New York Times*. "People seem to be jumping right past the issue of whether this should be a pedestrian space to what it should look like." Late-night television host David Letterman, whose studio was on Broadway just uptown from Times Square, was nonplussed. Times Square had become "a petting zoo," he said, that "encouraged [tourists] to bring coolers and sit in the intersection."

The fact that beach chairs made headlines and not traffic marked a victory in the global movement for public space. Once completed, there was no longer much argument about whether it was a good idea. The chairs lasted barely a month before they were replaced with more durable bistro chairs and tables. Those that survived the sit-fest were sold on eBay, but I keep one of the original beach chairs by my desk in my office. It's a simple affirmation, not just in New York but anywhere: in a city without seats, a beach chair can be king.

Alas, occupied beach chairs aren't themselves metrics for a successful transportation project. We needed data. Bloomberg wanted to know the measurable impact of the project on traffic, safety, and local businesses. Our forecasting model projected that traffic would move better. We had won the public relations campaign as the plazas immediately became as much a part of New York as Central Park or Rockefeller Center. But how did it stack up as the traffic project we had promised?

We produced what was then one of the most sophisticated evaluation reports created by a city transportation department for a single project. It also marked a shift in how we would measure out streets and projects from this moment on. Traffic data are traditionally gathered by transportation professionals driving cars dozens of times through an area before and after a project, measuring how fast they traveled on average—a practice known as the floating car technique. Bloomberg was skeptical of this approach. Traffic can change dramatically from

Miracle on 34th Street and Broadway: New pedestrian plazas turn a triangular

minute to minute. Maybe a driver would hit an unlucky string of red lights or a lucky string of greens, skewing the results. Maybe the driver would deliberately drive slowly before the project and then floor it afterward to prove that traffic moved faster and that the project worked. Knowing that our data had to convince the mayor, we searched for a better traffic yardstick less susceptible to bias. We discovered the best traffic measurement device a transportation commissioner could ask for: the humble yellow taxicab.

GPS units recently installed in each of New York City's thirteen thousand yellow taxis were already producing troves of taxi data daily. Multitudes of cabbies drive in and around the Times Square area, transmitting data about the distance and duration of every trip, allowing an analysis of average speed—and providing a virtual MRI of real-time

firing squad of traffic into a dense new pedestrian hub.   NYC DOT

traffic. If you had asked any of the cabbies in those taxis, you would have gotten a unanimous, almost violent answer: *Times Square traffic got worse!* Cabbies told any reporter who would listen that the reworking of Broadway through Times and Herald squares caused traffic jams, slower speeds, and fewer fares. Yet our study reviewed data from 1.1 million of these cabbies' own taxi trips through Midtown and determined that traffic overall moved 7 percent *faster* than before Broadway closed. Uptown traffic moved better in west Midtown, centered on Sixth Avenue at 34th Street, which was simplified from three streams of traffic to an orderly two. So traffic was moving better, despite the fact that we had created two and a half acres of pedestrian space.

Traffic was the first hurdle. The most important data point is how much safer it is to walk around Times and Herald squares these days. There are now 80 percent fewer people walking in the street. The redesign changed the street to follow pedestrians' desire lines. With fewer people walking in driving lanes, the number of pedestrians injured in car crashes dropped 35 percent. The safety effect extended well beyond the plazas as injuries for *everyone*—including people in cars—plummeted by 63 percent. Simplifying the street makes it safer to walk and also made it a safer place to drive, bike, and take buses.

Other analyses and surveys supported the project. In a Times Square Alliance survey, 74 percent of New Yorkers said that Times Square had improved dramatically. When they asked retail and business managers, 68 percent said the plazas should be made permanent, and this pro-business sentiment wasn't just based on anecdotes. The Real Estate Board of New York found that per-square-foot rental rates for ground-floor properties fronting Times Square doubled in a single year, a figure that would eventually triple. Five major retailers opened new stores in Times Square, and by the fall of 2011, Cushman & Wakefield announced that, for the first time in its rankings, Times Square was one of the top ten retail districts on the planet.

But just as beach chairs became a proxy for negative feelings about the redesigned Times Square, the report's data became a stand-in for the media debate. The issue was not that traffic didn't improve—it did, as measured by the more than 1.1 million Midtown GPS-tracked cab trips—but that the project didn't improve traffic *enough*. We had forecast a much greater traffic improvement, and, next to the cardinal political sin of hypocrisy, the next most devastating sin is that of unmet expectations. In particular, one metric from the report found that traffic moving southbound near Times Square moved 2 percent slower. Not only was such a slight decrease statistically insignificant, it was offset by traffic moving better in every other direction, making trips faster overall. Had we merely promised that the project would not diminish travel times, we could have been granted a clearer victory. Instead, some reporters immediately concluded that the project was "disappointing" and "fell short" of its goals. There was no such talk from Bloomberg or his deputies. The mayor read the report and asked a hundred questions before deciding unequivocally that Times Square was improved. He announced that the project would be made permanent.

The report was a critical step in this process, challenging the basic premise that changing streets is risky and that plazas and redesigned roads are bad for business. In fact, the plazas saved a Times Square that had already been lagging behind other commercial corridors of the city. What started as a public realm innovation succeeded as a traffic and safety project that helped even those who had criticized it. The long-term economic benefit of the project would have international implications, and it created new ways to talk about changing the street, setting the table for every project that would follow. These changes weren't just quality-of-life improvements. They opened a city to its people and through that expanded its economic prospects. All this was accomplished not in years but in months, with hundreds of thousands of dollars, not millions.

The plaza life cycle: From barrels and beach chairs to café tables and paint, the final stage in the plaza's development culminates in street redesign with attractive tiles, permanent seating, and modern drainage and power systems for Times Square's many annual events. Nick Mosquera

The critics claimed that the project would create traffic chaos, city-paralyzing traffic. Carmageddon. We were told that no one would want to walk in the plazas or visit Times Square, that the change would strip the area of its character. The gridlock never came, and today the plazas are one of the most visited spots in the city. The mere suggestion of returning the pedestrian spaces to cars is enough to unleash a torrent of criticism greater than the uproar over building them in the first place. This is the new "before."

Emboldened by the Times Square project and the evidence that it produced, we set in motion more than sixty plazas in the five boroughs, in parts of the city without quality public spaces. We established new public spaces beneath the elevated train tracks on New Lots Avenue in Brooklyn's East New York neighborhood and along Roosevelt Avenue in Corona, Queens, and we connected sidewalks and traffic islands to create space for seating along an underused service road at the Bronx Hub.

Had we tried to convince everyone in New York City that the Times Square project would work before we took the first step—answered every cabbie's doubt and refuted every newspaper columnist's armchair analysis—it would have taken five years just to break ground, and even longer for the dozens of other plazas. Instead, on December 23, 2013, at the last press conference that Bloomberg held as mayor and I as commissioner, we cut the ribbon on a new Times Square. After Bloomberg's 2010 decision to make the project permanent, we set in motion a redesign from the ground up to make the plaza a true pedestrian space, not just painted asphalt. Times Square had already been scheduled for a road reconstruction to replace water mains and sewers and remove the streetcar tracks that had been buried beneath layers of asphalt for more than half a century. As city contractors rebuilt the streets, they could rebuild them as world-class pedestrian plazas. We selected the powerhouse architecture firm Snøhetta to redesign the former road space, eliminating curbs and elevating the street surface to sidewalk level. Instead of asphalt there are now pedestrian pavers lined with embedded shiny metal discs, which glint with the lights of Times Square, reflecting Broadway's lights, energy, and excitement. Today there are 480,000 pedestrians, up from 356,000 a few years earlier. As work continues on the plazas, there's room for many, many more.

Times Square became a new touchstone in the annals of city streets, one that is already invoked on every habitable continent. Instead of nibbling around the edges, cities are attempting their own Times Squares—transformative projects not in the periphery but in the heart of their downtown districts, where the politics and competing traffic demands for streets are the most volatile.

A high-profile example like Times Square transcends the crossroads where it is located and represents models for streets big and small, near and far. Cities can never succeed in transforming their streets if they never try. There is no courage, no achievement, and no triumph in avoiding the attempt. As my father taught me, if you are not constantly trying something new, you are not trying hard enough.

7

Stealing Good Ideas

The public domain is in the public domain.

This obvious fact is a godsend for those of us in global street design and transportation practice; otherwise I and dozens like me around the world would be sitting in the stockade at The Hague for grand theft, transpo. Some of the best ideas on New York's streets were inspired, imported, borrowed, or flat out stolen from other cities—London, Montreal, Copenhagen—and many other places where we sourced our ideas. Cities are inspiring one another and choosing from the menu of options that other cities provide, and sometimes a borrowing city puts the ideas together in bold and unexpected ways, as Medellín, Colombia did.

Among the planet's 7 billion people, the city of Medellín probably doesn't ring many bells. It's likely that those who recognize the name know it more for its drug-laced reputation than for its culture or geographical beauty, let alone its transportation innovation. During the 1980s, Medellín was the seat of Pablo Escobar's drug cartel, the cocaine trafficking empire that epitomized the bloody drug wars. Wedged between two ridges of the Andes mountains, the city's population of 2.4 million *paisas*, as residents call themselves, was governed less by the government than by the cartel, as Escobar offered bounties for the heads of police officers and other rivals. In 1991, two years before federal authorities gunned down Escobar, 6,800 *paisas* were killed in largely drug-motivated homicides, a rate of 381 people for every 100,000 inhabitants, at the time the bloodiest murder rate of any city in the world. By 2014, the number was one tenth that figure—65 killed, or 26 per 100,000 inhabitants.

Medellín's leaders over the last decade have worked to change the city with a strategy of transportation and public realm improvements. Thirty years ago, a child kicking a soccer ball or skipping rope around in the Santo Domingo neighborhood would have seen only a hazy sky, tree-topped ridges, and an uncertain future. There were few ways in and out of some neighborhoods, and limited options to reach the city center.

Today, a child kicking the ball or riding a bike around Santo Domingo looks up and sees a gleaming transportation gondola gliding along a cable fifty feet overhead—the Metrocable—and doesn't give it a second glance. This is not an amusement park novelty; it's public transportation as the gondolas rise 1,300 feet up from the valley below and one mile into the barrios. They make stops along the way, at clean, well-lighted stations. People pay fares and pass through turnstiles, hopping on and off with bags of groceries. The gondola on Line K, which stops in Santo Domingo, connects the neighborhood with a Metro station in the valley, where commuters can easily transfer to a train and be whisked along the river into the commercial core. By connecting these inaccessible neighborhoods, the Metrocable cut the two-hour commutes in half. Since the system started in 2004, streets near the stations have flourished with new shops, banks, and vendors who serve a steady stream of customers.

The Metrocable system of gondolas is a transportation technology more at home at theme parks but is daily transit for thousands of Medellín residents.
Seth Solomonow

Banks of public transportation escalators in Medellín provide a cost-effective and simple transportation solution for a previously isolated, poorer neighborhood.   Seth Solomonow

Medellín today is a vivid inspiration for an enlightened social urbanism that provides a model for cities twice its size, ten times its average income, and one hundred times its density. A big part of Medellín's success stems from perfecting the practice of transformative transportation—investing in people by investing in the networks they use to get around.

Escalators are mass transit in Medellín's hillside neighborhoods and are designed into the streetscape, alongside vibrant murals.
Seth Solomonow

In Comuna 13, a poor hillside neighborhood in the western part of the city, three and a half miles from the central Plaza Mayor, residents had to descend and climb hundreds of steps to get to and from their homes. Their lives have changed dramatically not with new, municipally backed roads, diesel-belching buses, or upscale high-rises atop formerly affordable housing, but with connected banks of simple electric escalators that carry thousands of people up the mountain face to their neighborhoods. Four batteries of escalators, enclosed by tinted glass to keep out tropical sunrays and downpours that could soak commuters and short circuit the system's electronics, are connected to landings adorned with vibrant murals painted by neighborhood artists.

The gondolas and escalators might seem like old-fashioned technology, but they allow residents to make a trip to the city center and valley neighborhoods with the same kind of blasé attitude as urban commuters approach their daily bus ride. (To be sure, Medellín in 2011 introduced its first bus rapid transit system, which now carries sixty thousand passengers a day on two routes.) But these extraordinary public space and infrastructure projects go beyond transportation; they are also instruments for social and economic mobility. The network doesn't merely take *paisas* to the next station; it can transport its people to a better station in life.

"Public space is the space of equality," Medellín mayor Aníbal Gaviria Correa told me, squinting in the sunlight on a roof deck atop Medellín's city hall, where he prefers to meet visitors and tell the story of his city. Gaviria spoke to me in early 2015, nine months before his last day in office, a time of rapid transformations and building atop the progress of his predecessors. Mayor Gaviria calls attention to the equal access to public transit and freedom from urban bleakness as "the ethics of aesthetics," an attempt to restore social equity and dignity through inclusive and strategic public works programs. "Everybody wants beautiful things," Gaviria says. "People want their homes to be beautiful, not ugly. I want that for the entire city."

Urban ugliness is often a by-product of municipal structures and utilities that were built with function, not people, in mind. In the poorer hillside neighborhoods, desolate lots with massive cisterns that held clean water for the community for decades have over the last decade been turned into landscaped community centers called UVAs (Articulated Life Units; in Spanish, the anagram cheerfully spells the word for "grape") with outdoor water spouts where neighborhood kids can splash around. Included are recreation rooms for arts and crafts, dance lessons, and computers where kids can surf, research, and write.

If Medellín was like Mexico City, it would sprawl into the mountain forests. Medellín's leaders instead established a greenbelt that preempts development from the forces of both gentrification and sprawling poverty. A Hollywood-style sign is visible from the nearly alpine slant of streets leading to the hillside neighborhoods: Jardín. It refers to the Jardín Circunvalar, a lush, Andean envelope that is starting to wrap the entire city. Instead of more development, the green space will provide a continuous foot and bike path, connect hillside and recreational areas, where locals can play basketball and soccer, and allow for designated agricultural areas, where local residents can grow fruits and vegetables to supplement their diets and incomes.

Mayor Gaviria and his deputies are the first to admit that they have far to go to retrofit their city for a new age. "We are endangered by our own success," Jorge Pérez, the city's planning director, admitted to me during a visit to Medellín. While their accomplishments are breathtaking, so is the growth of private car ownership, which officials estimate at about 15 percent a year, a symbol, to their owners, of economic and social advancement. To accommodate this surge, the city is on a tear to build overpasses so that cars don't have to stop at intersections, frequently leaving pedestrians with no place to cross. And despite a nascent bike-share system, Medellín has few bike lanes, and the few cyclists I saw were mostly race cyclists or road warriors. Far away from the Metrocable and greenbelt, upscale apartment towers are accessible almost exclusively by private cars.

In his final months in office, Gaviria set in motion a multibillion-dollar plan to redevelop the Medellín River waterfront and dismantle the waterside highways. The project will stretch twelve miles along the river, connecting to forty-four neighborhoods across 808 acres of former roadway. Near the riverside park, Gaviria wants to see mixed income housing and the removal of physical and social barriers to public space. During my visit to Medellín, city planner Pérez sketched out the project area on a beer coaster—which I furtively pocketed— showing how the design would bring people of all classes together. Breaking ground months before the end of the mayor's term and starting with the most difficult construction left the project well under way by the time he left office and his successor more likely to see the project through to completion.

Medellín isn't the first city to be transformed socially, economically, and politically by its transportation system—it's not even the first city in Colombia to undergo such a rapid reshaping of its public realm. And as we've seen throughout these chapters, it can take very little to transform a street's use. The clearest example I've seen of this was during one of my first trips abroad as commissioner, to Bogotá, Colombia's capital, 154 miles southeast of Medellín. Bogotá spent much of the last decade reclaiming its streets from cars and building one of the world's great bus rapid transit networks, but the most enduring example of how easily the city changed its streets is an idea called Ciclovía. A Bogotá tradition since its origins in the 1970s, Ciclovía (Spanish for bikeway) is simply the act of closing streets to cars, in Bogotá's case from seven a.m. to two p.m. every Sunday and also on holidays, and letting city residents take to the streets on foot, on bikes and roller skates, roller blades— however they wanted to get around.

The Ciclovía idea didn't take hold until the early 2000s, when Bogotá mayor Enrique Peñalosa's brother, Gil Peñalosa, left a lucrative post heading a television station to become the city's parks commissioner. At the time, Gil Peñalosa told me, Ciclovía was "just a few miles and a few thousand people," unloved by the transportation department that ran the car-free event. Department engineers were afraid that expanding the event would only underscore its unpopularity and cause traffic problems. Gil Peñalosa made them a proposition: give him control of the event for one day and see if he could increase attendance. For one day he expanded the route to fifteen miles. It attracted forty thousand people, a sharp increase from typical weekends, and he called his former media colleagues to cover the event. "It was the number one story on the news that night and the front page of all the papers the next morning," he told me, proving that expansion would give the event the critical mass it needed to be successful.

Peñalosa said his inspiration was Frederick Law Olmsted, who created New York City's Central Park and countless other North American parks. In the 1850s, he said, there was social and racial strife among blacks, whites, natives, and immigrants, rich and poor—social conditions that were reinforced by a physical stratification within the city. These New Yorkers didn't know one another, didn't live in the same buildings. Their kids didn't go to school together and they didn't move within the same orbit. Olmsted saw Central Park as a place where people of every social stratum could meet as equals. A century and a half later, that idea is still relevant. Peñalosa told me, "I thought that Ciclovía could be the Central Park of any city of any size anywhere. It could be an exercise in social integration."

Today, Ciclovía's route runs more than seventy miles and attracts more than one million people to the streets every Sunday and holiday. Car-free or "open streets" events have spread around the world, from Los Angeles and Minneapolis, to Johannesburg and several cities in India, in cities with populations ranging from twenty thousand to twenty million. Peñalosa says that the automotive dominance is instantly tamed by car-free events as people have an opportunity to connect again with their streets: "All of a sudden people see that the streets are public space and belong to all of us, and things start clicking into other possibilities."

Peñalosa saw Ciclovía as a kind of Central Park of the streets, but when I saw it in action during a visit to Bogotá in 2007, it seemed foreign to the image of New York City's streets. Still, I thought it worth trying back home. Our interpretation, which we gave the hopeful name of Summer Streets, would turn seven miles of New York streets from the Brooklyn Bridge to Central Park at 72nd Street into a human-powered late-summer causeway for riding bikes, running, walking, or curbside dance classes. At first I imagined what it would look like on Broadway, but Michael Primeggia, my traffic deputy, noted that nearby Park Avenue would be easier logistically, as it is wide enough, with a planted median in the center, which would let more people run on their own power in both directions. We picked three consecutive August Saturday mornings for the event, when traffic in New York City was at its lightest, and to avoid conflict with the countless parades, street fairs, and other events that close city streets through the summer.

Before the first Summer Streets event in 2008, our biggest concern was that no one would show up, that it would rain, that the closures would foul traffic and become a black eye for us and for the mayor. We wondered if streets themselves would be enough to motivate blasé New Yorkers to come out on a Saturday morning even if there were no food booths, live music, or festival rides. Instead of food and festivities, Summer Streets offered physical fitness activities—kickboxing classes, dance lessons, rock wall climbing. Not exactly the stuff people line up for. Perhaps most unknown was whether New Yorkers, banished from the street for a century, would continue to turn their backs on their own street out of force of habit. Closing the street would be one thing. Making people feel safe and welcome was another.

We shot for the stars to gin up interest in the first event, and were thrilled when hip-hop mogul Jay-Z agreed to turn out for a press conference, a connection made through my old friend and ace communications consultant Joe DePlasco, who had worked with me at DOT over twenty years earlier. We were pleasantly surprised that celebrities would be willing to lend their fame to get New Yorkers to the street. Lance Armstrong, long before his fall from grace, joined us at a press conference with Mayor Bloomberg to call on people to dust off their bikes and pump up their tires, and even the legendary musical genius and bike rider David Byrne signed on to give street cred to the effort.

None of us slept the night before the first street closure. I know I didn't, turning over every worst-case scenario in my mind and checking the weather report obsessively for any chance of rain. I checked my messages every five minutes from Dani Simons, who project-managed the event. Waking well before dawn on the first day, I rode my bike up and down the route before police had even closed off the hundreds of side streets. I made it all the way across the Brooklyn Bridge before returning to Foley Square downtown to fire the starting gun for a seven a.m. route run and officially start the first Summer Streets. I was frazzled and bleary eyed from the days of preparations and the early start.

As the runners made their way up the route and the morning sun shone through the cross streets and into the asphalt and glass canyons, I started seeing people. Maybe it was their routine to walk, bike, or run on Park Avenue on Saturday, but we never noticed them because of all the car traffic. Maybe they came out after seeing Jay-Z on the evening news or in the papers. But I realized I shouldn't have worried. New Yorkers knew exactly what to do with a car-free street, and they came out in droves for those three Saturdays, seeing views never before visible to a person on two feet or a bike. We were all giddy looking at the happy faces riding, running, or strolling on Park Avenue that morning. I ran into Clarence Eckerson, the indefatigable filmmaker at Streetfilms, who helped bring our street transformations to life with a series of video segments. We high fived, both of us grinning like maniacs.

Car-free streets in dozens of neighborhoods, like this one on Montague Street in Brooklyn Heights, showed how quickly and easily a street could be transformed into inviting public space, revealing the street's hidden potential using little more than artificial turf. NYC DOT

The video clips Clarence shot and posted online and the blog posts written by its sister division *Streetsblog* were hugely important in getting out the word. More than 150,000 people came to the three Summer Streets events that summer, a number that had doubled by 2013 as the annual event became a New York summer staple.

Removing cars for a few hours revealed the city hidden beneath and within. A statue of railroad magnate Cornelius Vanderbilt, for decades visible only from cars driving along the viaduct that wraps around Grand Central Terminal, became a surprise attraction. Dozens of people stopped to snap pictures and pose for selfies. Notorious shoe gazers, New Yorkers in these first summer Saturdays started looking up, unafraid that they would block traffic or get hit by a car. Once we saw the possibilities of car-free streets, the options were irresistible. We added new attractions like zip lines, and set up courts for tennis and basketball atop the blacktop, and added golf courses and sand castle contests in plazas. We teamed up with a local entrepreneur to bring "Dumpster" pools next to Grand Central, letting New Yorkers take a free dip in converted shipping containers that had been lined with PVC (and equipped with a high-performance filtration system). The demand to wade in the pools was so intense that we had to use a wristband system, scheduling swim times hours in advance.

The full transformative force of Summer Streets came in 2013 when we opened a car-only tunnel below Park Avenue to pedestrians for the first time. The tunnel, which runs from 34th to 40th Street, opened in 1834 and was first used for horse carts, then replaced with cars—but no pedestrians in all that time. Instead of blank concrete, the tunnel was opened to the public as a portal of sound and light created by artist Rafael Lozano-Hemmer, bringing the space to life with three hundred theater spotlights that flashed and pulsed onto the walls of the tunnel in time with a system of sound amplifiers.

Summer Streets brought New Yorkers closer to their city and also brought the people in our agency closer among ourselves. On the route, I remember seeing Leon Heyward, the resolute deputy commissioner for sidewalk inspection and maintenance. He was also tasked with overseeing special events and responses to emergencies, but the biggest part of his job that day was to enjoy the street and let the people do all the work. All the resources of the agency had been put into creating an opportunity to let New Yorkers experience their streets. I rode along the route with my son, Max, who shot free throws at a basketball clinic sponsored by the New York Knicks and was given pointers on his shooting style. My husband, Mark, Max, and I biked together and hung out by the Cornelius Vanderbilt statue, an opportunity for everyone at the agency to meet my family and for me to meet theirs. Coworkers brought their partners, friends, and family for a special moment when the professional and the personal merged.

Seeing streets in Manhattan opened for free-range activities, communities in every borough started clamoring for their own versions of the event. An application-based program called Weekend Walks was created so neighborhoods could nominate streets for closures. In 2011, the first year, eighteen neighborhoods held events; by 2013, the number had increased to twenty-four neighborhoods. Decades from now these car-free events should be as much a tradition as the Macy's Thanksgiving Day Parade and the New York City Marathon.

While we accomplished a lot with paint and partnerships to make changes quickly and cheaply, we also set up new administrative processes that put the power of public space and its long-term management more directly into the hands of communities. The application program for these neighborhood car-free events reflected the model of our plaza program. It wasn't about simple empowerment—letting people ask for a plaza or a car-free street—it was necessary to establish a community management plan to keep the new spaces and events alive, and to maintain and help pay for them.

"It turns out that changing the space from a place for cars only to a place that invites pedestrians is the easy part," Andy Wiley-Schwartz told me. "Making the space successful, maintaining it and keeping it active in the long term, that's where it's vital to have a process and a partner to sustain it."

Cities have different models for managing public space. Our model was based on the public-private partnership approach used by New York City's parks department. Taking a page out of their book, we set up a system that turned each of our plaza projects into a partnership between the city and local community or business groups. These organizations pooled their resources, which they put toward maintenance of a plaza: putting out tables and chairs, taking them in and securing them in the evening, and replacing those that become damaged or disappear; sweeping up trash left from hundreds of visitors, removing any graffiti, watering plants, and shoveling paths after winter snows. These groups perform functions that government is less adept at doing. "Programming" is what we call any activity that animates a public space, drawing in people with its own energy as opposed to passive recreation. Perhaps it is a food truck event that draws crowds and generates a little revenue that the local community group can use for plaza maintenance. Neighborhood groups host performances, lending libraries, holiday markets, and craft fairs.

Not all neighborhoods have a nonprofit group to represent them or the resources to hire staff to maintain their spaces. But a public space policy needs to include all communities, not solely areas that have economic strength. To address this and help fill the gaps in New York's neighborhoods, we helped establish a nonprofit Neighborhood Plaza Partnership (NPP) with the help of Chase Bank and local foundations. NPP is one of the legacies left by Wiley-Schwartz, who was the planning and logistical force behind the more than sixty plaza projects launched over seven years. This program continues to bring new plazas to the street. NPP advises neighborhoods with little green or public space, guiding them through the application and administrative process, training them on how to maintain a plaza, and connecting them with private sponsorship funding. The program is a marriage of the Association of Community Employment and the Horticultural Society and connects less-well-financed neighborhood groups with the manpower needed to maintain the spaces. It helps train people who have been previously in jail or homeless in landscaping and maintenance skills in the process, providing a transformative connection for communities that need help, a valuable public amenity and employment opportunity.

An underused service lane in Corona, Queens, became a community space in a matter of days, forming a stage for cultural performances and activities. View a time-lapse video of the plaza's creation at https://www.youtube.com/watch?v=nvkfXZfkn2o. Neshi Galindo

Along Avenida 20 de Noviembre in Mexico City, former vehicle lanes have been transformed into pedestrian space and a bike path at the gateway to the Zócalo, the central gathering place in the nation's capital. Nick Mosquera for Bloomberg Associates/Hector Rios for Mexico City

NPP is one of several programs that turned the public planning process on its head. Instead of government presenting ideas to communities, we established a process enabling community organizations, business and cultural groups, and others to request projects that would change their neighborhoods. Parents, schools, activists, businesses, and elected officials are now fluent in traffic calming, way finding, curb extensions, and road diets, even though they barely knew these concepts existed just a few years ago. Giving communities a menu of options and a way to request them also sharply reduced the feeling within communities that they have been "planned to." It's an inspiring example that other cities can borrow; they too can unlock the power of their streets by empowering people to change it themselves.

While we imported great ideas from around the world, we also exported them.

In 2009, San Francisco started experimenting with New York City–style rapid-implementation plazas, painting a plaza at Market, Castro, and Seventeenth streets, the first of several similar projects across the city. The design looked like any number of projects in the Bronx, Brooklyn, or Manhattan, right down to the buff color, planters, and stone barriers. In Mexico City, Avenida 20 de Noviembre was a high-volume traffic corridor delivering endless columns of cars north to the Zócalo, the nation's cultural and political epicenter, even though virtually all of them were bound for destinations far from the center. Working with Dhyana Quintanar, director of the city's public space department, my team at Bloomberg Associates came up with a plan to look at these old streets in new ways, and redesign them from the perspective of the most vulnerable people on the street. The new designs calmed the vehicle traffic approaching the Zócalo and opened large stretches of space for people to walk, establishing a true gateway to the nation's central square and extending its grandeur and inclusiveness farther south.

Beneath the city's highways in Coyoacán, the city cleared vacant lots and turned these spaces into food courts, bakeries, convenience stores,

A pocket park in Coyoacán, Mexico City, one of dozens that repurpose unused street space to extend sidewalks for seating, gathering, eating, and people watching. Seth Solomonow

and fitness areas. Quintanar's public space department is invigorating neighborhoods with new community plazas (*parques de bolsillo*, or pocket parks) to serve as bulwarks against invasion by parked cars. City leaders have also started to create a viable network of bike lanes as bike-share stations and protected bike paths have emerged along busy Avenida de la Reforma and in the areas around the historic city center. Five bus rapid transit routes today operate along sixty-five miles of dedicated bus lanes where cars used to sit idle, becoming part of the city's transportation network, moving 900,000 daily passengers at full speed past lanes of stopped cars.

Little by little, the redesign of streets creates spaces that invite people and opportunities beyond cars. These strategies are more than just novelties. They may ultimately be part of Mexico City's long-term salvation—and the salvation of all cities.

A problem in many cities is finding your way around. Plazas give pedestrians new destinations, but without a system of signs indicating where they are, neighborhood landmarks like these can easily remain off the grid. While streets are cluttered with street name signs, one-way signs, stop signs, and totem poles of parking information, many cities don't have so much as a sign or an arrow for people walking. But even pedestrians need infrastructure. We've all experienced the frustration of being lost or pointed in the wrong direction by a seemingly knowledgeable local. Taking a page out of London's successful wayfinding playbook, we put New York neighborhoods on the map with the city's first coordinated sign system for pedestrians. While digital maps can be called up on any smartphone, there's still enormous convenience in having physical, freestanding maps on sidewalks, like those that Transport for London positioned along city streets—known as Legible London. We placed the sleek, eight-foot-high monoliths mostly within the sidewalk curb zones, inviting people to determine their location and their next step without being stampeded.

WalkNYC put New York's neighborhoods on the map, showing local destinations and how long in minutes it takes to walk to nearby attractions. Pentagram and Hamish Smyth

It's a kind of dirty urban secret that city residents know the streets they know, but stray a block or two off the usual commuting route and the geography can get fuzzy. Even native New Yorkers get turned around when emerging from an unfamiliar subway station. Which way is uptown, which way is downtown? There are 1.3 million street signs in the five boroughs that provide a lexicon for streets from the drivers' perspective, but until recently there were barely any signs to tell the pedestrians where they are and what's around the corner. DOT conducted a survey of more than five hundred pedestrians to see how well they knew the city. We were surprised that 13 percent of residents and 27 percent of visitors couldn't name the neighborhood or borough they were in. Which was north? Thirty-three percent of New Yorkers didn't know.

The maps are displayed in "heads-up" format, oriented in the direction that a pedestrian is facing, eliminating confusion over which way is north.
NYC DOT—Alex Engel

Another 9 percent admitted that at some point during the previous week, they had been lost. And those are just the people who would admit it!

It's one thing if you're momentarily turned around in a car and GPS can recalculate your route. But if you're on foot, small smartphone maps aren't as user friendly for exploring and getting the lay of the land as an old-fashioned map. This isn't just a matter of convenience but of growing urban economic necessity. Cities that do not offer basic orientation for pedestrian visitors miss an opportunity to enlarge the foot traffic that infuses the tourist and ground-floor retail economy.

Master maps produced by a consortium of firms led by design giant Pentagram were radical for their ingenious layout. The near-universal standard for maps is to orient them so that north is always at the top of the page. The obvious problem is that you first need to know which way is north before the map is useful. If you're like one of the one third of New Yorkers who don't know your north from your south when exiting an unfamiliar train station, you're out of luck. But what if the map already knows which way you're facing?

Our wayfinding maps use a "heads up" format, pioneered by Transport for London, prepositioning the map so that the streets are laid out in the same direction the viewer is facing. The maps are equally intended to help people make connections, showing major cultural destinations, government and educational institutions, transit stops, and even bike-share stations. When getting around, people think in terms of time, not distance. They may not walk if the map says a destination is a quarter mile away, but if it says the location is just a five-minute walk, that changes the decision. Each map has radial markings to show pedestrians how long it would take to walk to any given point on the map. Translucent representations of landmarks, helping people gain their bearings.

As with so many other pedestrian improvements, the wayfinding maps are more than simple conveniences. Accessible, user-friendly maps unlock entire neighborhoods and help even lifelong New Yorkers discover new

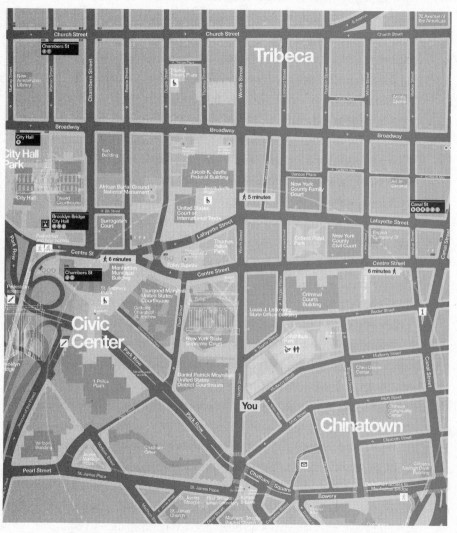

Blending a mix of landmarks, institutions, transit, and walkability, wayfinding maps can open more of the city for locals and visitors alike.

NYC DOT—Alex Engel

parts of their city. The MTA was so impressed with the design that it is now displaying neighborhood maps in subway stations, unifying the maps used both above and below the street. By 2013, the maps were installed on Select Bus Service kiosks and at each of the 330 bike-share stations, bringing a new visual vocabulary to the entire city's transportation network.

Combining these elements on our streets—prioritized transit, car-free streets, public art, and maps designed for pedestrians—gave New Yorkers new keys to the kingdom.

As we opened the door to let New Yorkers take back their streets, others were happy to climb through windows and hop fences to take them back in their own way. On a sunny New York City day in May 2010, a crew of three workers fanned out across the sidewalk along Fifth Avenue, just south of 23rd Street. Wearing bright orange vests, the official-looking squad carefully chalk-painted a line parallel to the curb, bisecting the sidewalk for about half a block. The sidewalk now had two lanes. To reinforce the point of these two lanes, the crew stenciled "New Yorkers" in one of the lanes and "Tourists" in the other lane. In a video of the act posted online, a crew foreman informed passing pedestrians to keep to the corresponding lanes. People seemed fine with it. Tourists seemed to accept that this was how things were done in the big city. A tourist protested that he walked fast enough to stride in the New York lane. The crew wasn't having it. "Statistically, you walk slow" came the retort. It's true that New Yorkers are notorious speed-walkers. And when we get stuck behind a pack of lollygagging tourists walking three abreast and blocking the sidewalk, we start to twitch and vibrate. But it turns out this "crew" was a local comic-art improv troupe, their DOT vests ersatz and their sidewalk lane work an unauthorized performance-art comedy installation. Their "work," perhaps intentionally, made an important point about how city residents relate to our streets. A small, even unauthorized change to the street can immediately change the use of a street, and even ordinary citizens—not traffic engineers, as city residents have assumed for a century—can design their own streets using household materials. And it's not just an inside joke.

In the dark of an early April morning in 2013, a group of urban guerrillas came to the block of Seattle's Cherry Street that runs below Interstate 5. Their tools were plastic posts, which they glued to a painted bike lane stripe to create a homespun protected bike lane. Reasonably Polite Seattleites, the group that claimed responsibility for the "attack," wrote to the Seattle Department of Transportation (SDOT) that their goal was "to demonstrate how an incredibly modest investment and a few minutes of SDOT's time is capable of transforming a marginal, under-utilized and dangerous bike facility into one dramatically safer for cars, pedestrians and bicyclists." City managers reacted as you might expect—they yanked out the posts. But they later installed new posts officially—and at a height that met specifications so bike riders wouldn't hit them with their hands.

These do-it-yourself interventions are indicators of the growing expectations people have for their streets, embodying a sense of ownership and the belief that their streets are once again within reach. There are thousands of examples around the world of city residents' reclaiming streets in largely unsanctioned but harmless ways, using only their own creativity and low-cost materials. They can be murals painted on neighborhood streets, artificial turf or chairs in a parking space to create a park for a day, or yarn-bombing parking meters. In the book *Tactical Urbanism*, Mike Lydon and Anthony Garcia document the efforts of one neighborhood group in Hamilton, Ontario, that placed unauthorized traffic cones to create a neck-down at an intersection residents felt was dangerous. The city immediately removed them, but the ensuing debate led to an official installation of markers to channel traffic. In Dallas, neighbors, artists, and biking advocates joined for a "better block" project. For two days, participants transformed a nondescript four-lane road into a kind of small-town main street, with benches, pop-up coffee shop and flower store, and a "New York style" protected bike path. The way the street was designed was illegal under Dallas building standards, but that was part of the point they wanted to make: livable streets are a virtual impossibility in many cities thanks to outmoded planning rules and manuals, which reject most uses for the street that don't involve moving cars and keeping obstacles—and people—out of the way.

These DIY acts reveal the power of signs, signals, paint—seemingly minor cues from the streets that shape our lives. It takes only a little bit of imagination to transform a sidewalk into a place-making feature of the street. In an increasing number of cases, city planners are being inspired and, in turn, inspiring these kinds of unorthodox strategies, blurring the lines between the sanctioned and unsanctioned and also erasing the barriers between the people and those who represent them.

There are countless eyesores within any city that offer opportunities for inexpensive interventions. With just a little initiative, ragged, never-visited medians and corrugated metal fences around construction sites can be transformed.

To bring this perspective to the streets I hired Wendy Feuer to run the agency's first Urban Design and Art Program. Wendy is a veteran with decades of experience in identifying and developing art and artists through the MTA's Arts for Transit Program, which injected a much-needed aesthetic into the underground network of pedestrian tunnels, platforms, staircases, and mezzanines of New York City's subway system. I wanted her to bring that same refreshing eye to the 6,300 miles of streets and in-between spaces to see what was possible.

One of my favorite art and infrastructure moments was in 2008, when I found myself seated next to musician David Byrne at an event at the Battery Maritime Building, which Byrne had temporarily transformed into an architectural musical instrument. I was a longtime fan of Byrne's and quickly discovered that he was also an inveterate bike rider and was writing a book about biking in cities during his travels around

Art meets infrastructure in bike racks custom designed by musician David Byrne for New York's streets. NYC DOT

the world. We became friends, sharing stories about how riding changes the experience of being in a city. Earlier that day I had been working to select a jury to decide on the design for the next generation of bike racks for New York City. Byrne was so interested he agreed to be on the jury and impulsively started suggesting his own ideas, which he scribbled on a napkin. The ideas were so fun and clever that on the spot we created a parallel bike rack program. Byrne would design twelve racks, to be custom built by his art gallery, and place them at strategic city locations. One rack was shaped in the silhouette of a woman's shoe, placed near the Bergdorf Goodman department store. Another, fabricated as a dollar sign, was installed on Wall Street. Times Square got a rack shaped like "mudflap Tammy," the bawdy, buxom silhouette that adorns the backs of some large trucks. Williamsburg got a rack shaped like a guitar in a nod to the neighborhood's hipsters.

People who create infrastructure don't always consider the contexts or visual appeal of their design, or think to bring artists into the design process. Yet artists can show us the hidden nature in our environments, and our work with the artistic community on bike racks was just the first in a series of collaborations that showed new ways that our streets could be used.

Broadway in Times Square was a canvas for a 2010 design competition to redesign fifty thousand square feet of roadbed. Artist Molly Dilworth won with a design inspired by the climatological heat island effect of cities. NYC DOT—Alex Engel (Artist: Molly Dillworth)

Jersey barriers: nasty, brutish, and short. Volunteers turn these blank barriers into anchors of a vibrant streetscape. NYC DOT—Jaclyn Jablkowski

Much public art is uninspiring because it is selected by committee. A piece of art typically must pass through hundreds of hands and thousands of eyeballs before winning approval from the city's design bureaucracy. In contrast, DOT's public art program avoided this institutional hurdle by placing works on the street for under a year at a time, the designated period before a work would require design commission approval. This created more adventurous, colorful, and constantly changing installations, ranging from lesser known but talented local artists to giants of the art scene, like Shepard Fairey.

A colorful mural beneath the Brooklyn-Queens Expressway brings life to a dark underpass while reinforcing the DOT's safety messaging. NYC DOT—Courtney Whitelocke

In one instance, we held a design competition asking artists to use the fifty thousand square feet of roadbed in Times Square, from 42nd to 47th streets, as a canvas for their imaginations. Artist Molly Dilworth won with a design inspired by the climatological "heat island effect" of cities. NASA's weather satellites show how city structures and blacktop absorb heat and make urban areas run hot. Dilworth interpreted a heat signature map, painting a white, gray, and blue asphalt stream along Broadway. The design visually cooled the space and recalled Manhattan's streams and ponds, which were drained or banished belowground centuries ago.

The Urban Art office worked with hundreds of volunteers to create designs and to paint miles of Jersey barriers (movable concrete blocks that transportation departments put on streets and highways to separate lanes of traffic), turning a traffic liability into a useful asset using little more than paint, and instantly transforming the streetscape for people on bikes or on foot.

We also partnered with neighborhood groups to create murals at underused spaces, such as on a wall beneath the Brooklyn-Queens Expressway. Tactics like these are what the modern, rediscovered city looks like. They are a living partnership between the public and the municipal leaders who serve them to recover a public realm that serves everyone. Public art makes the urban urbane. I still think back to a time when advertisements and graffiti were about the only color or design elements a New Yorker was likely to encounter on the street. Today, the next generation of art and design students walk through a city that can be a canvas for creativity and inspire them to take their streets into their own hands.

Brooklyn's Pearl Street plaza in DUMBO, at the foot of the Manhattan Bridge, the first place-making project from the New York City Department of Transportation. Completed in 2007, it required only the basic tools already in every transportation department's arsenal—paint and space— and became the first of sixty plazas installed citywide. Eight years later, some still believe these before and after pictures are renderings, too vivid and appealing to be actual images. NYC DOT—Ryan Russo

Ninth Avenue and 14th Street, on the border of Chelsea and the Meatpacking District, the first street intervention in Manhattan. By consolidating lanes, we created an asphalt triangle big enough for a community-maintained plaza. This project solidified the instant plaza design palette and showed how smart traffic management could reprogram street space without causing congestion.   NYC DOT—Ryan Russo

And then there was Broadway, where all of NYC DOT's tools came together. Just outside Madison Square Park and at the foot of the Flatiron Building, seven lanes of careering traffic became just two, and one of the longest crosswalks in New York City was made shorter and safer. NYC DOT—Heidi Wolf

In a great moment in livable streets history, students sat down with their sketchbooks just minutes after we redirected traffic. New Yorkers were hungry for new street space and this groundbreaking redesign was all the inspiration these aspiring artists needed. Courtesy of the Flatiron/23rd Street Partnership

The Crossroads of the World was a traffic crisis two hundred years in the making. Broadway, a pre-Colonial pedestrian path, sliced across the street grid, creating dangerous, irregular intersections and perpetual congestion. NYC DOT

In Times Square, 89 percent of Broadway was given over to cars, with just 11 percent dedicated to pedestrians, though their actual proportions were the opposite. The resulting sidewalk crush forced people into the street. NYC DOT

Above: The Green Light for Midtown project transformed Broadway and Times Square from the moment the construction barrels were placed in 2009. The new pedestrian space, formerly occupied only by automobiles, was filled instantly by hundreds of thousands of office workers, theatergoers, and tourists. NYC DOT

Right: To give people space to sit and take in the bright lights of the big city, we put out temporary beach chairs while long-term replacements were on order. Instead of debating safety benefits, congestion reduction, or the other merits of a remarkable urban transformation, many reporters instead kvetched about the beach chairs' kitschy color scheme.
Bruce Schaller

Before and after: The Times Square redesign was a smash hit on Broadway. With only paint, bollards, and smart traffic management, we provided a new gathering space for New Yorkers and sparked a local economic renaissance. After the redesign, retail rents for properties on the plazas tripled, six major stores moved in, and, for the first time ever, Cushman and Wakefield, a commercial real estate firm, listed Times Square as one of the top ten most valuable retail locations on the planet. *Left:* NYC DOT—Heidi Wolf *Right:* NYC DOT—Julio Palleiro

And the project went far deeper than asphalt. While the temporary plazas took off, we got the ball rolling on a world-class public plaza designed by one of the globe's leading architectural firms to reflect the lights and energy of the city. The economic and safety improvements of the groundbreaking redesign are now locked in, benefiting generations to come. The new pedestrian spaces make up just 2.6 out of the more than 180 acres of asphalt that have been repurposed for people over the last seven years. When construction is completed in 2016, this new direction for New York City streets will be set in stone.   Snøhetta

Slightly to the south of Times Square, at the epicenter of the Macy's Thanksgiving Day Parade in Herald Square, Green Light for Midtown proved that rethinking your streets doesn't mean Carmageddon. By reconnecting the threads of the street grid at the intersection of 34th Street and Sixth Avenue, injuries to motorists went down by 63 percent and travel times improved by 15 percent, facts we derived from GPS data on more than 1.1 million yellow cab trips. NYC DOT—Heidi Wolf

Better streets mean better business. When the city gets the fundamentals wrong, every other indicator of thriving, vibrant communities will also be out of balance. A more orderly First Avenue, complete with world-class bike and bus lanes, turned out to be a much nicer place to visit and do business, too: commercial vacancies fell by 47 percent thanks to an uptick in bus riders and a 177 percent increase in cyclists.

Top: NYC DOT—Julio Palleiro   *Bottom:* NYC DOT

Bikes were at the forefront of the New York transportation transformation. Over just seven years, we installed nearly four hundred miles of innovative cycling infrastructure, including the first parking-protected paths on the continent. While some projects were controversial, including one in Prospect Park West in Brooklyn, shown here in before and after photos, poll after poll demonstrated that some two thirds of city residents supported the expansion of the cycling network. New Yorkers love their lanes.   *Top:* NYC DOT—Julio Palleiro *Bottom:* NYC DOT—Nick Carey

Support came after we proved that bike lanes were safer for everyone. Streets with protected lanes brought injuries for all users of the street down by 50 percent, not just for people on bikes. And over the last decade, while bike ridership nearly quadrupled, the risk of injury to cyclists plummeted by 75 percent. Today, you can measure the success of a street by the number of women and children getting around on two wheels. *Above:* Plaza Street near Park Slope, Brooklyn. *Below:* Prospect Park West. NYC DOT

Planners can learn a lot simply by observing how people already use the street. Between Sixth and Seventh avenues in the heart of Midtown, hundreds of people would cross the street midblock to access a string of pedestrian spaces that run from 51st to 57th streets rather than walk hundreds of feet to cross at the corner. We built a series of intersections to connect these spaces and give people a safe way to cross. New York's newest thoroughfare—6½ Avenue—was born. NYC DOT—Julio Palleiro

Streets serve as tracks for the city's bus system—the nation's largest but, unfortunately, also the slowest, often moving more slowly than people walking down the sidewalk. To speed things up, we rolled out the red carpet with these eye-catching dedicated bus lanes. We also added fare machines that let riders pay before they board and gave buses priority at traffic signals and consolidated stops. Webster Avenue in the Bronx was one of seven Select Bus Service lines we launched in the five boroughs with the MTA, resulting in a 10 percent increase in ridership, a 20 percent reduction in travel times, and near-unanimous support from passengers. The improvements ease service daily for two hundred thousand passengers and annually save 620 years of cumulative commuting time.   NYC DOT—Taylor Reiss Gouge

We found incredible opportunities for artistic interventions to support the vibrancy of our streets. *Above:* This evolving mural in DUMBO—a space of constant reinvention since we installed the city's first pedestrian plaza there—was created with multiple layers of paint that would change with time and reveal new designs, letting us incorporate daily city street life into a part of the artistic process. *Below:* Aided by an army of volunteers, we breathed new life into concrete barriers like this one and other forgotten spaces that usually get lost in the urban shuffle.

Top: David Ellis, Pearl Street Triangle, 2012 (Two Trees Management and DUMBO Improvement District) (Location: Pearl Street Triangle at Water Street, Adams Street and Anchorage Plaza, Brooklyn). Photographers: David Ellis and Chris Keohane.
Bottom: Abby Goldstein, Fictional Landscape, 2012 (with NY Cares) (Location: Sands Street and Jay Street, Brooklyn). Photographer: NYC DOT—Emily Colasacco

The reinvention of our streets was about much more than aesthetics—we were providing new tools for New Yorkers. *Above:* When we installed the latest generation of parking meters that allowed drivers to pay by credit card, we converted the old coin-operated meters into bike racks among sixteen thousand new parking spots we created for 2-wheelers instead of 4x4s. *Below:* We also teamed up with musician and cycling advocate David Byrne to fabricate twelve stylized, neighborhood-specific bike racks.

Top: Designer: Maarten de Greeve and Ian Mahaffy. Photographer: NYC DOT—Alex Engel *Bottom:* NYC DOT Designer: NYC DOT

For the first time in the modern era, we brought each of the agency's 788 bridges into good condition or started reconstruction projects. The 60 plazas and 400 miles of bike lanes we built added up to just 1 percent of NYC DOT's capital budget for the state of good repair work.

Above: The replacement for the Willis Avenue Bridge connecting Harlem and the South Bronx is floated up the East River in August 2010 below the Manhattan and Brooklyn bridges.   NYC DOT

Left: We invested more than $1 billion to resurface more than 6,500 lane miles of streets, repair 2.2 million potholes, and produce innovative asphalt that uses 40 percent recycled asphalt from other city streets.

NYC DOT—Alex Engel

8

Bike Lanes
and Their Discontents

"**W**e are here today to talk about bicycles." The speaker was the chair of the New York City Council's transportation committee, and the committee room was packed. Reporters in that room far outnumbered members of the public, most of whom were sent to an overflow room down the hall to follow the proceedings on closed-circuit television.

"And believe it or not, few issues today prompt more heated discussion than bike policy in New York City," the speaker continued with an accent betraying his Bronx origins. "Biking is a good transportation alternative, but I do not believe that making it impossible to drive should be a policy our city pursues," he concluded.

By December 2010, the two-year, two-mile transformation of Broadway into a pedestrian and bike boulevard was complete from Columbus Circle to Union Square. The city's protected bike lanes had long since extended over the East River and into the streets beyond Manhattan, through Brooklyn, on to Brooklyn's Kent Avenue in Williamsburg, and, just five months before the council meeting gaveled to order, transportation crews installed a soon-to-be-controversial bike lane along Prospect Park West.

But this hearing wasn't a victory lap. It was a cross-examination. Just weeks before, the *New York Times* headline blared: Expansion of Bike Lanes in City Brings Backlash. "Surging bike ridership has created a simmering cultural conflict," the story claimed, with bike lanes in particular leading to "unusual scenes of friction." In blunt, tabloid terms, bikes were New York City's Public Enemy No. 1.

It's probable that as we spoke, attorneys at a white-shoe Manhattan law firm were waiting to read the transcript of my testimony as they prepared a legal challenge to the Prospect Park West bike lane. Three avowed lane foes involved in that suit were on the hearing's list of speakers that day, including Brooklyn's borough president. What happened in that hearing room was not just a debate about this or that bike lane, the loss of parking spaces, or a War on Cars. The hearing and its testimony was a major battle in the fight for New York City's streets and a challenge to an idea about what city streets are and who they are for.

You'd be forgiven for thinking that New York City had bigger issues to confront. Maybe there would be heated debate around transportation issues like the chronic underfunding of the public transportation network or what's needed to stop traffic violence, which killed 271 New Yorkers that year. But there were no transportation committee meetings on traffic safety that day. The focus was the Bloomberg administration's alleged obsession with bike lanes, of which I was the chief architect. The obsession, such as it was, amounted to about $8 million invested over three years to create the nation's best bike lanes. For perspective, earlier that year the Transportation Department started a $508 million project to paint the Brooklyn Bridge and rehabilitate its approaches. Another $612 million went for the replacement of the little-known Willis Avenue

Bridge crossing the Harlem River from Manhattan to the Bronx, which opened two months before the committee meeting. Together, these were just two of the DOT's 789 bridges, elevated roads, and overpasses. At this rate, it would take 195 years of bike-lane building to match the cost of painting just the Brooklyn Bridge. By the year 2433 we would have spent the $1.1 billion needed to paint just these two bridges.

But nobody asked about infrastructure investment in the carnival atmosphere at that morning's council hearing. The cross examiners were on to something: New Yorkers held very strong opinions about cyclists and bike lanes. The most-quoted testimony from that day came from Brooklyn borough president Marty Markowitz, who sang his statement to the melody of "My Favorite Things":

MARTY MARKOWITZ: [Singing]

> *Lanes fit for Fido and lanes made for lovers,*
> *hikers and bikers, significant others.*
> *A lane just for Santa, but please don't complain.*
> *These are a few of my favorite lanes.*
> *Strollers and schlepers and skaters and joggers,*
> *holiday lanes just for all the egg noggers,*
> *Let's not forget cars, it's getting insane.*
> *Welcome to Brooklyn, the Borough of Lanes.*
> *When the horn honks, when the dog bites, when the bikers stray,*
> *I simply remember my favorite lanes and then I just say, "oy vey."*
> *Thank you, members of the committee.*

The fight would get a lot worse. Just a few weeks later the most disabling snowstorm in many years would cripple the New York City region and embroil the administration in questions about its readiness. A long, dark winter was about to be lit up by blaring media headlines in a snow-encrusted backlash.

Oy vey indeed.

Never underestimate the anger directed at bicyclists. They ride too fast, terrorizing pedestrians. They ride too slow, dangerously obstructing drivers. They don't wear helmets or reflective bike gear, jeopardizing themselves. They look ridiculous riding around in those helmets and reflective bike gear, more like Mad Max marauders than human beings. They shouldn't ride in streets, which are hostile, car-only zones. They shouldn't have their own lanes because there aren't enough of them to take away space from cars. Yet there are so many of them that they're running down pedestrians and therefore shouldn't ride on sidewalks.

Bikes and the people who ride them elicit more passions than any other way of getting around. Tempers flare up on city streets every day on every continent, and the dispute over riders' presence on the street has spilled over into social science research, media coverage, and commentary. Anonymous attackers spread tacks on bike lanes to puncture the tires of cyclists in Melbourne. In New York City, saboteurs spread tacks on the Queensboro Bridge's bike path, in Central Park, and one attacker pulled a wire across the path of a cyclist in Brooklyn's Prospect Park, sending him over his handlebars, breaking six ribs and fracturing his elbow. Similar bike lane sabotage attacks have been recorded in London, Portland, Oregon, and in large and small cities, and violence erupting between drivers and cyclists has been posted on YouTube. Thousands of blogs, articles, essays, and Internet posts abound, tagged with variations on "I Hate Bicyclists." A Facebook community named "God I fucking hate cyclists using the road" claims 2,542 likes and growing as of October 2015. The bile is not just reserved for the trolling backwaters of the Internet. A columnist for *The Washington Post* found widespread sympathy when he debated running down loathsome cyclists in the District of Columbia: "It's a $500 fine for a motorist to hit a bicyclist in the District," he wrote. "But some behaviors are so egregious that some drivers might think it's worth paying the fine."

The antipathy doesn't end with people who ride bikes; it extends to the painted lanes that they ride on. Bike lanes don't simply rob taxpaying motorists of driving space that they bought and paid for. They seem to reward bike riders for their bad behavior. And bike lanes are a dangerous lure, giving would-be riders a false sense of security that it's safe to ride on streets. Streets are dangerous places, the thinking goes, *and they must be kept that way*!

"What I compare bike lanes to is swimming with the sharks," former Toronto council member Rob Ford said in 2010. "Sooner or later you're going to get bitten. And every year we have dozens of people that get hit by cars or trucks. Well, no wonder: roads are built for buses, cars, and trucks, not for people on bikes. My heart bleeds for them when I hear someone gets killed, but it's their own fault at the end of the day."

After being elected mayor and having the power to act on that sentiment, Ford in 2012 ordered the removal of a bike lane on Jarvis Avenue, an erasure that was delayed only briefly by protesters who lay in the path of work crews. Ford wasn't unique in his thinking, but rarely is this

Lane reversal in Toronto: Protesters delay but don't deter the removal of a bike lane on Jarvis Avenue in 2012. Shawn Micallef, Spacing Toronto

throwback perspective expressed so starkly: streets are places for cars, and people on bikes and walking must avoid them for their own safety. Instead of doing something about the sharks, Ford and transportation departments around the world have ordered people out of the water.

The cultural and political backlashes surrounding the growth of biking and new cycling infrastructure on city streets are not limited to New York City, Washington, D.C., or Toronto. New Orleans, Pittsburgh, Chicago, Sydney, Brisbane, Adelaide, London, and even supposedly progressive cities like Vancouver, Seattle, and San Francisco are just a few that have faced venomous opposition to bike riders and proposed lanes. The resistance often ranges from claims that biking makes streets more dangerous and congested at best to, at the other extreme, arguments that reapportioning streets for any use other than driving or parking is an ideological "War on Cars."

In the end, what you see on city streets depends on how you get around. Drivers see the street as a territory granted to them that is needlessly interrupted by signs, signals, and interlopers—pedestrians obliviously checking their Twitter feeds, lane-blocking buses, and dim-witted other drivers. From the view of those in the driver's seat, though, the tipping point into road rage is the new kid on the block: *F@$!ing cyclists and their bike lanes! They're the ones who are causing all the traffic.* From a transportation planner's perspective, however, the driver's victimhood isn't the whole story. Whatever annoyance or unpredictability pedestrians and cyclists pose on the street, drivers are the ones in each other's way. They are never stuck *in* traffic. They *are* the traffic they are stuck in.

Enter pedestrians. They are the antithesis of the car. Their only protection against a car's two tons of mass is the attention of the driver and the centimeters of flesh that protect their bones. Yet they have largely tuned out cars and the dangers they pose. Pedestrians have learned to read, and listen to, the street. They know when to dash across the street between waves of traffic. Mostly. Within those waves, a pedestrian is killed every two or three days in New York City, a small fraction of the 270,000 killed around the world annually, yet the term "pedestrian rage" hasn't yet caught on.

Enter the bike. Drivers and pedestrians may hate each other, but if they can agree on one thing, it's that they both hate cyclists. Drivers and pedestrians haven't learned to read the street and to see or hear bike riders. They aren't expecting them or aren't looking for them. Every pedestrian has a story about being nearly killed by an aggressive, wrong-way-riding, Lycra-clad ninja cyclist. From the view of a pedestrian stepping into the street, bikes are simply too slow, too sleek, and too silent to be as easily noticed as people in cars. Pedestrians have learned to detect an oncoming car, relying on peripheral vision and the sound of an approaching vehicle's engine. But people on foot still don't know how to read the presence of bikes. I've startled pedestrians on my bike even when I've been stopped, waiting for a red light. I've been cursed at for appearing "out of nowhere" when riding with the signal in a bike lane. But even when I've done nothing wrong, I can see that the fear and instinct for collective punishment are no less real. Bike riders exist on a totally different frequency, moving at speeds seemingly incompatible with people who drive. They're cheaters, cutting the line in front of law-abiding people behind the wheel, running lights as if the rules don't apply to them. The stereotypical urban biker rides a fixed-gear bike with a lock and chain slung across his One Less Car T-shirt, like a bandolier. A regular two-wheeled, holier-than-thou, rolling lifestyle protest. *And they seem so damn smug about it.*

A pedestrian killed by a cyclist is guaranteed front-page news status for days on end in New York City, with saturation coverage and outrage. It's likely because of its rareness that even a "near miss" is appalling to the point of backlash. But rarely is a bike rider's death beneath the wheels of a car, bus, or truck regarded with the same reverence or outrage. More frequently, the mere fact that someone dared to ride in the street in the first place is Exhibit A that the rider was "asking for it," especially if he or she wasn't wearing a helmet. After all, that's what you get when you swim with sharks.

As with most cities, New York City's streets were not designed to accommodate bikes. Riding atop two tires and just twenty pounds of steel, bicyclists feel invisible on the street, as vulnerable as someone walking yet expected to behave like a motor vehicle driver along one-size-fits-all roads, weaving in and among the cars, buses, and trucks, avoiding potholes and car doors swinging open. My advice to people annoyed by cyclists is not to judge them until you've ridden a mile in their lane.

So why would anyone want to ride in the first place? Just as Mayor Rob Ford declared in Toronto, many city leaders and residents think that riding a bike on city streets is suicidal. *Bikes don't belong on the road.* Some cities even require that bike riders wear helmets, and politicians and bike opponents routinely suggest that bike registration or insurance would make streets safer. I think what's crazy is that anyone would be content with city streets so dangerous that only a lunatic would ride a bike on them, or that some think the only way to deal with cyclists is to require that they armor themselves or to ban them from the road. If death-wish speed racers are the only ones lured to your streets, and if a helmet is the only counter weapon, the problem is a lot bigger than bike riders.

The fault is not in our cyclists, but in our streets. A century of bad design has left us with streets built for cars, trucks, and buses, yet serve everyone, but no one well. Road rage directed at bike riders obscures the underlying design flaws of streets that bring riders, walkers, and drivers into conflict in the first place. Bike riding shouldn't be an act of bravery, and transportation leaders should redesign their streets so that they don't depend on armor or surrender to survive. Arguing that streets are built for cars and are too dangerous to bike on is an argument for a safety intervention to upgrade those streets. Every epithet yelled at a passing cyclist is a demand for more and better bike lanes. Safe, inclusive street designs have the power to settle these arguments before they escalate into conflict and danger. Designs that protect people who ride bikes reinforce the variety of street uses, making the entire street safer by making people more visible and predictable. If cities really want to deal effectively with bike riders and create safer streets for everyone, they can start by building bike lanes.

In launching bike infrastructure programs, cities also embark on a controversial policy: daring to take street space that for decades has been used exclusively by vehicles and do something else with it. City planners will inevitably hear the International Bike Objection: "We're not Amsterdam! We're not Copenhagen!" This cry has been invoked in Washington, D.C., London, Auckland, Sydney, Pittsburgh, New York, and dozens of cities big and small. The rationale is that their streets are different. Too hilly, too spread out. We drive. Nobody bikes. It's too dangerous. It's too hot. It's too cold. It will cause traffic. It will hurt businesses. It's just not in our culture. We're different and we pride ourselves on not being like those fruity Europeans.

Having biked around Amsterdam and Copenhagen and seen the creative ways those cities have built biking into the street, I'm moved to ask, What's not to like? Hundreds of cities that aren't Amsterdam have bike lanes. Why would a city be proud *not* to attempt something that has been so successful elsewhere? Are Amsterdam and Copenhagen so freakishly well organized that their biking culture wouldn't roll in rough-and-unready car-based cities in North America and Down Under? Not exactly. Even Amsterdam and Copenhagen weren't always Amsterdam and Copenhagen. Both cities adjusted their streets for cars following World War II. It was only after public disgust and protests over traffic deaths in the 1960s that national leaders started to build bike lanes and bike parking facilities. European cities pioneered bike lanes that are completely segregated from car lanes and pedestrian traffic, and regulated by traffic signals timed so that cyclists need not come to a full stop. This in turn stimulated growth in ridership and infrastructure over decades, not overnight. This approach is the backbone for the incredible 48 percent of traffic in central Amsterdam who bike, and 36 percent of trips in Copenhagen. Neither biking nirvana was built in a day.

Bike commuting outside of European countries is so small that it could be tagged as a semisocialistic novelty. Portland, Oregon, has by far the highest bike mode share among big American cities, with 5.9 percent of commuting trips by bike. Many people see in these numbers the proof they need that there is no demand for cycling infrastructure and that leaders shouldn't even bother trying to catch up with the rest of the world. Yet despite the weighty burden of not being Amsterdam, dozens of cities around the world have launched ambitious plans for vast bike networks, some even inspired by what they saw occurring in New York City. Chicago mayor Rahm Emanuel announced plans to build one hundred miles of protected bike lanes, with protected paths already installed on Dearborn Avenue. Car capital Los Angeles installed its first protected paths on Reseda Boulevard and on South Figueroa Street, feats that would have seemed impossible ten years ago. Indianapolis used an eight-mile bike and pedestrian path to link its cultural attractions. Auckland, known as a "City of Cars," is trying to reverse the development that has emptied out the city center by adding new bike lanes, including the first bike path across the Auckland Harbour Bridge.

For its part, New York has had a long and bumpy relationship with bike lanes. The city designated the nation's very first lanes in 1894, along five miles of pedestrian walkway on Ocean Parkway, a tree-lined Brooklyn boulevard, perfect for pleasure cruisers. Mayor Ed Koch in the 1980s laid barrier-protected bike lanes during the first of his first three terms, which New Yorkers roundly blasted. Koch quickly ripped them out. Bikes were seen as bad politics—there was little constituency aside from the urban pioneers—and bike programs were jettisoned if they were inconvenient. By 2007, the 220 miles of bike lanes in New York City were little known beyond the small core of people who dared to bike New York's streets.

While New York City lagged, cities around the world started to wake up to the benefit of becoming great biking cities. Biking infrastructure is a basic feature in cities such as Paris, which in 2007 launched its Vélib' bike-share system with seven thousand bikes, or Portland, which more than doubled the number of bike commuters in half a decade.

Coming to the job in 2007, I saw no reason why New York couldn't also be one of the world's great biking cities. New York isn't Copenhagen or Amsterdam (as had been abundantly established), but New Yorkers are nothing if not proud. Why should we let European cities eat our lunch on safer, more bike-friendly streets?

New York is relatively flat and most trips in the city are less than three miles, making it perfect for biking. Riding on city streets was a pastime dating back to my childhood. As commissioner, I rode the forty-mile Five Borough Bike Tour around the city, biking along the FDR Drive, Queensboro Bridge, the Brooklyn-Queens Expressway, and the Verrazano-Narrows Bridge with Mark and our son, Max. We rode with the tour's savvy director, Ken Podziba, a former city sports commissioner, thrilled by the sensation of riding in bridge and highway lanes usually forbidden to anyone not in motor vehicles but for this one day a year. I also rode with my bike team, including Ryan Russo and Josh Benson, scouting potential corridors for new bike lanes, and seeing where just a couple blocks of connecting bike paths could close gaps in the network. PlaNYC in 2007 didn't mention bike share, a system of bikes publicly available for low-cost rentals that functions as a kind of public transportation. But it was specific about building lanes on New York City streets at a rate of about fifty miles a year.

In my first months on the job in 2007, I visited Copenhagen (New York not being Copenhagen, I had to travel there), taking with me my deputy commissioner for traffic management, Michael Primeggia, to see how the Danes built bikeways. We toured the city with Jan Gehl, the globally influential architect and urban planner. Gehl pioneered the idea of designing cities from the perspective of pedestrians and cyclists. This perspective, according to Gehl, generates the kind of intimacy and street life that makes cities into attractive places.

One of Copenhagen's bike lane designs is radically simple: curbside bike lanes protected by a lane of parked cars. Most American city streets allow parking along the curbside lane—probably even the street in front of your house or on the route to work—while a traditional bike lane is placed on the moving-traffic side of a parking lane. As discussed in earlier chapters, a parking-protected lane reverses the traffic syntax, placing the bike lane at the curb while moving the parking lane into what used to be a moving traffic lane. This puts bike riders next to a sidewalk on one side and parked cars in the "floating" lane on the other. It separates bikes and vehicles, reducing the chance that a vehicle will illegally block the bike lane and organizing the street better for pedestrians, with safety islands that reduce crossing distances.

I was convinced of this design. But it was critical to get the buy-in of the chief traffic engineer to make the changes I wanted in New York, and that's why he was with me on that trip. Primeggia at first seemed skeptical about this approach. With more than twenty years at DOT, he was steeped in the standardized engineering defined in manuals and reinforced by decades of risk-averse practice. With a new directive (PlaNYC) and a new commissioner, it was as if the shackles were off. This was no small change.

I was delighted during the trip to Copenhagen when Primeggia knelt down and measured the dimensions of a protected bike path along a main street. The wheels were turning as he mentally compared the Danish dimensions with New York's avenues. Cars parked along the curb were as common as parking meters in New York, just as they were in most big cities. I asked Primeggia if there was anything in his manuals that required parking spaces to be along the curb in New York. He admitted there was nothing that explicitly barred the Danish design. But there was nothing explicitly authorizing it. Primeggia knew that neither the engineering nor the manuals posed any problem for making a parking-protected lane work in New York. It would be with New Yorkers. Would they accept this design?

As expected, when we brought our Copenhagen-inspired idea home, many even within the agency thought it was crazy. Having witnessed it work well in another city, Primeggia and his team continued designing what would become the first parking-protected bike lane in North America. The location was Ninth Avenue, in Manhattan's Chelsea neighborhood. Ninth Avenue is not as famous as its avenue cousins, Fifth, Madison, or Lexington, yet it's always been a wide traffic workhorse, on the section we were targeting—from 23rd to 16th streets, near one of our first plazas.

Simply describing the bike lane design to the local community was difficult. I had to mime the design with my hands and fingers but eventually realized there was no avoiding the need for well-drawn street design renderings to show how the new street would look. The ten-foot-wide protected bike lanes were wide enough to accommodate fire trucks, ambulances, sanitation trucks, and the largest emergency vehicles. The new bike lane design needed citywide coordination and the support of the commissioners who were affected by the new designs. A key principle of the Bloomberg administration was to work together as a team—no silos. For example, many fire departments across the United States object to street designs that change the width of traffic lanes or alter the street's function, but Fire Commissioner Nicholas Scoppetta and his chiefs had no problem figuring out that the designs left ample room for their companies (it helped that Scoppetta's chief deputy was a bike enthusiast). Our engineers met with fire officials to run tests of their engines-and-ladders to ensure that they could actually make the turns that worked on paper.

We also needed the buy-in of the police department, which raised questions about signs, traffic flow, and enforcement. If a car was parked in a floating parking lane, could it still violate the rule against parking within fifteen feet of a hydrant? (Yes.) Did protected bike lanes require the installation of bike traffic lights? (Not necessarily; we built them on Ninth Avenue but not on most of First Avenue, and both ways seem to function well.) These changes are not popular with police departments across the country, and it took the leadership and support of Police Commissioner Ray Kelly to get the department's sign-off. Another player in the game was Sanitation Department Commissioner John

The first parking-protected bike path in the United States, on New York City's Ninth Avenue in 2009, placed a row of parked cars in a floating lane, offset from the curb,

Doherty, a bike rider himself, well disposed to bike lanes, and who bought the city's first snow plows to clear them.

The design was presented to the local community board, which approved it. While the plan was for a bike lane, our borough commissioner explained that it would also benefit older New Yorkers who lived in the neighborhood. The redesign would lop twenty-five feet off Ninth Avenue's seventy-foot crosswalks, dramatically decreasing the space in which they were exposed to car traffic.

By October 2007, the bike lane took shape. It wasn't an exact copy of a traditional Copenhagen lane. We used only markings, no street reconstruction that would raise the bike lane a few inches higher than the rest of the road, and no curb, median, or barrier aside from the row of parked cars. This was an only-in-New-York design using only paint for the lane and concrete for safety islands—the transportation depart-

and forming a barrier between the bike lane and moving traffic. The success of the initial lane led to its extension, pictured here. NYC DOT—before: Joan Scholvin; after: Inbar Kishoni

ment's stock-in-trade. Because it was a new design, we also made all of the lane markings as clear as possible, slightly narrowing and aggressively delineating all the remaining car lanes, including dashed lines through the intersection to give drivers visual cues that kept them from drifting.

The idea of altering the street for bikes seemed jarring at first. Most New Yorkers were so used to their streets that they had no idea they could be changed, and the idea of riding a bike was foreign. Some believed that bike lanes cut the space needed to process traffic and to park. Some businesses feared the lanes would make it harder to get deliveries. Others objected that the lanes disrupted the street code that delineated where pedestrians and cars were supposed to be. The street might be dangerous, it might be inefficient, oppressive, and counterproductive, but New Yorkers were used to it.

Yet the successful installation of the first bike lane—and the initial lack of opposition—led to a series of rapid-fire projects, with new bike lanes set in motion on nearby Eighth Avenue; Vernon Boulevard along the Western Queens waterfront; in the Greenpoint neighborhood of Brooklyn; on Staten Island's Bay Street; and Grand Concourse in the Bronx; plus a vital, interconnected system of feeder bike lanes connecting the East River bridges to local bike lane networks in Manhattan and Brooklyn. By 2009 we had completed the most rapid installation of bike lanes ever executed in any city, repurposing former car space to create two hundred miles of bike lanes in three years, nearly the equivalent distance of a bike lane running from the Grand Concourse in the Bronx to the Boston Common. Jan Gehl would later remark that more lanes were built during this transformative period of building bike infrastructure in New York City than in fifty years in bike-friendly Copenhagen. I guess Copenhagen isn't New York!

Another appeal of bike lanes is their low cost. Federal funding, particularly transportation clean-air funds that could be used to help build bike lanes, paid for 80 percent of our bike lane expenditures; the rest we paid for with a local match. For 20 cents on the federal dollar, millions of New Yorkers enjoyed redesigned streets for a fraction of the price of a single subway train.

While most of the first two hundred miles of bike lanes were welcomed or unremarked upon by New York's neighborhoods, the exceptions highlighted the tensions among New York's diverse communities and foreshadowed the coming bike backlash. One of the first bike lane battles ignited on Manhattan's Grand Street—a cluttered crosstown street that cut through SoHo and into Chinatown. Grand Street had one moving traffic lane, two parking lanes, and a bike lane. We converted the existing on-street bike lane into a bike path placed at the curbside, and we pushed the parking lane away from the curb, creating a Ninth Avenue–style floating lane and a protected bike lane. The street still had one moving lane, two parking lanes, and a bike lane, simply in a different order that all but eliminated the possibility of double-parking.

There were the same number of lanes before and after the change, but merchants and local residents claimed that we had removed a traffic lane and also eliminated a parking lane. Others claimed that the change was made unilaterally, without any public notice. A mayoral candidate, sensing an easy political win, declared, "I'm in favor of bike lanes but you can't put bike lanes in without speaking to the community." In fact, the bike lane had been duly presented to the local community board, which supported the project in a 33–1 vote. This bears repeating: the street had the same number of traffic and parking lanes before and after the project, but with better organization. We sent reporters pictures and copies of the authorizing resolution from the community board. Reporters quoted local business owners who claimed the design eliminated a lane, despite clear, photographic evidence that this wasn't the case.

A protected bike path on Grand Street through Manhattan's SoHo and Chinatown helped organize a chaotic street but led to one of the earliest bike controversies. NYC DOT—Heidi Wolf

Some voices whispered that the change stopped fire trucks from turning—exactly the eventuality we had anticipated and engineered into our plans. Still, the headlines blared "'Grand' FDNY Pain." Despite official FDNY statements that the lane had no impact on their trucks' response times, anonymous firehouse sources allegedly claimed that the bike lane "is a problem, [and] it's something we've been talking about. We've been changing our routes when we're driving around this area." In reality, the changes on Grand Street were comparable to the width of thousands of other city streets. Fortunately, these concerns got no further than a one-day headline, nor did the political candidate win any elections with his comments.

Across the East River in Brooklyn, a lopsided 39–2 community board vote supported building a bike path on Kent Avenue, which runs parallel to the rapidly developing Brooklyn waterfront at the edge of the Williamsburg neighborhood. Historically populated by Hasidic Jews, Puerto Ricans, and Dominicans, Williamsburg's population burgeoned during the 2000s with an influx of younger professionals and hipsters. The Kent Avenue bike lane would be a bike superhighway connecting with DUMBO, Fort Greene, and Greenpoint, and become a local link in a biking greenway that one day will link neighborhoods along Brooklyn's fourteen-mile waterfront. Kent was a notorious late-night speedway. It was too wide for two-way traffic, particularly at night, when the long, dark corridor lures thrill-seeking drivers. Yet it was too narrow to add bike lanes while keeping parking on both sides. The greenway plan for Kent envisioned a two-way bike lane that was physically protected from moving traffic with curbs and plantings, creating a waterfront route for bikes and, by narrowing the roadway, slowing down the speeders.

Because a separated lane would require long-term construction, we implemented an interim bike lane project to provide an immediate two-way connection. That design eliminated two hundred parking spaces to give riders enough buffer from passing vehicles, compensated for by modifying parking regulations on side streets to provide more spaces. These spaces would have been removed eventually in the community-approved greenway design. Still, manufacturing industries along Kent protested that they couldn't make or receive deliveries and had nowhere to load trucks.

Even worse, there was the issue of women. *On bikes.* They were lured by bike lanes to Williamsburg's neighborhoods of observant Jews dressed year-round in conservative, body-covering outfits. "Hasid Lust Cause" read the headline. "It's the Hasids vs. the hotties in a Brooklyn bike war." Reporters fanned out all along Kent Avenue to shoot pictures of the Ladies of the Lanes, no doubt because the lanes "are popular with North Williamsburg hipsters—many who ride in shorts or skirts."

A cultural and parking battle flared up before David Woloch, who ran DOT's intergovernmental office, pulled together the threads. While industrial shop owners on Kent objected to the loss of parking, the problem for Jewish leaders with scantily clad *shiksas* wasn't on Kent but on a parallel bike lane on Bedford Avenue, one installed well before my tenure. The Bedford bike lane ran even more directly through religious Williamsburg. In meetings with the agency, Jewish leaders were clear that they would gladly turn Kent Avenue upside down so long as it took the tank-topped and stretch-panted women cyclists away from Bedford Avenue.

We mapped out a redesign for Kent Avenue, including a parking-protected, two-way bike path alongside two parking lanes. In a single stroke, the plan reinstated hundreds of parking spaces and restored loading zones. We expected pushback to the proposal, which also changed Kent from a single traffic lane in both directions to a one-lane, one-way car traffic street. But that didn't seem to faze neighborhood opponents when they saw how much parking would be restored. Through community consultation, a street design was negotiated that was more radical than the one it replaced. Had we started by proposing what we ultimately built on Kent, we would have been tossed from the Williamsburg Bridge.

The downside to the redesign was the controversial erasure of the bike lane on Bedford. It was hard to explain how this seeming retreat actually advanced the biking agenda. But with the new Kent Avenue lane, we have the best bike lane in Brooklyn just a couple of blocks parallel to the one we removed from Bedford, which still connects riders with the Williamsburg Bridge. Today, it is one of the most heavily used sections of bike infrastructure anywhere in the city, or in the nation. I would have loved nothing more than to have won every battle and side skirmish. But this single action instantly stanched a potentially deep political wound and made possible hundreds of miles of future bike lanes in New York City. And to this day, hundreds of people still bike down Bedford Avenue daily in the blank space where the bike lane used to be—just as it is legal to bike on any other city street. Stretch pants, short-shorts, miniskirts, and all.

The biggest bike controversy of all—one that engaged some of New York City's most powerful political figures in a highly public, bitter, and vitriolic battle—centered not on busy Times Square or on any of Manhattan's raucous avenues but miles away, in Brooklyn, on an otherwise quiet street, Prospect Park West. A nineteen-block, .9-mile stretch of road jutting southwest from Grand Army Plaza, Prospect Park West runs alongside the park for which it is named, designed by Frederick Law Olmsted and Calvert Vaux, the creators of Central Park and dozens of other city parks. Tree-lined and home to upscale co-ops and multimillion-dollar town houses, the five-lane street somehow never feels crowded even when full of families pushing strollers or locals hitting the park's running or biking paths or filing out for its summer concerts, food events, and fireworks displays.

Speeding on Prospect Park had been an issue for years, and the transportation department had previously floated plans to convert the street to two-way traffic. As neighborhoods started to see the changes coming to city streets, a new generation of urban activists were starting to trickle into the New York City's Community Board system. These unelected bodies are appointed by borough presidents and city council members and given authority to conduct meetings and advise city agencies on local issues. Though they lack the actual authority to approve or veto projects, their support is widely viewed as important. Community board meetings often end with resolutions addressed to the city agencies demanding action. It was at one such meeting that the community board representing Park Slope called for a bike lane to be implemented immediately on Prospect Park West to provide room for people on bikes while slowing down drivers.

Backed by these resolutions, our bike team came back to the community board with a fuller analysis of the problem: 74 percent of cars monitored on the street were speeding, making the street feel more like a highway than a grand boulevard. Forty-six percent of bikes that used the one-way street rode illegally on the sidewalk. Cyclists didn't want to be on the sidewalk. They were frustrated onto it because the street didn't offer the route they wanted to use—traveling north toward Grand Army Plaza, in the opposite direction of traffic on Prospect Park West to reach adjacent neighborhoods and destinations. The presence of people riding bikes on the sidewalk was as much a frustration line as a desire line, a signature of how the street failed to keep up with how people used it.

Following the people along the street, we designed a two-way protected path, similar to that installed on Kent Avenue, by converting one of the street's three vehicle traffic lanes into a two-way bike path and narrowing the remaining car lanes to calm traffic and also provide a few extra feet for a buffer between the bike lane and the parking lane. We anchored the crosswalks with our now-standard pedestrian safety islands, where people crossing the street could wait for a break in the traffic before crossing two lanes of moving car traffic instead of three. The board voted to support the proposal, reinforced by a petition signed by 1,300 people. As implementation day drew closer we held open houses to present the proposal to reach an even wider public audience. This support on its own would have been more than enough community involvement to implement a project in any other neighborhood. But not this time.

Prospect Park West before and after: Two lanes of traffic and better-timed traffic signals work as well as three lanes, where cars would speed from red light to red light. In the after photo, right, the two-way bicycle lane takes bike riders off the sidewalk, where 46 percent of riders on Prospect Park West would ride illegally among strollers, and helps connect neighborhoods along the one-way network of streets bordering the park. NYC DOT—Julio Palleiro

"She is a zealot" came the voice on a local radio station one morning. The deep, Brooklyn-blunt voice was unmistakably that of the borough's president, Marty Markowitz. The "she," I realized over my morning coffee, was me.

"I have supported bicycle lanes, throughout the borough," Markowitz continued. "But where I feel bicycle lanes would have an adverse effect my job is to speak up for it."

Local cheerleader Marty Markowitz is known for his mouth. Whether he's sinking his teeth into a Junior's cheesecake, extolling the virtues of the Brooklyn Nets, or, in this case, leading the charge against bike lanes, Markowitz used the same vocal intensity to cheer on projects or to bury them, with all the subtlety of a shovel in the face. Borough presidents have little actual authority, legislative or otherwise, save for a small discretionary budget. But then there was his mouth.

This was the same guy who sang his bike lane version of "My Favorite Things" to the City Council four months earlier. Speaking with a reporter in a local paper, Markowitz questioned, "What is our objective in this city? To stigmatize the use of cars? To make it difficult to park? *Do we want Brooklyn to replicate Amsterdam?* These are legitimate policy issues" (emphasis added).

With the "zealot" thing, Markowitz shifted the terms of the debate. The impending construction of a bike lane on Prospect Park West, Markowitz's turf, wasn't a safety issue or a neighborhood-requested project. It was about me and my purported personal war against cars: "I'm acutely aware that she wants to make it hard for those that choose to own their automobiles," Markowitz said. With one well-timed, well-modulated bark into an all-too-willing reporter's microphone, the nature of this game was established: it was my bike lane in his backyard.

Despite Markowitz's preconstruction denunciation, the building of the bike lane in Prospect Park West went ahead in the early summer of 2010 with little drama. I heard reports that my predecessor as transportation commissioner, Iris Weinshall, who lived in a well-appointed high-rise along Prospect Park West with her husband, influential United States senator Charles Schumer, was skeptical about the lane. We had heard that some locals planned strategy sessions to mount an organized opposition to the lane, but nothing much materialized that summer.

The bike lane was a sensation from the moment work started. The design reconfigured one of Prospect Park West's two parking lanes into a two-way bike path. The parking lane was moved away from the curb, taking one of the three vehicle travel lanes. Combined with retimed traffic signals, the same amount of moving traffic would rely on two lanes instead of three. Having seen the "less is more" model work well in Midtown, and with so many streets in Brooklyn moving more traffic on as many lanes, we were confident that the new design would work on Prospect Park West. Reducing the number of lanes changed only the speed of traffic and its impact on the neighborhood, not the street's ability to process all vehicles. The new, broad cycling lane took riders off the sidewalk, giving them a direct route to and from Windsor Terrace, Crown Heights, Park Slope, Prospect Heights, and points in between that were previously circuitous scrambles. By July, when the paint on the lane was still barely dry, Prospect Park West was a different street. None of the prophesied traffic pileups came to pass, no chain-reaction crashes, no reports of people mowed down by bike riders in the lane. Anyone watching the street might be lulled to sleep by the gentle traffic cycles. We succeeded in making the street better for everyone.

Enter two groups of local residents, Seniors for Safety and Neighbors for Better Bike Lanes, both apparently formed for the sole purpose of opposing the Prospect Park West bike lane. Such great names. Who could be against seniors or safety, or oppose neighbors who want better bike lanes? In the new lane these groups saw an aesthetic calamity that spoiled the grand avenue and made it harder for people crossing the street to see oncoming cars and bikes. A better alternative, they offered, would be a two-way bike lane on a road within Prospect Park itself. There were three major holes in this modest "compromise." Putting the lane inside the park would do nothing to reduce speeding on Prospect Park West or prevent people riding bikes on the sidewalk, the project's two original goals. And there was only one bike-accessible park entrance on the street between the extreme ends of the park. Riders would need a new bike lane on the street just to reach the bike lane in the park. This would be capitulation, not compromise.

In the bike lane's fledgling months, these two groups cobbled together a strategic campaign against the lane, targeting reporters and news outlets with allegations about the lane. The anti-laners alleged that we had dodged community notification and approvals. Yet the lane had been requested and approved by the neighborhood's community board numerous times. The subsequent public process made Prospect Park West the most thoroughly vetted and enthusiastically supported bike lane in human history. Plus, the lane worked, and so it stayed. So did the controversy.

Newspapers and local blogs ginned up the drama with claims and counterclaims by local residents. Anyone who learned about Prospect Park West from the headlines might think that children were being run over by city bulldozers and speared by bike riders carrying lances. "It's a Bike Lane War on Prospect Park West!" "Bike Lane Controversy Spurs Shouting Match." "Pedestrians Argue That Zippy Cyclists on Prospect Park West Bike Lane Put Safety at Risk."

The most illuminating coverage during the period came from *Streetsblog* and its sister platform, Streetfilms, which was run by Clarence Eckerson. Eckerson used his storytelling talents to create short, energetic, but documentary videos about transportation projects, cooling the rhetoric that surrounded the lanes by showing how they really looked and operated. Street designs lose something in the translation to print. But the videos that Eckerson and his team produced, including a four-minute segment about Prospect Park West in late 2010, a few months after the bike lane's construction, showed the peaceful coexistence of pedestrians, cyclists, and drivers.

The new lane brought new riders to the streets. Women were attracted to it in increasing numbers. People no longer thought it was crazy to ride with small children. "I can ride safely with my daughter," one rider told Streetfilms, "and not have to worry about traffic and being hit by a car." A young woman in the video reported that she was a relatively new biker on city streets because she was "pretty scared of cars." The design of the new bike lane, protected from moving traffic by parked cars, meant she wasn't frightened of "someone dooring me; I'm not scared of someone parking in the bike lane or pulling into the bike lane."

"People who are critical of the bike path have claimed that it was sprung on them in the last couple of months but nothing could be farther from the truth," Eric McClure said in the video. McClure lived near the bike path and helped lead the fight to build and keep the lane. "The truth is that the community has been asking for traffic calming on Prospect Park West, including a protected bike path, for at least four years."

Six months after the lane was finished and a month after my city council cross-examination, Assistant Commissioner for Traffic Management Ryan Russo attended a meeting in a Park Slope church two blocks from the lane. Relying on the data about how the street had held up in the months since the lane had been installed, he was ready to answer questions from the community board that requested the project and ready to face the dozens of bike lane supporters who came out in force alongside a cadre of anti-laners.

Walking in about halfway through the meeting was my predecessor as commissioner, Iris Weinshall. She took a seat a few rows behind the rest of the crowd. Her name had appeared in news reports as an ardent opponent of the bike lane. Just weeks earlier, Weinshall had cosigned a letter to *The New York Times*. "When new bike lanes force the same volume of cars and trucks into fewer and narrower traffic lanes, the potential for accidents between cars, trucks and pedestrians goes up rather than down," she wrote. "At Prospect Park West in Brooklyn . . . our eyewitness reports show collisions of one sort or another to be on pace to be triple the former annual rates."

The statistics told a far different story. Russo clicked through the presentation as reporters lurked around the auditorium. Speeding on the corridor—the original impetus behind the project—bottomed out, from 74 percent of cars on Prospect Park West speeding before to just 20 percent after. Sidewalk bike riding dropped from 46 percent of riders on the sidewalk before the project to just 4 percent after—and many of these stragglers were children, who are legally allowed to ride on the sidewalk. The number of crashes actually resulting in injuries dropped 63 percent, from an average of slightly more than five for every six-month period to just two in the six months since the lane was installed. Traffic volumes and driving time remained unchanged. Before the redesign, cars sped from red light to red light. Now they cruised at a slower, steadier pace with few, if any, stops. A survey conducted by Brad Lander, the community-minded council member for Prospect Park West's district, found that most people surveyed who lived near the park supported the changes.

Some of the meeting attendees wanted to make constructive adjustments, such as installing concrete pedestrian refuge islands, adding raised stripes to the bike lane that would cause bikes to "rumble" as they approached crosswalks, and changing parking regulations to provide more drop-off zones. Weinshall didn't speak at the meeting, and the opponents were strangely muted. That night, we celebrated a successful meeting that had gone even better than our best-case scenario. It looked like the lane was there to stay.

The community board said it was going to review the data we presented and issue a resolution regarding the lane's future. Opponents of the lane were also looking at the data that night and had already given their take on it to a reporter. "B'klyn Nabe Disputes Lane 'Success'" read the next day's tabloid headline. The story continued: "A battle over a Brooklyn bike lane is in high gear," with a group of well-organized residents accusing the city of "fudging the numbers of bicycles using the lane to support the city's drive to make the pathway permanent." No mention of the community request or support for the lane. Opponents of the lane had collected their own "data" (video of the lane shot from the penthouse of a resident) and said they saw vastly fewer riders in the lane than our counts. Their counts were collected at only one extreme end of Prospect Park West, the equivalent of counting the number of passengers riding a train by counting how many are on at the last stop, but the tactic played well in the media and riled up bike lane opponents. The underlying bike lane battle wasn't a factual, data-based argument but a cultural and political fight that was rapidly devolving into a backlash, one that, as we soon discovered, would be resolvable only in a court of law.

The bike backlash of early 2011 peaked with the fight over this project, and they were the toughest months I've ever endured professionally. Newspapers, radio stations, and blogs delivered damning quotes from shopkeepers, people in cars, schoolteachers, and crossing guards to inflame the debate. We were accused of ignoring community views and ramming projects down communities' throats, making streets dangerous and killing businesses. Every day brought new stories of misery, not just about Prospect Park West but about every bike project old or new, plazas already constructed, and phantom projects that hadn't even been proposed. "Don't worry, Sis," my brother John Sadik-Khan told me, "you know the scouts always get the arrows."

A reporter questioned a bike lane project on Manhattan's Second Avenue that ran near the Israeli consulate. "Imagine if the man on the bike was a terrorist!" On Columbus Avenue on Manhattan's Upper West Side, store owners organized around a protected bike path, prompting elected officials to call for changes to address concerns that the lane made deliveries and parking more difficult. The dialogue over this controversy was constructive, but it was represented in the media as an acrimonious fight. We updated parking regulations and established more metered parking spaces on side streets.

A writer for *New Yorker* magazine lamented that city officials "sometimes seems intent on turning New York into Amsterdam, or perhaps Beijing." These policies, however noble, represented the views of "a small faddist minority intent on foisting its bipedalist views on a disinterested or actively reluctant populace." Another columnist had no patience for such fussy language and dubbed me the "wacko nutso bike commissioner." The backlash landed on the cover of *New York* magazine with a photo illustration containing every urban streetfight cliché: two aggressive men riding bikes the wrong way; horrified pedestrians; a car blocking a bike lane; and the headline "Not Quite Copenhagen. Is New York Too New York for Bike Lanes?" For the record, a bike lane opponent answered: "We will never be Amsterdam, never be Copenhagen."

The stories were as thick and immobilizing as the frozen snowdrifts from a destructive blizzard that winter, all centering on the same theme: a commissioner, as loved by some as she is loathed by others, faces backlash for her radical bike agenda. One local magazine put my face on the cover with multiple-choice boxes: Love or Hate. I worried about what the mayor thought about the tsunami of bad press and asked Marc La Vorgna, our media contact at city hall who became the mayor's press secretary, what he made of the love/hate dichotomy.

"Whatever. I checked love," he shot back. The article "says you have big ideas and don't accept the status quo."

It was hard to take comfort in these kind words as still more stories landed. One tabloid harshly criticized me for what it viewed as a lackluster response to a devastating blizzard that winter, and saw my defense as a criticism of Police Commissioner Ray Kelly, a close ally of mine. Blistering critiques of the bike backlash and my starring role in it fueled a major story in *The New York Times*. The lead quote in that piece came from Anthony Weiner, a Queens congressman and candidate for mayor to replace Bloomberg, who said that during his first term, "I'm going to have a bunch of ribbon-cuttings tearing out your fucking bike lanes." Talk about going off half-cocked.

Opponents of the Prospect Park West bike lane took to the courts, filing legal papers that claimed the transportation department's decision to build the bike lane was "arbitrary and capricious." The suit accused the department of giving false or misleading bike lane data to the public and claimed that the lane should have been studied for "various environmental impacts, including but not limited to exhaust and noise pollution," and possible violations of the city's landmarks preservation code.

The news reached every part of the city. My son, Max, asked me if I was being sued, saying that all the kids at his high school in Brooklyn were talking about it. My husband, Mark, a law professor at New York University, helped me explain to Max how the law worked and that I was being sued in my official capacity as commissioner. Not exactly the kind of conversation I ever expected to have with my child, especially about a bike lane. I counted on Mark's counsel and humor more than anyone. Every night we talked through the issues of the day. Mark told me that many of his colleagues at the law school had seen the story in the *Times* and were impressed, thinking that I must have been doing something right to be given such prominence in the papers. Others pointed out sexist assumptions they saw in the story. Another common refrain, only half in jest, was that "as long as the story doesn't include the word 'indictment' and has a good picture, it's a winner."

As the stories mounted, the administration closed ranks. Bloomberg's director of public affairs, Frank Barry, told *New York* magazine, "Janette is doing exactly what the mayor expects of all his commissioners: pioneering innovative new ways of serving the public, no matter what the politics. . . . There will always be some who resist change, but in the case of bike lanes, the community boards have strongly supported them—and the safety numbers show they're saving lives."

In response to a *Daily News* editorial that alleged that many projects were forced upon unwilling communities, we sent a memo to the paper pointing out that despite vocal opposition to some bike lanes, local community boards supported and specifically requested them. The paper brushed aside the message and the PDF copies of the board resolutions and authorizations. "You can dismiss all this as inaccurate if you like," the editorial writer e-mailed us, *"but people are saying this."* Contradicting factually inaccurate claims wouldn't eliminate them from public discussion; it only helped keep the controversy alive.

Deputy Mayor Howard Wolfson was the best colleague, friend, and bike lane defender I could ever hope for. He became an inveterate bike commuter as deputy mayor. People in the administration jokingly accused me of being responsible for his Lycra attire at city hall, rolling his bike past security. Nope. It was all Howard and he was the person you wanted on your side when things got tough. And they did.

He shot back with a memo to reporters filled with statistics documenting our extensive outreach on bike lane projects and the majority support they enjoyed with New Yorkers at large. "It's official," he added in a separate post. "Bike lanes have become a metaphor. For some they symbolize the 'nanny state' run amok—as if the City were forcing drivers out of their cars and compelling them to get around on two wheels instead. But to paraphrase that great cyclist Sigmund Freud, sometimes a bike lane is just a bike lane." Wolfson's memos and tweets were the media equivalent of air support, strategically helping us in the debate and also boosting morale.

Newspapers that hoped to harass Mayor Bloomberg or whip his aides into a froth to fire me and tear out the bike lanes were bitterly disappointed. "I've always said that if you want lifetime employment in our administration, you just get the *Post* to demand that I fire you," he said.

As that was apparently the tabloid's goal, and because it was obvious that the mayor made decisions based on facts and data and not headlines, the *Post* responded in kind with a sarcastic, reverse-psychology editorial entitled "We ♥ Janette," demanding that I be kept on as commissioner.

"This one's a keeper," it concluded. "*Pleeeeease* don't fire her."

He didn't, and I kept that editorial at my desk for the remainder of my tenure.

As the Winter of Bike Discontent thawed into spring, there were fewer hit pieces, and broadcast media moved on to other drive-by topics. The advocacy community also pulled together, just as they had at Prospect Park West. Paul Steely White and Caroline Samponaro from Transportation Alternatives spoke out at community meetings, drafted op-eds and letters to the editor, and always made themselves available to reporters writing about bike controversies. Supporters delivered 1,700 thank-you letters at an event on the City Hall steps, thanking the mayor for the string of street changes. They were led by savvy leaders like Kate Slevin, of the Tri-State Transportation Campaign, and Gene Russianoff, from New York's Straphangers Campaign, and backed by officers of the Natural Resources Defense Council and the New York League of Conservation Voters. "We're here today to say thanks to Janette Sadik-Khan and Mayor Bloomberg," Slevin said. "It's safer to get around New York City today than at any time since record-keeping began."

There may have been a more practical explanation for the end of the media frenzy: the polls started coming in. A Quinnipiac University poll found that 54 percent of New Yorkers said that bike lanes were "a good thing." This was the first of many polls that would be released in the coming months, two putting bike lanes' popularity as high as 66 percent—higher than the approval numbers for most New York politicians. Judged by the polls, most New Yorkers either didn't read the papers or didn't relate to the controversy. What sounded like a chorus of opposition in the media was actually a small but determined section of the population. Influential news columnists also began to take up the issue, as headlines about conflict were replaced with kinder words like "Thanks," and "Bicycle Visionary" from *Times* columnist Frank Bruni, who helped expand the media vocabulary.

It became clear that the fight wasn't about me or Bloomberg, and we didn't win the public debate by outwitting the opposition. The battle was won by the projects and by New Yorkers themselves. New Yorkers were way ahead of the press and the politicians. They took to changes on the street with an enthusiasm immune to the government that built them, to the advocates pushing for the changes, and to the opponents arrayed against them. They were just looking for new ways to get around and saw in the transformation of the streets the fulfillment of a long-dormant promise. *Change is possible.* They weren't Lycra warriors or ideologues out for blood, and in fact there was less blood on the street than there was at the start of the process. And it wasn't about bike lanes. It was about an idea about our streets and who they are for.

We succeeded in building as many bike lanes after the bikelash as before it. The number of riders doubled from 2007 to 2013, representing a fourfold increase measured over a decade. Judged from the street and by the sight of ordinary people riding bikes as basic transportation and not as a political statement, a new road order for cities had become a self-evident fact on the streets of New York.

"The biggest mischaracterization about the infamous New York Cycling War is that there's a war at all," wrote a columnist for *The Wall Street Journal*. "Look all around you. The bikes have won, and it's not a terrible thing."

A final victory wouldn't arrive until September 2016, six years after the lane was installed and nearly three years after I left office. The chief plaintiff of the Prospect Park West lawsuit withdrew the suit, citing its low prospects for success.

You can fight it, you can lie about it, you can say that the sky is falling, but you can't keep a good bike lane down.

9

Bike Share: A New Frontier in the Shared Economy

Just after eleven p.m. my e-mail inbox exploded with messages from viewers tuned to *The Daily Show with Jon Stewart*. I was out that night at an event and had missed the entire show, but quickly figured out that Stewart had just given Citi Bike the full comic treatment.

"There are a lot of important stories in the world right now," Jon Stewart said to open the show, and "one of the most important is happening right here in New York City."

Then came the footage of Citi Bikes. "Oh my god," Stewart said, anticlimactically. "We have basically imported Europe's most boring idea." Stewart unspooled clips from recent news reports that Citi Bike had launched amid concerns that the system was buggy, that bike-share riders don't have to wear helmets, and that locals had complained that the racks were ugly and arbitrarily placed in neighborhoods.

"Oh, they're not safe," Jon Stewart mocked. "They don't work. Looks like shit. Blah blah blah. You know, we used to say the same thing about the Irish!"

Jon Stewart's Citi Bike routine was just getting started, and so were we. Citi Bike launched at a Memorial Day press conference, six years to the weekend after we had first shut down Broadway through Times Square. But unlike hundreds of other projects we had nurtured from idea to implementation, Citi Bike existed on a different political and emotional scale. On May 27, 2013, we launched a new public transportation system for New York City, a bike-share system with six thousand bikes docked at 330 stations. Fifteen thousand annual members had signed up for the system by the first day. They were the only ones who were allowed to use the system during its first week of operation. The soft launch of about five thousand rides on that first day gave us a chance to work out the kinks while the city was emptied out for the holiday.

And there were kinks. We were smiling in front of hundreds of media, drenched in brilliant sunlight for Citi Bike's launch, but inside I was afraid the entire system might crash. Biker and writer David Byrne walked along the perimeter of the massive pool of reporters from New York and around the world attending the event, a familiar face and supporter whom I sorely needed. In the hours before the press conference, out of eyeshot of cameras and reporters, I repeatedly tested the docks, checking out bikes with my own key. It worked most of the time. But I was dismayed that some bikes took ten, fifteen, twenty, and even thirty seconds to unlock after swiping my key in the dock. That function was supposed to take a few seconds at most.

I stood at the lectern with the mayor as he announced the official start of the system, marked by the trilling of bike bells by dozens of transportation department staff bike-share workers. As the cameras rolled, Bloomberg stuck his key into the Citi Bike dock to pull out a bike. I stood behind him, praying hard that it would work. It did. It was a giddy moment. I was thrilled and exhausted, but most of all, as I steered a Citi Bike across the plaza amid hundreds of people, I just wanted to ride. Deputy Mayor Howard Wolfson, Jon Orcutt, Seth Solomonow, and I set off along Centre Street, each on a Citi Bike.

We rode past Petrosino Square, home to a thirty-three-dock bike rack, where a group of artists staged daily sketch-ins, drawing seminude models posing to protest the installation of the station. We rode by Bicycle Habitat, the SoHo bike store opened in 1978 by Charlie McCorkell, a huge supporter of our work who sold bikes to generations of New York City riders long before anyone conceived of New York as a biking city. High on press conference adrenaline and warm, late spring air, we

Artists stage a sketch-in at Petrosino Square, protesting the installation of a bike-share station in 2013. A lawsuit over the racks was dismissed. Jen Chung/Gothamist

navigated uptown on First Avenue's protected bike path. The city seemed to open up. From the bike path, the normally chaotic First Avenue gave us room to breathe. Buses zipped along a painted red lane on the opposite side of the street; cars plied uptown in their own lanes. Pedestrians waited safely at islands for the light to change. In my mind's eye, I saw rainbows and heard birds tweeting as in a maudlin scene from a Disney movie. We completed this victory lap in Times Square, beneath the glare, even on a sunny day, of the electronic billboards. We exchanged hugs and high-fives, wondering how we had forgotten to pack a bottle of champagne. But we felt so good, who needed it?

It was just 238 days until the end of Mayor Bloomberg's third and final term, at the end of 2013. The bike backlash was two years behind us and there was a sense of finality and tension to every action, of getting as much into the ground as possible in the short time remaining. Launching Citi Bike was the culmination of years of work, delays, and disappointments and a dream that one hundred times I thought was dead. Even as I coasted along the First Avenue lane that day, I knew that some of the hardest days lay ahead, as the fabulously popular new transportation mode collided with its own still-buggy software and lackluster private management and funding. The euphoric buzz of the launch would wear off—though not so fast that I wouldn't appreciate the extraordinary work my policy director, Jon Orcutt, and the bike-share director, Kate Fillin-Yeh, had done to get us there. But the remaining days would be an ordeal to keep the program from collapsing and rescue it from the self-inflicted wounds of its own management.

Years before Citi Bike's launch, the knock on bike lanes in New York City was that no one would use them because no one would be crazy enough to ride a bike in the first place. After installing more than three hundred miles of bike lanes by 2013 and with bike ridership exploding by a factor of four over a decade, the complaint was that the streets had now become overrun by people riding bikes. In building bike lanes, we had built demand for biking, creating demand for new and better bike infrastructure. Within seven weeks of launch, riders had logged 1 million rides on Citi Bikes, blowing the pedals off bike-share systems in other cities. It took just over a year to reach 10 million rides. At its height, more than 100,000 people held annual passes. We had to ask ourselves, for all the backlash and battles, had we built *enough* bike lanes to keep up with the hundreds of thousands of New Yorkers who were now getting around on bikes?

The runaway success of our May 2013 bike-share debut was incredibly affirming, but it wasn't surprising. The rise of the urban generation means a rise of the "zip" generation. Younger Americans are turning away from car ownership and driving less. The number of younger Americans getting driver's licenses dropped from 87 percent of nineteen-year-olds in 1983 to just 70 percent in 2010, and Americans overall are driving fewer miles on average than a decade ago and taking transit more than at any point since the Interstate Highway System took off in the 1950s. In the same way that desire lines provided incentives for place-making investments in cities, the search for an alternative to needing a car to get to every destination, whether commuting or running errands, has prompted the public and private sectors to find a new transportation model.

Many younger Americans, particularly those in cities, see driving as a frustrating, time-wasting chore, and are stressed out by traffic, incivility, cost, and the difficulty finding a parking space. Car ownership is a huge up-front financial commitment, and once you own a car for one purpose—say, for commuting—it's a natural and seemingly cost-effective step to start using the car to shop, visit friends, and set up other habits that prompt even more car trips. The new transportation model says that cars are still helpful, even necessary for occasional tasks—shopping at a distant location, a day trip beyond city limits—but they aren't worth the 24/7/365 commitment, expense, and hassle of car ownership. Starting with Zipcar and followed eventually even by traditional rental companies, companies now offer car rentals for just a few hours for an all-inclusive price. Once you're done with your errand or finished visiting your grandparents on Staten Island, you park the vehicle at its designated parking lot and need not think about it—or move it on street cleaning days—again.

The trend of young people turning their backs on car ownership has greater ramifications in cities where travel distances are shorter and transit more developed and where even a shared car is inconvenient. It's easy to think of travel simply in terms of the primary mode of transportation that gets you from place to place—airplane, car, bus, subway, taxi, Uber—but over the course of a day, for many city residents, trips are complex combinations of these modes. People walk from home to the train, then walk from the train to work. A store employee might drive to work but walk to a nearby deli or food cart for lunch or to run errands. A businessman in downtown might take taxis between appointments before walking to transit or driving home. When you add up the many trips in between, bikes suddenly offer to play a more significant role, even for people who drive. This practicality has been at the heart of bike share's rapid growth across Europe, Asia, and in the Americas during the 2000s, reaching 712 cities and more than 806,000 bikes by mid-2014. The principle of bike share is based on an accessibility that car share can't reach: ubiquity. Hundreds of bike-share stations located every couple of blocks throughout the city, either on the street or in parks, plazas, or other public spaces, can be checked out and returned to any dock for a nominal fee. Virtually immune to traffic and resilient to parking problems, bike share greatly expands a person's reach in the city.

From our first day in office we knew that bike share would be a perfect fit for our city. About half the trips in New York City are less than three miles, and its relatively flat topography makes it easy for most people to bike a mile or two in ten minutes without breaking a sweat. While New York is a transit-dense city, not all development is concentrated along subway lines, leaving huge swaths, and hundreds of thousands of New Yorkers, just beyond walking distance of subway stations or bus transit. Bike share could be used for short trips, extending the reach of New York's existing transit options. It could make the ten-minute walk from the subway a pleasant three-minute cruise on sturdy bikes with always-running lights. If deployed well, bike share could reassign millions of annual trips from cars to bikes, boost transit, and give people an alternative to driving or taking a cab for longer trips.

A 2009 city study envisioned a ten-thousand-bike system with easily available bikes on sidewalks, plazas, and curbsides in the densest parts of New York City. Based on models in cities like London, the system could be paid for by sponsorship funds and member fees—no taxpayer investment. Using new wireless and solar systems, stations could be installed without having to dig into city streets. New Yorkers would have access to these bikes for $95 a year, a price that brings them an electronic key in the mail and grants the rider unlimited forty-five-minute rides on bike-share bikes. "Unlimited forty-five-minute trips" means that riders can make as many trips as they want without incurring an additional charge, so long as each ride lasts less than forty-five minutes. This lets members bike to a dock at a subway station, catch a train, then grab another bike when emerging on the other side. You could bike to the store, dock the bike, shop, then jump on another bike once you leave the store to go out to lunch. You can leave work and grab a bike to reach a neighborhood a few blocks away, then bike back to the office, all with no charge on top of the annual member fee.

The most famous system operating in the world at the time, Paris's Vélib' system, launched in 2007 with ten thousand bikes at 750 stations, had greatly expanded and was a success by the time we announced our own bike-share plan, but it wasn't without a fight and a public-relations struggle. A design flaw in the bikes' locking system made them targets for theft, and media carried reports of thousands of bikes plucked from the streets of Paris annually and dumped in the Seine, ridden down the steps of Montmartre, winding up on the streets of North African cities, or sold on the black markets of Bucharest. Nevertheless, Paris's system, operated by a multinational outdoor advertising company, grew to twenty thousand bikes as of early 2015.

Based on an analysis of New York City's market, the cost estimate for implementing a program like this—with enough bikes to keep people rolling and with enough docking stations so that a bike would always be available within a block or two in the densest part of New York City—came to about $50 million. Given the pushback against funding bike lanes, we knew there would be little will for spending tens of millions of dollars in taxpayer funds to implement a new system, particularly as the economy was still recovering from the 2008 financial crisis. But seeing how successfully bike-share programs were operating elsewhere in the world, we were confident that this would be a great opportunity for private sponsorship. A lot of companies would love to have their name on thousands of bikes cruising around the middle of New York City and would pay big money for it.

Many companies would be attracted to the prospect, but it takes time for such a major deal to work its way through the city approval process, and time was running out to get a program up and running before the mayor's term ended. In a crucial legal maneuver, DOT's general counsel, Phil Damashek, proposed structuring New York City's bike-share program as a revenue contract. This gave the transportation department the authority to select a prospective vendor while also ensuring that deciding where to place each bike station wouldn't become a political free-for-all, bogged down for years in the city's land-use process. Franchise contracts, which some city legislators might have preferred, would no doubt have delayed or even killed the program, with requirements for city council review and approvals. Instead, our contractual strategy would let the council hold oversight hearings without opening the bike-share contract and every station location up for negotiation with each of the fifty-one council members.

We were nervous as we approached launch date and hadn't sealed the deal with the eventual sponsor, which was supposed to be secured by the bike-share operator, Alta, a Portland-based company that ran bike-share systems in Washington, D.C., Boston, and elsewhere. We were running out of time before the planned summer 2012 launch of the system, and New Yorkers wanted to know whose name would be on the bikes. Frustrated by the bike-share operator's lack of progress, I intervened in that process personally, developing pitch presentations for likely sponsors such as Citibank, Apple, Puma, and MasterCard.

The selection went to Citi, which put up $41 million for the naming rights for the bike-share system for five years, and augmented by $6.5 million from MasterCard, which agreed to be the payment sponsor and have its logo attached to station kiosks. Citi's name and the Citi Bike moniker seemed like a match made in marketing heaven, an opportunity not lost on Ed Skyler, the former Bloomberg deputy mayor who joined Citi in 2010 and helped land the deal for the bank. We announced the selection at a city hall press conference in May 2012, introducing New Yorkers to the freshly wrapped new Citi Bikes.

Relief at selecting Citi was short-lived. Earlier that spring, news reports stated that Alta was having software problems with its bike-share systems in Chattanooga. No problem, Alta and its supplier, the Montreal-based PBSC, assured us. Chattanooga used a different software system. They would patch up that problem and New York wouldn't be affected.

To our horror, we discovered there was more to this story. Much more. PBSC was embroiled in a legal dispute after firing the software vendor that had provided the proven, high-capacity network that worked in Boston and Washington, D.C. PBSC was so confident that it decided to develop its own software system. Brand new. From scratch. Without telling us. And despite the company's opacity, we eventually discovered that Citi Bike was slated to receive the same software system that was foundering in Chattanooga. The problems were enormous. Docks wouldn't unlock bikes. Transactions took too much time to process. And that was a thirty-station system. What would happen when we started putting two hundred times that number of bikes on the streets of New York City? Reporters started asking the same question.

On the transportation department's team, Chief Technology Officer Cordell Schachter helped rescue the bike-share program by assessing the scale of Alta and PBSC's bike-share meltdown. He traveled to Montreal and Chattanooga to learn the technical guts of the system—investigating deep enough to understand how bad PBSC's new software system really was. He was our eyes and ears in our meetings with Alta and cautioned us to avoid launching the buggy system. He also developed protocols for testing the new software and helping to stabilize it.

I was furious at Alta and PBSC executives who, despite their conclusive failures, repeatedly averred that Citi Bike would be ready to launch in summer 2012, and seemed unconcerned by a buggy rollout. They claimed they could iron out kinks in a few weeks. Knowing how unforgiving the New York City public would be for a botched rollout, I had no appetite for putting bikes on the street that might or might not work or might take customers' money without giving them bikes. I dragged the leadership of Alta and PBSC in for meetings and daily conference calls in the late spring and summer of 2012, raking them over the coals as they missed deadline after deadline and their homespun software system failed test after test. As the summer progressed and we lost the best part of the bike-riding season, we were faced with a choice: either postpone the system launch until the fall, when Alta and PBSC claimed the system would be 100 percent, or pull the plug on a 2012 launch, building in six months of buffer time that would allow us to start with a clean slate in the spring.

As we weighed our options, the Alta team promised me and senior city leadership gathered at increasingly tense city hall meetings that the system would be ready to go live on time. They may have been representing their company's legal self-interest, as to admit that the system wasn't ready to launch would put them in legal default. Or they may have been deluding themselves into thinking that New Yorkers could muddle through if the system didn't work in the first few months. Regardless, they were either out of touch with the truth or had no concept of how to conduct the public's business in New York City, where a botched launch could be fatal to even the best ideas. We kept radio silence with the public as we warred, leading some reporters to question what was happening behind closed doors.

As our meetings and failed system tests carried us deep into July, we closed the door on the possibility of a summer launch. The only thing remaining to be done was reformat the contract with the revised start date. The choice was painful and obvious. Mayor Bloomberg broke the news on his weekly radio interview show on August 17, 2012. The delay wasn't the result of some kind of skulduggery. "The software doesn't work, duh," he said, reflecting the exasperation we all felt. "We're not going to put it out until it does work." New launch date: March 2013.

The arrival of Superstorm Sandy, which rolled into the eastern seaboard later that October, put us even further underwater—literally. Thousands of bikes stored in the Brooklyn Navy Yard, along the East River waterfront, were damaged in the flood. New launch date: May 2013.

Delaying the bike-share rollout created a news vacuum and left plenty of time for the plan to be criticized and proposed locations challenged. If the system was not ready by spring, and that was a big "if," there wouldn't be enough time for us to get back on our feet and launch a successful system before Bloomberg's term ended. The delay meant that, at a minimum, Citi Bike would launch in the middle of the campaign to elect the mayor's successor. We'd seen what happens when bikes collide with electoral politics. In 2009, Bloomberg's Democratic opponent, William Thompson, spoke out against a community-approved bike lane on Grand Street. It was a cheap shot that ignored the public process, but politicians looking for an edge often attach themselves to local controversies in search of votes.

The presumptive frontrunner in the 2013 race to replace Bloomberg as mayor was Council Speaker Christine Quinn. She told a reporter, "Bike lanes, I put that now in the category of things you shouldn't discuss at dinner parties, right? It used to be money and politics and religion. Now in New York you should add bike lanes," she said as the campaign was starting to heat up.

Just two days after Bloomberg announced the delay in launching the bike-share system, another candidate, Public Advocate Bill de Blasio, complained to a newspaper that I was a "radical," and that, as mayor, he would take an "incrementalist" approach. "Incrementalism would say we want to make progress, and we have to do it with communities, and we have to be realistic," he said.

De Blasio immediately had to walk back his words after an outcry from advocates who feared he was signaling a change in policy away from bike lanes and plazas. After being elected mayor, he has expanded bike share, bike lanes, rapid bus service, and virtually all of the safety programs we initiated. "We don't do incrementalism," he said after becoming mayor. "We don't take on small and easy plans."

One city official raised alarm that the Citi Bike system did not require riders to wear helmets. In fact, very few cities require helmets because there is evidence that whatever safety benefit helmets provide riders, it is erased by discouraging people from riding in the first place, making streets less safe. In Paris, where there is no helmet requirement, seven people riding Vélib' bikes died in traffic crashes, three of them in the first year of operation. But data on bike-share riders in London, where there also is no requirement, found that riders of the Barclays bike-share system were safer than riders on private bikes. And we had an important safety asset on our side: we had spent five years developing—and fighting for—a network of safe, interconnected lanes, including thirty-one miles of protected bike paths. The number of people killed or injured in New York City hadn't changed despite millions more bike trips every year.

By the time the brackish water from superstorm Sandy had dried in spring 2013, the pending launch of Citi Bike started to stir up many of the passions that had lain dormant since the bike backlash. Retrofitting dozens of neighborhoods in Manhattan and Brooklyn with the bike-share system's 330 docking stations—perched on sidewalks or nestled in parking spaces and plazas, next to subways, and the largest of which would shut a block of Park Avenue next to Grand Central Terminal—provided all the necessary ingredients for yet another backlash.

This time, we were ready. We had spent several weeks documenting the intensive bike-share location siting outreach process in a twenty-nine-page report, which we blasted out to hundreds of journalists. We bludgeoned city transportation reporters with the facts: over eighteen months we had held 159 public meetings, a number that grew to nearly 400 when counting additional face-to-face meetings our staff had with elected officials, civic groups, business owners, property owners, and others about where to place the stations. We unfurled detailed maps at these meetings that New Yorkers could mark up, denoting where they did and didn't want stations. These meetings, which alone constituted the greatest public outreach effort for almost any single transportation project in the city's history, were supplemented by an online outreach portal where people who couldn't make our meetings could weigh in on where they wanted stations. All told, the portal received 65,000 suggestions and indications of support on the portal's geo-coded map— the most advanced form of crowdsourcing we had yet used. By the time the first station would have gone in, station locations would have been public for nearly a year.

In placing the six thousand bikes in 330 stations, we saw an opportunity to tip the scales of the street, both by clawing back some of the streetscape for use by something other than cars and by placing mil-

Bike-share systems have become part of the streetscape in London, left, and in Paris, right, and helped provide early guidance on system equipment, different models for revenue, and requirements for bike density, influencing the establishment of new systems around the world.   Jon Orcutt

lions of riders a year on the street. While biking is often dismissed as an elite fad, it's actually the cheapest way around town, We specifically sited stations at public housing complexes, with at least one station within a block of all twenty-nine city-owned public housing properties in the bike-share area. A steep discount was offered for public housing residents—sixty dollars for an annual subscription, versus ninety-five dollars for other users at launch. Even the more expensive membership for an entire year of rides was less than the cost of a transit card for one month of unlimited rides on the city bus and subway system.

The community outreach report fell on deaf ears. "DOT bike-share report finds DOT outreach 'most expansive public process in transpo history,'" a *New York Times* reporter chided in a Tweet, adding the dig, "In case anyone was asking."

It seemed that no one cared about these 159 meetings. But this dismissal was in fact a good sign. We knew from the punishing backlash two years earlier that meetings and supporting resolutions and letters of support from community boards, elected officials, and civic and business associations would not be enough to keep back critics. We directed the public and reporters to bike share presentations we posted online, and dedicated an entire team to identifying bike station locations and conducting door-to-door outreach to businesses near stations. We had to call attention to our meetings to the point where reporters and the general public had gotten sick of hearing us describe how nauseatingly great our outreach was. The events leading up to the launch in spring 2013 proved this strategy right.

The morning of April 6 started in the chillier part of the thirties. As the sun rose on the corner of Fulton Street and Grand Avenue in Brooklyn's Clinton Hill on a quiet Saturday, a crew was already working to snap, screw, and shimmy Citi Bike's first station into place, setting dock segments onto the sidewalk. In a moment of semifrozen exhaustion, we

New York's Citi Bike system used batteries and solar power, allowing stations to be placed on city streets in minutes without an electrical hookup that would have turned every station installation into a potential construction zone. The bike-share team hoists one of the first into action.   NYC DOT—Alex Engel

stopped the work crew from lifting the fifteen-foot-tall solar power–collecting antenna into place, setting it upright ourselves.

The station at Fulton and Grand wasn't controversial. We had the bike-share company start installation of bike-share stations in Brooklyn, not on Manhattan's more provocative real estate, staving off confrontation for at least a few weeks while also giving installation crews time to hone their skills before they attempted Manhattan. Instead of a single bike lane on a single street or corridor, bike share promised a minefield with 330 potential flash points. If a bike-share station was on the sidewalk, neighbors would protest that it impeded walking. If a station was in the street, businesses might bemoan a loss in parking for customers or deliveries. If it was in a park or plaza, there would always be someone to grumble about a loss of space for fun, art, or recreation. Residents in brownstone neighborhoods saw the stations as commercializing eyesores, while residents in high-rises lamented that the stations left them no room to place their garbage at the curb. We had fifty-one days between the first station installation and the system launch on May 27, a political eternity when there would be only the invasive docks and bikes and none of the benefit of being able to use them. New Yorkers might get grumpy.

Because we had already undertaken such extensive community outreach and vetting, the first flashes of antibike hysteria turned comical and hyperlocal instead of threatening. Those who made the inevitable claim that we hadn't enlisted enough community involvement didn't win as much charity with many reporters to whom we had sent the outreach report—even the one who questioned if anyone was asking. The owner of a bistro in TriBeCa, outraged when a crew started to install a station next to his restaurant, sat down in the parking lane. "I'm all for bike sharing," he said, according to the *New York Post*, "but the Department of Transportation did not inform us this was going to happen." He backed down when police told him that his protest could land him in jail.

On Bank Street in the West Village, residents claimed that a new bike-share rack "presents a serious threat to public safety." "This is a cobblestone street," the building's lawyer told the *Daily News*. "The bicyclists will go on the sidewalk." Residents filed a lawsuit to remove the station. The lawsuit was dismissed.

A half mile away, at East 13th Street in the Village, residents told the *New York Post* that a bike-share station in front of their apartment building blocked paramedics from reaching a ninety-two-year-old patient in the building. "The ambulance couldn't even come up to the building," his wife told a reporter. Residents filed a lawsuit to remove the station. The lawsuit was dismissed.

Across town in SoHo, local residents opposed a location in a curb-side lane on the grounds that it would block emergency vehicles. When the dock was relocated into the tip of tiny Petrosino Square, it aroused the ire of local artists who claimed the park space as their own. "We're livid," a local advocate said. "That area was supposed to be reserved for art exhibitions, not bikes." This prompted another lawsuit—filed by the same lawyer who was the lead litigator in the case against the Prospect Park West bike lane. The lawsuit was dismissed.

In Brooklyn Heights, a bike-share dock purportedly blocked a patch of sidewalk where apartment building managers placed trash and garbage bags. "We feel this is not the right spot," a resident told the *Post*. "There are other places in the neighborhood. We have a very crowded neighborhood. We were never consulted. We didn't find out about them until they were put in." Yes, another lawsuit. Yes, another lawsuit dismissed.

Next to Central Park at the famous Plaza Hotel, hotel managers claimed a Citi Bike station across the street from their front door was too blue, taking away from the hotel's aesthetics. Lawsuit. Dismissed.

Locals complained that a bike-share rack at Dag Hammarskjold Plaza in Midtown was dangerously close to the United Nations. One resident at a public meeting recounted how terrorists in Jaipur, India, used bombs hidden in bikes to kill fifty-six people and injure scores of others in the 2008 attacks. The speaker shared the story "because it appears that bombs inserted on or in bike parts could become a tool of global terrorists in our city under a citywide massive bike program." Bike-share terrorism? Please. You can't even sue for that one.

On the day of Citi Bike's launch, one tabloid reported that a bike-share station was too close to a neighborhood bike shop on Manhattan's Lower East Side, competing with the shop's rental customers and leaving the owner "struggling to survive." The shop is still there as of this writing, two years after Citi Bike launched.

In the end, the five lawsuits amounted to a challenge on 1.5 percent of the 330 stations. Our worst-case scenario—if we lost all the lawsuits and had to move the five stations—would leave the system virtually unaffected.

One station that passed almost entirely under the radar is right next to Grand Central Terminal. This was the system's single largest station, on a two-lane section of Park Avenue that connects 41st and 42nd streets, known as Pershing Square East, where two mega-racks combined for 118 bike docks. The station's footprint required closing both lanes and converting the street into a combination pedestrian and bike street. Every day, some 750,000 people pass through Grand Central; the passengers on a single train or subway car could deplete all 118 bikes at once. Yet the day we closed the lanes—a development advertised well in advance to property owners and community representatives—hardly anyone noticed. Crews laid down 171 gallons of epoxy and 8,400 pounds of crushed gravel on the asphalt street surface. The road has been closed ever since and as of this writing is on its way to being a true plaza.

Instead of prompting another Prospect Park West–size backlash, the panicked reactions and lawsuits barely passed the laugh test for the overwhelming number of New Yorkers who, like Jon Stewart and Stephen Colbert, were amused by all the fuss. When critics said the bike stations would violate the character of historic neighborhood streets, blogs like *Brooklyn Spoke* posted pictures of dozens of beat-up cars parked on those streets that no one complained about.

Critics did have one thing right: the New York bike-share system didn't work as well as it should have at launch. When a customer swiped her bike key or entered the code to release a bike, it could take upwards of twenty or thirty seconds to unlock, an unacceptably long time. Locking mechanisms sometimes failed to engage and hold bikes securely, or wouldn't let riders lock them up when the ride ended. Entire stations

Yellow cabs, subways, the Staten Island Ferry, and now Citi Bike. New York is a city of transportation icons. Jon Orcutt

went dark, what we called losing a "heartbeat," simply shutting down without letting bikes go or accepting them until the station was manually rebooted. A downloadable bike-share app designed to give customers real-time information about available bikes and docks barely worked, causing confusion for customers. Some stations were perennially empty and others always full, a function of uneven biking supply and demand. Alta was understaffed and unable to keep pace with the demand to "rebalance" the bikes, loading bikes onto trucks from full stations and taking them to empty ones so bikes and docks would always be available.

In a few nail-biting episodes, system inspectors found some station locking systems failing entirely, leaving all bikes unsecured. If someone grabbed one of the bikes and rode off, it would be the last we would see of it. When our DOT bike-share team came across these stations on the street, they physically guarded the unlocked bikes until technicians could get the station back online, warding off legitimate would-be riders in the process.

A problem related to the software snafus caused bike stations' display screens to eat up each station's battery life, which was identified as a big culprit in stations' losing their heartbeats and shutting down. Working with Alta, a system was developed to replace station batteries more rapidly. Technicians also reprogrammed screens so they would go dark when not in use and not shine brightly throughout the night, draining the battery.

With a system this big, these issues were no secret, as the media gleefully reported. But the glitches obscured a more significant reality: the bikes were in huge demand, and within the first eleven days, 100,000 riders successfully used the system, a number that would grow ten times in the next six weeks. Reporters in that first week detailed the program's success even as they gave prominent attention to its problems.

On May 31, just four days after launch, there was a game-changing event in how people talked about Citi Bike in New York City. And it had nothing to do with any media, operational, or political strategy we put together. *Wall Street Journal* editorial board member Dorothy Rabinowitz, a Pulitzer Prize–winning writer and conservative columnist, appeared in a *WSJ* opinion video interview titled "Death by Bicycle," in which she gamely responded to an interviewer's questions about Citi Bike.

Was Citi Bike even necessary, the interviewer asked? Are people so fat that they need to ride bikes? "Do not ask me to enter the minds of the totalitarians running this government," Rabinowitz replied, in all seriousness, claiming that she represented "the majority of citizens" in New York City who were "appalled by what has happened" with the launch of Citi Bike.

She was clearly relishing the chance to speak out on the carnage. "We now look at a city whose best neighborhoods are absolutely *begrimed* by these blazing blue Citibank bikes," which she said were "sneaked under the radar."

Whoa, did she say "begrimed"? Is that still a word in the twenty-first century? Was it even a word in the twentieth? And I thought New York City had been grimed a long time ago.

Rabinowitz kept going: "I invite the mayor and his ideology-maddened traffic commissioner Janette Sadik-Khan to stand on Lower Fifth Avenue and to see exactly what happens every day. There is nobody who doesn't blow by every traffic light." These marauding cyclists were emboldened, Rabinowitz said, by Bloomberg city government apparatchiks. "The bike lobby," she warned, "is an all-powerful enterprise."

Wrapping up the five-minute segment, the interviewer, amused by Rabinowitz's oratory, summarized, "New York is not London or Paris."

"Or Amsterdam," Rabinowitz added.

With that interview, the landscape shifted sharply. We laughed about the segment, thinking it was so much inside baseball. But the response to the tirade from outside the agency was heartening. Bloggers and tweeters ridiculed Rabinowitz, and mainstream news reporters picked up on it. Whatever people thought about Citi Bike, loved it or loathed it, whether it was unsafe or a panacea, Rabinowitz represented an incoherent extreme that neutralized much of the vitriol over bike share. Her reaction seemed so out of touch that the entire line of criticism could no longer be taken seriously. She might as well have been arguing against too-short skirts, long hair, and naughty song lyrics. Bike supporters embraced the paranoia, creating buttons that said Official Member—All Powerful Bike Lobby.

"They're just f**king bikes, lady," Jon Stewart mocked Rabinowitz on *The Daily Show*. A *Daily Show* correspondent talked to bike-share opponents who complained that the racks were installed without adequate notice.

"Apart from the 159 meetings, they didn't say a word," the reporter deadpanned to a bike-share foe, quoting our outreach report.

Stephen Colbert fully engaged his mock outrage in support of Rabinowitz on *The Colbert Report*. Using archaic language, Colbert pointed out that New York City was already famous for a different kind of grime, so singling out the bikes was playing unfair favorites: "Begrimed!" he cried. "Befouled! Be-dirtied! Now, as you're ambulating about the historic West Village, a gaudy blue rack of bikes will take away from the simple beauty of the Cherry Boxx discount dildo shop." Minutes later, Colbert's guest, legendary rocker Paul McCartney, who had clearly been following the show from backstage, humorously recalled his post–Beatles days in the early 1970s as he started his solo group, Wings.

"There were times when I was begrimed," a smirking McCartney confided to Colbert.

Bike share carries the rewriting of the street to its full potential, using its infrastructure as an intervention that changes the street and helps achieve more expansive goals. The presence of hundreds of stations sent the message that bikes and the people who ride them are important and as much a part of the streets and the city's transportation network as the buses or cars that dominate them. The bikes in turn would carry riders, filling the streets and bike lanes with lifelong New Yorkers, recent arrivals and visitors, businessmen and students, tourists or people just getting from the subway to the West Side—and by doing so, invite more people into previously forbidden street space and inspire still others to ride. More riders create demand for more biking infrastructure and invite more people to ride and to walk on increasingly safer streets in an increasingly virtuous cycle. Seen this way, bike share was transformative transportation for New Yorkers, not just getting them from place to place but bringing more of the city and its streets within reach of more people.

The New York lesson offers an example to prospective, nascent, or even established bike-share systems: station location can be its own exercise in changing the street. We used bike-share stations to protect bike paths and to increase visibility on the street for pedestrians. Involving New Yorkers in the station selection process helped guide where we placed the racks in the first place and ensured that each location had a kind of local ownership. Density is destiny for bike share. Stations must be densely distributed in an urban network or the entire system will fall apart. Bike-share riders must have a variety of station options where they can pick up and drop off bikes. Station density provides redundancy, reliability, and peace of mind to riders that they won't be left stranded with a bike but no dock or station to return it, or with no alternative stations if a station is out of bikes. Would-be bike-share cities that think they can dip a toe into bike share with a small-scale system in one neighborhood shouldn't be surprised if that system fizzles. Transportation isn't about one neighborhood, and a one-neighborhood bike-share system would be as effective as a one-neighborhood bus or train system. When it comes to bike share, bike big or go home.

Bike share should never be viewed in isolation as an alternative to driving or public transportation. Bike share works well when it serves both those who use it solely to commute as well as those riding to and from transit hubs. The 66,500 bikes in Hangzhou's system in China are specifically geared to solve the "first mile/last mile" problem to get people from their homes to the city's transit system. This is a big gap in many cities with lower but still moderate densities that could serve transit if residents had an effective means to reach bus or rail without driving.

And bike share is a physical, irrefutable alteration of the city, breaking the bike-brain barrier that makes people think that streets can never be wrested back from the combustion engine. The ubiquity of bike share changes the need that people have for the street. Bike share wasn't about one bike lane on one street or one plaza at a three-way intersection. The network of stations changed the language of the street, and with it the entire political landscape.

It was clear in New York that public opinion shifted decisively after the backlash. I remember the press conference where we announced the Citi Bike sponsor, an event covered by *The New York Times*'s transportation reporter, Matt Flegenheimer. We jubilantly coaxed the reluctant reporter into riding one of the new bikes, realizing too late that the Manhattan native had never quite gotten the hang of riding. He nearly wiped out during a wobbly, twenty-foot ride outside City Hall. I blanched. Reporters taking headers on bikes in front of City Hall make for terrible optics. To his credit, Flegenheimer signed up for riding classes with Bike New York, turning the lessons into a funny page-one story in the *Times* under the headline As Easy as . . . Look Ahead! Turn! Oh, No!

Flegenheimer's front page transformation from biking wallflower to participating New York City bike rider reflected the evolution of what many New Yorkers assumed about themselves and what was possible on their city's streets. Media and popular attitudes adjusted to the new rules of the road. The headlines about bike-share terrorists were replaced with elected officials outside of Manhattan demanding to know when bike share would reach their neighborhoods. *The New Yorker* magazine featured Citi Bike on its cover, with a drawing of a woman docking a bike outside a gym where people rode stationary bikes. Celebrities—Leonardo DiCaprio, Seth Meyers, Louis C.K.—were spotted riding the bikes among the businessmen, supermodels, and ordinary New Yorkers. All the lawsuits against Citi Bike were eventually dismissed, with judges citing the outreach report. Under Bloomberg's successor, Citi Bike would expand far beyond its original launch area, moving up the Upper East and Upper West sides and into Long Island City, Queens, and Park Slope, Brooklyn. The Great Bike Panic could no longer be reported with a straight face. The bikes had truly won, forging a new frontier in the shared economy.

The city's waterways are an extension of its road network. We invested heavily in the Staten Island Ferry system, the nation's busiest, serving some twenty-two million passengers, the largest number in forty years, maintaining a critical lifeline for the borough. NYC DOT—Alex Engel

The $175 million federally funded reconstruction of the St. George ferry terminal completely overhauled a hub serving the seventy thousand riders on the ferry, twenty bus lines, and the Staten Island Railway. Julian Olivas

My new job at Bloomberg Associates is to bring the lessons we learned on the streets of New York City to other ambitious urban hubs around the world. In Mexico City, our partnership with Mayor Miguel Mancera and Dhyana Quintanar at the public space authority is producing dramatic results for the largest city in the Americas. On Avenida 20 de Noviembre in the city's historic center, we aided in the redesign that created thirty-two thousand square feet of new pedestrian space—more than half a football field—extending south of the zócalo and opening the corridor to weekly pedestrian events. The project will serve as a model for communities across Mexico City and is sending the message that the status quo is not welcome on city streets.

Moritz Bernoully

Another Bloomberg Associates partnership in Los Angeles helped bring new life to streets where the car once reigned supreme. LA is punching holes in the old myth that no one walks in that town, with safety projects like this one on Broadway in the heart of downtown. When even Los Angeles is learning to put people first, you know there's been a tectonic shift in priorities. Melani V. Smith—Meléndrez

Even before I left NYC DOT, we were seeing the lessons we learned applied to streets in cities across the globe. You can see telltale signs of our experience with road diets and transit improvements on Avenida 9 de Julio in Buenos Aires, Argentina. Often referred to as the widest street in the world, the transportation department completed a redesign in 2013 that included a new bus rapid transit line and new pedestrian space, reducing the distance that pedestrians need to cross.

GCBA (Gobierno de la Ciudad Autónoma de Buenos Aires)

When the San Francisco Municipal Transportation Agency carved out street space for a pedestrian plaza at the irregular intersection where Seventeenth and Castro streets meet Market Street, they credited New York City's newest public space as inspiration. The lesson for planners is to figure out what your city needs; see what other cities are doing to solve similar problems and then adapt what works to your own streets. San Francisco Planning Department

Today we're seeing the next generation of urban innovations in cities that in years past haven't been hotbeds of smart street designs. On the far side of the globe in Auckland, New Zealand, leaders are looking to undo decades of damage caused by urban planning that valued car-based sprawl more than people. From waterfront revitalization to transit expansion to shared street projects like this one on Elliott Street downtown, the so-called City of Cars is remaking itself into a twenty-first-century city of people. Auckland Design Office, Auckland Council

There's no better example of the transformative power of transportation on communities than Medellín, Colombia. Once the seat of Pablo Escobar's notorious drug cartel, the city has transformed itself over the last twenty years with efforts to reconnect neighborhoods.

A twenty-eight-story series of escalators connects the Comuna Trece area built into a ridge in the Andes with the city core.

The three lines of the Metrocable system connect the steep, hillside barrios to the city's metro, cutting in half a two-and-a-half-hour commute and breathing new life into once-crime-plagued neighborhoods.

Having transformed the heights of the city, planners are now rebuilding from the ground up, building out a network of safe bike lanes to complement the ever-expanding transit system. Seth Solomonow

Cities constantly need to update the hardware that keeps their transportation systems moving. At NYC DOT's Traffic Management Center in Queens, *above,* staff is able to monitor traffic conditions across the city and make real-time changes to traffic signals to clear up gridlock. Thanks to the agency's Midtown in Motion project, traffic speeds in the heart of the city improved by 10 percent.   NYC DOT

We also invested in sustainable infrastructure, like this bioswale, one of 5,700 planned by the city to capture rainwater and prevent runoff into New York Harbor. DOT is also exploring permeable pavement and other treatments to ensure that New York's streets—28 percent of its public land area—can help create a more sustainable city.   NYC DOT—Stephen Mallon

By changing how city streets were used, we changed New Yorkers' expectations for their city. Our annual Summer Streets series opens seven miles of streets from the Brooklyn Bridge to Central Park, drawing a hundred thousand visitors a day, and allows us to open two spaces that are usually seen only from the backseat of a taxi cab.

A sound and light installation by Rafael Lozano-Hemmer drew thousands of people to a tunnel that had been closed to pedestrians since the early twentieth century.

Rafael Lozano-Hemmer, Voice Tunnel, 2013 (Location: Park Avenue Tunnel, Manhattan). NYC DOT—Stephen Mallon

Aboveground, the world-famous Park Avenue viaduct around Grand Central Terminal provides cyclists and pedestrians with a brand-new perspective on their city. NYC DOT—Alex Engel

A system of pedestrian wayfinding maps help New Yorkers and visitors alike decode the street with local landmarks and show how long it will take to walk distances.

Designer: PentaCityGroup.
Photographer: NYC DOT

Real-time bus arrival information helps take the guesswork out of how long the wait will be, and if there is time to grab a cup of coffee.

Designer: PentaCityGroup.
Photographer: Christopher Herwig, City ID

The city bench system for the first time brought more than fifteen hundred attractive and durable benches to a city without seats, giving New Yorkers the option of stopping to take it all in.

NYC DOT—Randy Wade

Street transformations don't have to be high-profile plazas and bike lanes. Simple changes to road geometry can improve safety and street life for decades. In just seven years, we implemented safety design on 137 street corridors and 113 intersections, set in motion 29 residential slow speed zones and 189 schools with reduced speed zones, added red light cameras at 50 intersections, and installed the city's first-ever radar cameras at 20 locations near schools. *Top:* NYC DOT—Heidi Wolf   *Bottom:* NYC DOT—Julio Palleiro

If Robert Moses had had his way, Delancey Street would have been part of a highway system to take cars from the Williamsburg Bridge across Manhattan to the Holland Tunnel. Though the plan was defeated in the 1960s, local streets remained dangerous and depressing. From 2006 to 2010, 742 people were injured along the street, and 9 people died from 2005 to 2012.   NYC DOT

A redesign in 2012 created twenty-one thousand square feet of pedestrian space, not simply making the street safer to cross, but also connecting neighborhoods divided by the street.   NYC DOT

In Corona Plaza, Queens, the Neighborhood Plaza Partnership helped connect a local community nonprofit with private financing to clean and coordinate events in new city-created public spaces.   Neshi Galindo

New York's communities become city partners in public space, with local businesses underwriting and maintaining street seats built in a curbside lane, where passersby can stop and sit down along streets with limited sidewalk space.
NYC DOT—Ed Janoff

Citi Bike, the nation's largest bike-share system, launched in 2013, with 6,000 bikes at 330 docking stations in lower Manhattan and parts of Brooklyn. The system extended the reach of transit and opened up new swaths of the city to commuting and exploration.   Kate Fillin-Yeh

New York City's first new transit system in more than sixty years, Citi Bike was supported entirely by private sponsorship funding. In a city that people said no one biked in and where biking was an act of suicide, New Yorkers took Citi Bikes for more than twenty million trips in the first two years without a single rider fatality, and overwhelming demand forced the system operators to double the network size. NYC Mayor's office—Kristen Artz

Transforming a city can start by changing its streets. In 2007 there was no public vocabulary in New York City for public space design, for bike lanes and bike share, or for innovative transit and safety. By 2013, when this picture of Madison Square was taken, millions of New Yorkers were fluent in their streets and the changes were just another part of the streetscape. Today, these transformations are being translated around the world.

10

Safety in Numbers

Early on a Thursday in late February, six-year-old Amar Diarras-souba and his older brother approached the intersection of 116th Street and First Avenue in East Harlem, the final crosswalk in their daily walk to Public School 155. When the light turned green, the driver of a tractor-trailer on 116th Street started to turn right onto First Avenue, into the crosswalk where Amar started crossing with his brother. The driver claimed he never saw the boys and didn't notice anything as he drove through the intersection and over Amar. He continued driving before someone flagged him down two blocks later to tell him what he had done.

The tragedy of Amar is heartbreaking, but not unusual. Amar was one of 177 people in New York City in 2013 killed by drivers while walking. The total was 293 fatalities, including drivers and their passengers. What was unusual in Amar's case was that the New York Police Department issued two citations to the truck driver, one for failure to exercise due care for his vehicle and the second for failure to yield to a pedestrian in a crosswalk, both punished with fines comparable to parking tickets. A driver's claim that he "never saw" the person he hit and killed with his vehicle is often all that's necessary to be excused from criminal prosecution in New York and many American cities.

Another singular feature of the death of young Amar was that it was news at all. The media report on only a handful of the most upsetting stories, usually the ones with particularly horrific circumstances. Traffic crashes, injuries, and deaths are so routine that they rarely make news. We learn little about the details beyond the body count and the effect on local traffic. Circling choppers during rush hours matter-of-factly describe roadside wrecks and the arrival of emergency crews, but rarely any comment on the causes and the physical and emotional horror that these crashes inflict on victims. Smartphone apps and computer maps translate crash investigation scenes into graphics and offer alternative routes around the crash scene. Local radio stations reinforce this notion of traffic-as-immovable-force by bundling "traffic and weather together." In many ways, traffic violence is viewed the same way as weather: a passing, potentially inconvenient condition over which we have no control. Even the word "accidents" blunts the impact of these deaths and obscures the causes and our responsibility to end them. A closer look at each incident reveals specific human factors that contributed directly to them such that they don't warrant the euphemism "accident" at all. They are preventable deaths.

Nearly 17,000 American servicemen were killed in 1968, the single bloodiest year of the Vietnam War. In the United States in 2014, an estimated 32,675 American lives were snuffed out—not by war but in ordinary car crashes. Numerically, this death toll is the equivalent of a jetliner packed with 300 passengers falling out of the sky every three days for an entire year. It's more than three times as many people killed in one year as died on 9/11, plus the American service people killed in combat in Iraq and Afghanistan combined in the decade and a half since, and nearly three times the number of Americans killed annually in homicides by guns. Most of these crashes involve simple and preventable actions such as speeding, which was a factor in 29 percent of traffic deaths in 2013, or drinking alcohol (31 percent). Yet there is no corresponding revulsion or even sustained outrage at the persistence of needless and preventable deaths. It's unimaginable that such a toll would go almost unnoticed in any other field, industry, profession, or practice.

Just as we don't notice people walking on the street, Americans don't see their traffic deaths as an imminent or headline-worthy health threat like Ebola. In 2013, the most recent year for which data are available, 4,735 people were killed while walking in the United States and another 66,000 were injured by motor vehicles. Almost half of those pedestrian deaths involved alcohol. In New York City, failure to yield to pedestrians in the crosswalk was a factor in 27 percent of fatal or serious crashes, and driver inattention 36 percent.

The claim that "I never saw" somebody before hitting him or her should be tantamount to an admission of error and responsibility. People—even those who walk—are not invisible. Many crashes could be eliminated simply by the driver's slowing down, paying attention, and staying sober. Yet traffic deaths are one of the few categories of death for which there are rarely criminal consequences.

In New York City, from 2000 to 2006, 2,464 people died in crashes with motor vehicles, about one person killed every day. Yet New York's transportation department, like those of other cities, had been relying on outdated manuals and strategies. It focused on keeping traffic moving and didn't see safety as its primary department goal or as part of its essential identity, but rather as a list of check-the-box, minimum-standard mandates. The first priority of every city should be the physical and psychological safety of people on the street. Hundreds dying on city streets would be classified as a public health crisis in any other field.

City officials would be hauled before the court of public opinion to account for the crisis and explain their plans to reduce and eliminate the danger.

There is a lot to be optimistic about when it comes to safety. Although some 275 people die annually in traffic crashes in New York City—counting those in cars and on motorcycles as well as those hit by them—accounting for cities' populations, New York's death rate is a fraction of the national rate, making the Big Apple by far the safest big city in America. And the number of traffic deaths nationally is decreasing, by more than one third since 2001. Some comes from advances in automotive design—airbags, steering, and brakes—and the awareness and police enforcement around behaviors like drunk driving. But if car safety and enforcement were all that was necessary to make American cities safer, why did dense New York City, crawling with vulnerable people on foot, in taxis, on bikes, and pushing hot dog carts in the street, have a traffic death rate a third of car-dominated Atlanta or Houston? New York's enviable traffic safety ranking isn't despite all the pedestrians; it's because of them.

Most people think of safety as protection from crime and violence. Today, safety incorporates this same notion but expands the meaning to capture the fundamental *feeling* of safety from traffic. Both ideas of safety—traffic and crime—are served by the same quality: people, and their eyes on the street. Sidewalks busy with pedestrians are a crime deterrent. More people on the street—including on bikes—creates safety in numbers, a human system of indicators, signs, and signals.

But most New Yorkers weren't prepared when DOT finally decided to make safety the agency's prime directive—in word, in design, and in action. Recognizing that New York's dense population is a natural traffic-calming asset, we devised strategies to increase the number of walkers and bikers on city streets. We started by doing something the transportation department had never done before: we resolved to cut city traffic fatalities in half, to 135 by 2030. This goal, the centerpiece of the first chapter of DOT's 2008 strategic plan, was the first time the transportation department expressed a specific target and metrics for reducing traffic fatalities in New York City.

At the time, even having a goal to reduce traffic deaths aroused skepticism within the department. The agency's engineering and safety offices questioned how we could promise to reduce traffic deaths when so many crashes were caused by reckless driving, drinking, and blowing through traffic signals and signs. They couldn't engineer for bad judgment. Through a productive dialogue, we reached agreement that many strategies can be brought to bear in addition to street design—such as enforcement, education, and an emphasis on personal responsibility. But the street, in its diverse splendor, we could control. Designs could physically change the street to prevent or reduce any benefit to driving dangerously, and tip the balance of the street in favor of the pedestrian so that a mistake on anyone's part doesn't become a death sentence.

Measuring safety is the crux of this approach, because what people fear and what actually threatens their lives on the street are rarely the same thing. As we saw in earlier chapters, what people see depends on how they get around, and what they believe makes streets dangerous hinges more on emotion and snap judgments than on data. Media headlines seem to bolster almost any opinion: clueless or drunk pedestrians texting in the street, marauding wrong-way cyclists, crazy cabbies, cracked roads, brake failures. None of these is actually responsible for killing most New Yorkers.

In the same way that people who drive believe more roads can solve traffic congestion, local residents believe that signals and stop signs can solve traffic safety problems. When a young boy like Amar is killed crossing the street on the way to school, people immediately assume that a red light, a stop sign, a school crossing guard, or a speed limit sign will solve the problem and prevent future crashes. Yet signs and signals on their own are bad at regulating anything much more than the right-of-way, and ineffective at preventing tens of thousands of serious crashes that still occur every year. Amar had the green light—and so did the turning truck driver. A crossing guard was assigned to the intersection where Amar died but she was not present at the time of the crash. Instead of assuming that traffic signals and signs will keep the peace, traffic engineers must instead place safety at the center of street designs and change the geometry of urban streets to slow drivers to the speed of life. Knowing how and where to do that takes the right kind of data to prioritize safety improvements according to the danger and not the annoyance.

We launched the largest traffic safety study of a city ever undertaken. Our action plan targeted not the superstitions, annoyances, or pet peeves about what made streets dangerous, but instead the actions that were actually killing and injuring New Yorkers. The 2010 study looked at seven thousand serious crashes over five years and took a multilayered analysis into where, when, and how they were occurring to find patterns. While New York's traffic fatality rate is the smallest of any American big city, pedestrians represent half of those deaths, far higher than the rate in many other cities. That's not surprising considering how swarmed New York's streets become during the busiest times of day. But the study revealed a different source of blame. As our safety engineers pointed out, most deaths were caused not by a *lack* of signals and signs; they occurred after people driving vehicles have *ignored* these controls or violated numerous other rules of the road. These crashes are also costly. A review of data from the U.S. Department of Transportation helped estimate the true cost of traffic crashes in New York City: $4.2 billion in property damage, medical costs, and lost wages annually. If a city was hemorrhaging that kind of money over any other chiefly human activity, auditors, investigators, and prosecutors would demand accountability.

Other details in the study were less obvious. The way many transportation departments and the media talk about traffic danger is by ranking the "Top 10 Most Dangerous Intersections" or similar, headline-grabbing snapshots. Our report looked beyond this frame for two important reasons. First, safety studies often look at raw crash data that include everything from an incident when one car driver dings another in a parking lot to another where someone on foot is run over by a drunk driver. Both are considered "crashes," but that's a false equivalence. Second, looking only at specific intersections can obscure high rates of serious crashes dispersed over many miles of a particular street. Intersection X may have the highest single number of serious crashes, but Street Y has far more people dying and suffering injury.

The transportation department's report took a corridor view, geo-coding only crashes that resulted in death or serious injury and heat-mapping their locations. These maps turned seemingly less-threatening corridors into more visible danger zones, and prompted us to take on blocks-long redesigns of streets instead of diluting our efforts on an intersection-by-intersection basis.

Because New York City is known for its congestion and gridlock, you would assume its traffic hotspots would be where the greatest number of New Yorkers cross the street on foot and where vehicle traffic is busiest. But speed, not crowds, is a deadlier ingredient in traffic. Wide streets, like sprawling Queens Boulevard (infamously referred to as the Boulevard of Death), are as likely to be deadly for people on foot as Manhattan's pedestrian-dense 42nd Street. The reason is that drivers are more likely to reach deadly velocity on a wide avenue than in congested Midtown. The deadliest time of day for pedestrians isn't rush hour, when the most cars and pedestrians are wedged together, but from three to six a.m., when the city's wide, empty avenues, particularly in the outer boroughs, combine with young men behind the wheel, revved up with alcoholic bravado.

A poll included with the study revealed that most New Yorkers didn't even know that the city speed limit was 30 miles per hour, unless a street sign said otherwise. While that speed might seem to be a fantasy on the city's traffic-choked streets, there's an elastic tension to traffic. Slow-moving congestion and driver frustration builds, then suddenly uncoils into speed the moment there's a clear one hundred yards of roadway.

The findings unexpectedly exonerated the default villains of New York's streets. Taxis, trucks, and bike riders are typically perceived as loose cannons on city streets, yet 79 percent of crashes in the study involved private automobiles as opposed to cabs, buses, or trucks. Considering that the average taxi racks up a lot more miles on the road than most private cars, taxi drivers are, statistically speaking, some of the safest drivers in New York City.

The safety data are even more definitive on streets with bike lanes, where serious crashes are 40 percent less deadly for pedestrians. In separate studies of streets with protected bike paths, injury rates plunged as much as 43 percent for cyclists, pedestrians, and people in cars. Citywide, the number of bike riders involved in crashes remained virtually unchanged over a decade when the number of people riding exploded. Accounting for the fourfold growth in riders, the rate of people riding who were killed or seriously injured dropped by nearly 75 percent. Despite the explosion in people riding bikes, there was no increase in the number of pedestrians killed or sent to hospitals after being hit by bikers. None were killed in more than four years at the height of the bike boom from 2009 to 2013.

Perhaps the most sobering statistic is the overrepresentation of older New Yorkers among traffic deaths. People sixty-five years or older are less likely to be hit by a car while walking, but they are far more likely to die from their injuries if struck. Research found that while they make up just 12 percent of the city's population, older New Yorkers accounted for 38 percent of pedestrian fatalities, far higher than the national rate.

The safety report was a transformational moment for the agency. When releasing the document with Mayor Bloomberg in the summer of 2010, I called it a "Rosetta stone" for safety because it provided the language and framing of the urban problem in a way that would translate into all of our projects. The report marked the first time that a traffic safety plan for the five boroughs had made the front page of *The New York Times*, a sign that public opinion was evolving, turning traffic safety into an essential question of government's responsibility to its people.

Taking the basic elements of our operations—markings, signs, asphalt, and speed bumps—the transportation department launched the largest traffic-calming campaign ever undertaken in an American city. We built the city's first-ever residential and senior safety zones that reduced local speed limits to 20 miles per hour, with speed warnings stenciled directly on the pavement and eye-catching signs posted at the gateways to these zones. The first call for applications for residential slow zones yielded nearly 100 responses from neighborhoods ranging from Staten Island to the Bronx, a number that increased to 173 by the second year. Instead of requesting stop signs and traffic signals, New York City's neighborhoods were demanding new tools to drop the boom on speeders and take back their streets.

The safety data didn't give us Top 10 lists of dangerous intersections but a road map that prioritized the redesign of 6,300 miles of streets, like Delancey Street at the foot of the Williamsburg Bridge. Delancey moved traffic off and onto the bridge, forcing people on foot to leg it across wide streets filled with speeding cars and trucks. A total of 742 people were injured in car crashes on Delancey between the bridge and the Bowery from 2006 to 2010, a consequence of cars flooring it to get to and from the bridge. A 2012 redesign brought 21,000 square feet of space atop massive tracts of former asphalt space and shortened crosswalks at fourteen locations.

We went beyond Delancey and wrangled traffic from the streets that

A safety redesign of Delancey Street in Manhattan narrowed the street and expanded the use of the road at the foot of the landmark Williamsburg Bridge.
NYC DOT—Julio Palleiro

Shorter crossings for pedestrians and improved traffic patterns made car trips more direct and eased lane changing, which contributes to traffic congestion.
NYC DOT—Julio Palleiro

fed it. The previous, outdated traffic pattern forced cars from the FDR Drive that wanted to reach the bridge into a four-block detour along one-way streets. We converted Clinton Street into a one-way feeder lane and created a new entrance to the bridge direct from the street. This barely noticeable nip-and-tuck shortened the trip to the bridge by four blocks and took traffic away from high-rise residential buildings on Norfolk Street and off Delancey itself. A review of safety data in 2013 found that there were 21 percent fewer crashes than before the redesign.

While we changed the streets, we also wanted to change the conversation about safety. Re-educating city drivers to see traffic death as

The Delancey Street redesign shortened pedestrian crossings, reclaiming 21,000 square feet of former roadbed in the process and creating safe pedestrian idylls where cars once ranged.   NYC DOT

Normally relegated to forgettable ads, safety gets an in-your-face treatment in New York with a simple physics lesson about deadly speeding. NYC DOT

a preventable public health crisis takes more than a finger-wagging media campaign that scolds: "Don't speed" or "Don't drink and drive." Safety used to be the stuff of low-budget, easy-to-ignore public interest announcements during TV after-school specials. We took a different approach, using drama and humor to get messages across. Our first was an aggressive 30 miles-per-hour antispeeding campaign with a simple, deadly physics lesson that we licensed from the city of London: If you're hit by a car moving 40 miles per hour, there's a 70 percent chance that you'll be killed; if you're hit by a car moving 30 miles per hour, there's an 80 percent chance that you'll live. The difference of just 10 miles per hour is literally the difference between life and death.

Humorous ads that aired on local television networks and on the Internet blared, "Don't Be a Jerk," with examples of jerky bike behavior provided by celebrity chef Mario Batali, actor John Leguizamo, and super-model Paulina Porizkova, riding bikes the wrong way, on sidewalks, or through crosswalks. Ads on buses and bus shelters targeted drunk drivers and told pedestrians and motorists to get their heads out of their smartphones. We also took a page from London's streets and stenciled Look on the ground to get New York pedestrians' heads into the game.

The safety campaigns and projects made a difference. At locations where major engineering changes were made citywide, fatalities dropped 34 percent, and the safety results were seen in every borough. Injuries at one of the most dangerous intersections in the city, 33rd

With U.S. Transportation Secretary Ray LaHood, a great safety advocate, on East 42nd Street, site of one of the city's first Look! decals to help give distracted New Yorkers a nudge to pay attention on the street. Similar campaigns targeted people who drive and bike. NYC DOT—Alex Engel

Street and Park Avenue South in Manhattan, decreased by 88 percent following a 2008 project that made the Park Avenue Tunnel one way and improved pedestrian crossings. After converting Jewel Avenue in Queens from four lanes to two lanes of vehicle traffic, crashes with injuries decreased 37 percent. A redesign with consolidated lanes and pedestrian islands on the Bronx's Southern Boulevard reduced injury crashes by 28 percent. On Staten Island's Luten Avenue, outside of Tottenville High School, where a senior was run down in a chain-reaction crash, a traffic-calming project brought a painted median to the street, along with pedestrian islands and turn lanes, helping to reduce speeding by up to one third.

As cities design and build safety projects, opponents often make the counterclaim that these same redesigns make the street *less* safe. Adam Clayton Powell Boulevard, as Manhattan's Seventh Avenue is known north of Central Park in Harlem, was one of the most dangerous avenues in the city. Although no individual intersection along Seventh Avenue would have cracked the top ten, the street as a whole ranked in the top 12 percent according to severity-weighted corridor rankings. In the seven years from 2006 to 2012, twelve pedestrians died in motor vehicle crashes along the thirty-five-block stretch from 118th to 153rd Street. Despite the death toll and local demands to do something about it, the local community board objected to transportation department proposals to remove one of three lanes of through traffic to create a better-organized street. Some claimed that one fewer lane for through traffic would create congestion, frustrating drivers into driving dangerously and contributing to asthma by bringing traffic to a standstill. Community board members claimed they needed more information or proof that the project would work. One resident questioned whether painting a bike lane on the street would strip the street of its historical character—as if twelve people dying alone weren't enough of an affront to the neighborhood. The DOT team spent hundreds of hours and attended endless night meetings with local groups and residents along the boulevard to high-light its dangerous design and build support for the project. By this point we had completed enough projects to know that we could reduce the number of lanes on the streets without halting traffic and also save lives. There were no examples of streets redesigned for traffic safety that suddenly became traffic dangers, no asthma clusters around bike lanes or plazas. There were no more studies to be done or information to give.

Still, some in the community suggested that a redesign was unnecessary, and they blamed pedestrians for their own deaths, caused by reckless walking. They had no substantiation for this allegation. "We just don't understand it yet," a local official demurred to *The New York Times* about the proposed project. The objection seemed grounded more in a fear of possible traffic safety than in actual traffic danger. Opposition from the community board also ran counter to urgent demands from residents' associations, churches, and senior groups along the corridor to push aside the board's delaying tactics. After four years of deadlock with that board, we finally moved ahead with the support of this coalition of groups representing the neighborhood. We changed twenty blocks of the street, converting three lanes in each direction to two lanes, with turn lanes at alternating intersections. The redesign delivered the "more information" we needed: Speeding and serious crashes during the evening and nighttime dropped by 33 percent. Traffic moved fine, even better during rush hour. I have no doubt that had we continued with more outreach we would have gotten nowhere, and the street would still be as deadly as it was a decade ago. The project itself was the proof that we needed.

As cities around the world launch bike-share systems and bike lane networks, safety objections are often used against bike lanes and cyclists in the form of mandatory helmet laws and proposals to register bikes and insure riders. These are all solutions in search of problems and attempts to legislate against perceived annoyances, not according to actual safety data. In New York City, a university professor from the area boldly predicted "a doubling or even tripling of bike deaths" in 2012 with the imminent launch of bike share, which carries no requirement that riders wear helmets. He provided no evidence to support this claim, only the assumption that helmets reduce a given risk of injury, so therefore more people riding around without helmets would be splitting open their heads in increasing numbers. In fact, the opposite occurred because we were able to reduce the underlying risk of injury for all riders, regardless of whether they wear helmets.

Bike ridership in New York City quadrupled from 2000 to 2012, while the number of severe injuries or deaths remained virtually unchanged. In 2013, the year that Citi Bike added six million trips to the traffic mix of New York's densest business districts—and the year the university professor forecast bike blood on the streets—bike deaths plummeted to a thirty-year low, from eighteen to twelve. In the more than twenty-three million bike-share trips in the entire United States one year after Citi Bike launched (and counting), none resulted in a traffic fatality. Not that I have anything against helmets. I wear one and encourage other people to wear them too while we continue to build more and better infrastructure. We supported the voluntary use of helmets, fitting one hundred thousand New Yorkers with them, and created a program that required professional deliverymen who ride bikes to wear helmets, lights, reflective gear, and identifying numbers, which the restaurant industry and riding public generally supported. But focusing on helmets for all users perpetuates the misimpression that biking is an inherently dangerous activity and obscures the underlying problems with our streets. When it comes to the hard-core mechanics of what makes people safer, we had learned long before that the answer lay in the design of our streets and not in how well we wrapped our heads.

There is much hyperventilating about helmets in cities around the world, but there is no evidence that requiring riders to wear bike helmets is more effective in decreasing injury and death rates than the very real effect of safety in numbers—the cumulative safety effect of having more people on bikes riding the streets. On the contrary, there is growing evidence that cities with helmet laws succeed only in significantly decreasing the number of people riding bikes, reducing crashes but forfeiting the safety benefits of more riders.

As more people bike, their visibility on the street increases. When drivers see more bike riders, they learn to expect them, to anticipate their movements. They slow down and look around when they have to share the road, which also protects people who walk, completing a virtuous cycle. By the logic of helmet proponents, European nations like Denmark and the Netherlands, with vast numbers of cyclists riding without helmets, should see sky-high rates of head injuries. Yet they are far safer than other countries and are becoming only more so as the number of cyclists increases.

Helmet laws, meanwhile, create a barrier to spontaneous riding in order to prevent an extremely rare—one-in-a-million, statistically speaking—bike death. People would have to carry a bike helmet with them wherever they go on the off chance that they might use bike share once or maybe twice, and then for only a ten-minute ride, at some point during the day. Imagine carrying around your own dinnerware in order to eat in a restaurant. Requiring helmets would effectively eliminate biking as a transportation option in a wide swath of situations.

Australia's mandatory helmet laws have contributed to the poor usage of bike-share programs in Melbourne, a city with a fraction the use of similar-size bike-share systems elsewhere in the world. Meanwhile, other cities, such as Mexico City, Tel Aviv, and Dallas, specifically repealed helmet laws in order to encourage use of their new bike-share programs. In findings that echo New York's experience, the United States as a whole saw bike riding more than double from 2001 to 2012, yet the number of cyclists killed remained stable, despite there being no adult helmet laws in any but a few big cities.

If governments sincerely believe that their streets are so dangerous they must compel people who ride bikes to wear armor, they should instead immediately redesign their streets to make them safer so people don't need that protection in the first place. Failing that, municipalities concerned about their citizens' heads should enact and aggressively enforce laws that require pedestrians to wear helmets too. Some 270,000 pedestrians die globally every year after being hit by cars, 4,735 of them in the United States. As far as I know, none was wearing a helmet.

Just as there is often a vast difference between what people fear and what actually endangers them, there is also a chasm between what is safe and what feels safe. Safety isn't just an absence of threats on the street. It's also a feeling that people on foot, on a bike, or in a car have when they are recognized, respected, and securely positioned on the street. We heard fears at the height of the bike backlash that bike riders are a safety menace to pedestrians. As we saw in earlier chapters, streets with bike lanes are not simply safer for people on bikes; they are safer for pedestrians as well. But there is one metric that cannot be calculated: what people call near misses. I have personally fielded dozens of angry reports of people "almost hit" by bikes. The passion is palpable, the anger and frustration with cyclists as a collective group more acute than for anyone else who uses the street. Yet this anger and frustration is misplaced. Cyclists may annoy, anger, or even deeply scare you. More cyclists might result in more near collisions with pedestrians, but they protect pedestrians from the far greater threat posed by drivers. Every day, ninety Americans wind up in morgues as a result of crashes with cars, not bikes.

The problem resides in poor street design. Instead of adapting the street so people can use it safely, transportation officials opt for strategies that adapt people to the street, leaving the road and its dangers unchanged. Nothing represents this surrender of the streetscape to cars with as much inconvenience as a pedestrian bridge. Walkways and

Bridges can be second-class transportation for pedestrians by forcing people on foot to walk long distances to make hair-raising crossings over highway lanes. These inconvenient crossings compromise safety instead of enhancing it, frustrating people on foot and tempting them to cross streets, dangerously, via the most direct route. Nick Mosquera

ramps over city streets are the pedestrian equivalent of trying to build your way around congestion, yet they typically succeed only in cluttering the streetscape and dividing neighborhoods. In Mexico City, pedestrian bridges force people to walk often a quarter mile out of their way, to a long, circuitous climb up stairs inaccessible to those who have difficulty walking.

Another poorly thought-out safety feature is pedestrian buttons at crosswalks. Many urban and suburban crosswalks will never get a Walk signal unless someone at the corner presses one of these "beg buttons." It's not surprising to find that many people get tired of waiting or don't realize there's even a button to press, instead taking their chances by crossing against the light. And once you're crossing there's no guarantee

Asking pedestrians to carry high-visibility flags like these in Salt Lake City is seen as a way to increase safety at dangerous crossings but they obscure the underlying street design problems that make the crossing dangerous.   Seth Solomonow

that motorists will respect your right-of-way, leading some municipalities such as Salt Lake City and Fort Lauderdale to install safety flags. The first time I heard about these safety flags, I thought it was another farce from *The Onion*. Pedestrians preparing to cross the street are instructed to grab a hand flag from utility poles at the crosswalk to make themselves more visible so that motorists will respect their right-of-way. The joke, however, is on the pedestrian. City officials may as well replace the bright orange flags with white flags of surrender.

Another example of counterproductive safety policies is pedestrian fences on busy streets like those in Rome, Athens, and London, which have barriers more suited for farm animals than quality street safety amenities. On Via dei Fori Imperiali, dense groups of people walking to and from Rome's ancient Colosseum are penned in on the sidewalk to keep them from spilling into the street and into the path of passing buses and cars. Confining people to the sidewalk misses the opportunity to do something about the street and to follow the desire lines that have led us through this book. These are last resorts, and one hopes they will be followed soon by redesigns that would render them unnecessary.

Pedestrian fencing on Via Fori dei Imperiali, Rome, pens in pedestrians on the sidewalk and then blocks pedestrians walking in the street from reaching safety from passing cars and buses. Seth Solomonow

Above all, streets should be safe and simple to use no matter your age or ability. City residents should expect and demand streets safe for people who are eight or eighty years old, and those who walk with canes or use wheelchairs. People shouldn't feel defenseless in streets, afraid to cross a road, or forced to press a button to get a walk signal, or wave a neon flag. On top of all the fears people have of their streets, they shouldn't also be afraid to demand that they be safer. Safety critically depends on public attitudes and expectations. The street is lost when we cease to believe that it can be better.

Traffic deaths plague our city streets, but American roads are actually safer than those in most of the world. While the legislative bodies of Western nations have gathered around traffic safety in the second half of the twentieth century, only 7 percent the world's population is subject to effective traffic safety rules that touch all of the top risk factors for global traffic deaths: speeding, alcohol, motorcycle helmets, and child restraints in vehicles. The World Health Organization estimated in 2013 that road traffic injuries were ninth on the list of global causes of death—and expected to rise to seventh, ahead of HIV/AIDS—and the number-one killer of people ages fifteen to twenty-nine.

In 2011, Mayor Bloomberg and I joined United Nations Secretary-General Ban Ki-moon, who had just announced a Decade of Action for Road Safety, in a campaign to challenge cities and nations around the world to start taking traffic violence seriously and pursuing policies and strategies that could save 5 million lives by 2020. A key part of this campaign required enacting and enforcing comprehensive legislation that addresses traffic deaths and punishes dangerous driving, combined with infrastructure investment that pays attention to people who walk and bike. Global road safety continues to be a big priority for Bloomberg since he left office. Bloomberg Philanthropies, under the inspiring leadership of Patti Harris, has dedicated $250 million over ten years to help cities around the world implement safety strategies.

While working on global safety issues, I've been surprised by the dearth of data in many cities, a sharp contrast to the incredibly illuminating information that we have in our possession here in the United States. Some cities wrestle to collect any usable data at all. Many cities keep incomplete statistics on traffic deaths and have difficulty prioritizing investments and interventions. Data are sometimes kept by multiple organizations, and the crash-reporting metrics don't always contain the granular detail needed to make tactical safety decisions in local communities—where the body count is growing. Cities need to answer specific questions. Was the crash in the crosswalk or in the far leg of the crosswalk? Was the vehicle speeding? Was the light red? How serious was the injury? Knowing the details from the vantage point of the person on the street can help cities direct limited resources to the most effective safety strategy instead of trying to unleash citywide campaigns that attract headlines but have no effect on traffic accidents. And as we will see in the next chapter, having this information is vital both for targeting interventions in the first place and for providing the baseline to measure the effectiveness of these changes.

The nearly seven years I served as commissioner recorded the seven fewest annual traffic fatalities of any years since records were first kept in 1910. If people still died on city streets at the rate they did in 2001, there would have been 1,113 more New Yorkers killed over the last decade. That's 1,113 lives saved. Of all of the achievements in New York City, this is the one I am proudest of, and the results provide more than enough proof. Mayor de Blasio and Transportation Commissioner Polly Trottenberg, my successor, longtime friend, and former policy guru at the U.S. Department of Transportation, doubled down on these gains with the announcement of Vision Zero: the goal of eliminating traffic fatalities entirely. They have encountered many of the same timeworn objections in attempting to implement safety projects. And they've been criticized, both for their successful lobbying of the state legislature to authorize lowering the city speed limit to 25 miles per hour, and also for the city's subsequent efforts to enforce it. But there's no doubt that the public outrage over the carnage on our streets from traffic violence has changed the status quo. Vision Zero campaigns and goals have been adopted in a growing number of cities, including Los Angeles, Boston, Chicago, and Seattle, and softer, safer street designs are becoming the new norm.

The nationwide breakthrough now under way in traffic safety is the direct result of years of work by advocacy organizations like Transportation Alternatives (TA), of which Jon Orcutt was the executive director long before working with me. His appointment as the policy director at DOT was critical for transforming the spirit of the advocacy campaign into the practice and policies of government. TA continues to be an unstinting voice for biking, walking, transit, and safety under the leadership of Paul Steely White. Both before and during my time as commissioner, TA has been most effective when bringing a human face and voice to public policy and the safety agenda. It was through TA that I met Mary Beth Kelly, whose husband, Carl Henry Nacht, was struck and killed in 2006 by a police tow truck as he rode his bike along the Hudson River Greenway. Kelly's loss inspired her to become an advocate for safety, joining TA, becoming a member of its advisory council, and a public voice as a witness for safety and not just an advocate. The same is true of Steve Hindy, a force of nature and owner of the famous Brooklyn Brewery, whose son, Sam, died in a 2007 bicycle crash on the Manhattan Bridge. He turned his sadness into positive action as vice chair of TA's board. There's nothing so powerful in the fight for safer streets as the passion of a person who has lost someone to senseless traffic violence. Reorienting public attitudes toward these preventable deaths and shattering the routine of "dull" automotive deaths is as important as the changes we make to the streets, and making the connections between engineering, education, and emotional loss can help close the circle on traffic violence.

While my vision has always been aligned with TA's, our relationship was rocky at times. It can be hard for any advocacy group to deal with an administration that in many respects was ahead of the advocates' agenda. Moving from a combative role criticizing the city for not doing enough on street safety before I became commissioner, to one of support for our aggressive safety agenda, took several years, though I'm happy to say it worked out in the end. Judith Rodin of the Rockefeller Foundation was characteristically prescient about the tension and the importance of bridging the divide, and I am grateful for her counsel on working it out. Steve Hindy in particular deserves a lot of credit for mending the rifts over "beer summits" at his home.

Every fight that DOT took on had key allies within the neighborhoods where the projects were built, and I'm so grateful to them all.

Now that I'm no longer commissioner, I'm struck by how the call for complete street projects has taken on a life of its own. A few years ago, reorganizing New York City's traffic was labeled "controversial." Now you see elected officials, schools, senior centers, business owners, and parents uniting to demand changes to streets, inspired by the street life they've seen in pedestrian, bike, and bus lane designs on other streets like First, Second, Eighth, and Ninth avenues. The transportation department has evolved into an entity focused on saving lives. Combining fierce advocacy with smart policy—and using statistics as a weapon to take action on the street—is part of a campaign to get people to understand what really endangers them. The statistics show that bike riders actually protect pedestrians by altering the behavior of drivers. But safety is not simply a matter of numbers. If we don't fear what is most dangerous—the driver and not the cyclist—we are left chasing public phantoms, fatally compromising the essence of traffic engineering.

11

Sorry to Interrupt, but
We Have to Talk About Buses

I get it. A lot of people don't like to ride buses. So why would you want to read about them here? When writers and film producers dream of an urban future, they imagine hovercrafts cruising through sleek cityscapes. Never lines of cars. Certainly no people walking or biking. And fast, reliable, or demand-based buses would truly be science fiction or a doomed ride, like Keanu Reeves in *Speed*.

A dazzling transit dream for many cities still conjures images of a modern, driverless metro, high-speed monorails, and maybe high-speed rail or hyperloop connecting major cities. In *The Simpsons*, a shyster sells the residents of Springfield on a monorail system before absconding with the city's money. What is it about monorails that prompts people to bring them up in community meetings as potential panaceas for transportation problems? Monorails are what we thought the future would be like at the 1964 World's Fair. Even that *Simpsons* episode was from 1993. Mayors and transportation departments are just as guilty of this fantasy, and old-fashioned transportation like buses aren't the stuff of dreams. If it's not expensive and doesn't require significant construction, the proposed project doesn't seem like a serious solution to transportation ills.

Buses are as sexy as Amish dresses. American commuters regard them as a poky transportation throwback that they left behind with their last school bus ride. In many large American cities, they're seen as the transportation choice for people who have no choices because they can't afford the expense of a car.

But buses in the twenty-first century have been transformed from transportation-choice-of-last-resort to become the surface subway of the world's cities, as fast and reliable as trains, and more convenient and economical than a car. Bus rapid transit (known as BRT) has exploded in popularity since the 1970s when, in Curitiba, Brazil, Mayor Jaime Lerner created a network of buses that ran in dedicated lanes with passengers who paid their fares at train-like platforms. Today, more than 561,000 residents take bus rapid transit daily in Curitiba, 30 percent of the city's population. This success helped inspire similar systems in Bogotá, Melbourne, Seattle, and Ottawa. BRT systems now operate in 194 cities worldwide and move 32 million daily passengers along 3,200 miles of streets, overwhelmingly in Latin America and Asia. As every city is different, each city's rapid bus system must be customized for its geographic and demographic situation. But each city can take advantage of the fact that buses only require roads and avoid the construction costs and land use issues that come with rail. Cost is why so much of this innovation came from less economically developed nations, which have fewer resources and greater incentive for planners to design efficient, inexpensive networks.

Bogotá's bus rapid transit system, TransMilenio, was a pillar of Mayor Enrique Peñalosa's administration, and its effects resonate beyond the bus route. In his first term, Peñalosa combined TransMilenio with strategies to

Bus Rapid Transit station in Curitiba, Brazil. Passengers enter and depart like a surface subway onto high-capacity buses, paying their fare beforehand and boarding via all doors. Mariana Gil/EMBARQ Brasil

increase public space, reduce car circulation on city streets, and improve traffic in Bogotá. "An advanced city is not one where poor people drive cars," Peñalosa says, "but where rich people take public transportation."

TransMilenio operates like a train, with buses moving in dedicated lanes separated by barriers that keep out general traffic. Passengers pay their fare before they get on the bus, avoiding delays. They get on the bus via any of its three doors, reducing the time spent at stops. They board at stations where buses don't have to pull over and then wait for a break to remerge into traffic. The system costs around 5 percent of a new metro system. Since the launch in 2000, Bogotá's TransMilenio has grown to carry 2.2 million daily passengers on eleven routes, an incredibly large transportation mode share in a city of 7.7 million people.

New York is known as a subway town and it's assumed that's how most everyone gets around. But there are vast sections of the city, particularly outside Manhattan, far from a train station or otherwise lacking a direct connection from one neighborhood to another. To fill this gap, New York's Metropolitan Transportation Authority (MTA) runs a 5,667-bus fleet, the largest in North America, carrying 792 million people in 2014, or about 2.5 million passengers on an average weekday. It also has the slowest average bus speeds of any big city. In 2011, a comedian riding a big-wheeled children's tricycle outpaced a bus traveling crosstown along Forty-second Street from Tenth Avenue to Madison Avenue. Average speed: 4.7 miles per hour. Michael Primeggia, my former traffic deputy, commented on this, saying that the only way to get crosstown was to be *born* there.

The jokes would be funnier if it wasn't so sad that taking public transit can be slower or less reliable than *not* taking it. We cannot persuade more people to take buses without making them faster.

Working with the MTA, we developed the city's first rapid bus network in all five boroughs, a network called Select Bus Service (SBS). The SBS plan was the culmination of a years-long effort to identify New York City neighborhoods underserved by transit, with an initial rollout of at least one line in each of the five boroughs. We also created an SBS task force that included the city's foremost transit advocates, Gene Russianoff from the Straphangers Campaign, Joan Byron from the progressive and community-minded Pratt Institute, and Kate Slevin from the Tri-State Transportation Campaign. The group's final report proposed more than twenty bus lines, based on feedback and recommendations from communities and advocacy organizations. The task force also identified transit deserts—neighborhoods where tens of thousands of people lived just out of reach of the city's subways.

Changing bus performance starts with the street, which I see as the rails for urban bus networks. PlaNYC called for one rapid bus route to be established in each borough along densely populated but poorly served neighborhoods. But it didn't spell out how those corridors should be designed. The fundamental problem with bus service isn't that the buses are incapable of higher speeds. Even though a single bus can take the equivalent of fifty cars off the road, buses are forced to operate at the same creeping pace of crosstown traffic as people who drive private cars. More than a quarter of the delay in bus times comes just from passengers' boarding and paying fares. To persuade people to take buses, we needed to speed up bus operations so they provided a convincing transportation alternative.

We were starting with totally different raw materials from Bogotá: narrower streets and an existing, developed mass transit network. Our work began on streets with the highest bus ridership, reaching tens of thousands of commuters on routes with demonstrated demand. Unfortunately, these streets were some of the most difficult to separate bus lanes from general traffic lanes without bringing all lanes to a halt. The transportation department and transit authority combined to set up a system for people to pay at the bus stop and receive a receipt before boarding the bus. We worked with the MTA to secure low-floored buses that make it easier to get off and on. Our road marking contractors painted high-visibility red bus lanes, but we needed a mechanism to keep them free of cars.

It is a New York City traffic principle that any street space not occupied by a car will become occupied by a car unless protected by a physical barrier or law enforcement agent. Since 34th Street was too narrow to let us build a barrier to keep bus lanes free from interlopers—and it's impossible to enforce the lanes with officers without creating its own traffic jam—we needed another solution, in this case, cameras. It was in our quest for state legislation to authorize the use of cameras to enforce bus lanes that we learned how transportation politics make for strange bedfellows. Kevin Sheekey, the brilliant political strategist and architect of Bloomberg's three successful mayoral bids, suggested I talk to Dan Cantor, the hard-working leader of the city's Working Families Party. I recall meeting Cantor at his cluttered offices in downtown Brooklyn, unsure if he would take much interest in the bus portfolio. Skilled at identifying and convincing qualified candidates to run for office—and to be effective once they win—Cantor took an immediate interest in faster transit. He cast it as an equity issue important to his constituency of union members who drove the city's buses, and of working people who depended on them. Within minutes, he was on the phone with the state assemblyman chairing the committee where the bill was stuck, getting it moving on the way to passage.

We lined the SBS routes with enforcement cameras that issue tickets to cars that drive, stop, or dawdle in the dedicated bus lanes. We also installed the city's first transit-signal priority technology that aligns buses and traffic signals. Using infrared signals, traffic lights can be altered so that buses can proceed more quickly through intersections. Riders need not show the driver their receipt. Instead, teams of enforcement agents board buses to randomly check passenger receipts and hand out stiff fines to fare evaders. The SBS lines also have strategically located the stations. Just as subways don't stop every other block, neither should buses. SBS buses can travel up to a quarter mile between stations.

Such extensive collaboration with the MTA was new for the transportation department. Through my previous work at the U.S. Department of Transportation, I was close to the leaders of the MTA, a relationship that became key to getting the bus program off the ground, especially when things got tough—which they did. Thanks to my long-term friendships with the chairs of the MTA—whether Lee Sander, Jay Walder, or especially Tom Prendergast—I could pick up the phone and they would help resolve problems that inevitably come with new programs. That easy interaction and reciprocal respect made seemingly impossible things happen quickly, and it's a key to success for transportation departments around the country. Whether figuring out how to adapt the MTA's fare machines to work aboveground or integrating the system with the DOT's equipment, the project could not have been implemented without our collaboration with the MTA.

SBS is a special high-performance system that needs its own special fleet of buses to set it apart from the rest of the network. That required branding. The city's marketing and branding team came up with a slate of options for the bus design, selecting interior patterns for seat covers from among hundreds of choices. The MTA won design awards for the distinct look.

Our first SBS bus line was on Fordham Road in the Bronx, a winding route from the Co-op City housing development across Fordham's commercial strip and into Upper Manhattan. The freshly painted bus lanes were easily recognized by their terracotta color. I will never forget seeing Joe Barr, the tactical genius who ran our SBS program, nervously awaiting the first bus along Fordham Road. He was a planner, presenting at public meetings and working with the traffic engineers and bus operations staff. But on the first day of service on Fordham Road, he was suddenly a full-time bus ambassador, pacing in front of the banks of bus fare machines installed on the street while handing out informational brochures to passengers. We needed to educate New York's bus riders about the route and its benefits, teaching them that, unlike on every other bus in the city, they now had to pay *before* they got on this bus or risk a ticket. Much to our relief, riders quickly mastered the off-board fare payment process, and despite fears of fare evasion, scofflaws were no more present than on ordinary bus and subway lines. Fordham Road was a big success from the start: travel times improved by up to 20 percent and ridership increased 10 percent. The effectiveness of the new route helped it speed from skepticism to acceptance even faster than plazas and bike lanes.

Likewise, our rapid bus service on First and Second avenues, launched in 2010, delivered an immediate advantage to the fifty-four thousand local bus riders along the route to Manhattan's subway-starved East Side. The bus runs in the area where, as of this writing in 2015, the Second Avenue Subway remains under construction, at a cost of several billion dollars. The M15 SBS took less than two years of planning and an intensive community outreach plan. Although it took longer to win support in the high-end neighborhoods, the project, which also included protected bike paths, eventually won approval even on the Upper East Side. That success came about in no small part through the efforts of DOT's Manhattan borough commissioner Margaret Forgione, who pushed back on the bogus claims that the street redesign would cause congestion, pollution, and asthma. While the project elicited pockets of opposition, Forgione helped forge an alliance of elected officials from the East Side to win community approvals.

Our most controversial SBS project was on a corridor that most needed a transit upgrade: 34th Street, one of Manhattan's busiest streets and one of the few two-way corridors across town. Some 300,000 people work within a quarter mile of 34th Street and nearly 900,000 transit riders start or end their trip at subway stations along 34th or at Penn Station. Penn Station alone provides access to the Long Island Railroad, six subway lines, New Jersey Transit, and Amtrak trains serving cities up and down the Northeast, making it one of the busiest and best-served rail destinations in the entire country. Above-ground, however, the scene changes. Pedestrians and bus passengers, who make up 90 percent of the traffic on 34th Street, were crushed together—people on foot crowded into impassable clusters at cross-walks while buses mixed in with cars on the street. Buses averaged 4.5 miles per hour and spent a third of their time stopped so people could board and pay their fares—not even counting the time spent stuck in traffic or waiting at red lights. The street was functionally broken,

Up, up, and a transitway. The car-free option for 34th Street.
URS, now AECOM, for NYC DOT

unable to serve anyone well. If ever there was a case for transportation equity, this was it.

Our work began in 2009. We painted red bus lanes on 34th Street from First to Eleventh avenues to speed the way for the thirty-three thousand passengers who use the local buses daily. On a parallel track, we developed three different long-term options that could make the street into a surface subway line—operating at higher speeds with no interruptions—and presented them to local community boards, businesses, and property owners. One option, which had never been attempted in New York City, involved the closing of 34th Street entirely to private vehicles between Fifth and Sixth avenues. In its place, a new transitway would be created—dedicated lanes on the street where only buses could drive, with the remaining space allocated to pedestrians. Outside of that one-block stretch, two-way bus lanes would occupy one side of the street, and the other would be used by one-way car and truck traffic, speeding buses while providing an outlet for Midtown traffic.

Though one of three options, this proposal became the only one that the public, local developers, and building owners talked about—and not in a good way. Local businesses and residential properties objected to eliminating two-way traffic and were terrified that tinkering with the crosstown corridor that links the Queens-Midtown Tunnel to the east with the Lincoln Tunnel on the west would cause a traffic chain reaction. Critics said that placing bus stops farther apart would be a burden for older and disabled residents, while the bus lanes would supposedly make it harder for people to be dropped off in front of their buildings by taxis and paratransit services.

We attempted to convince newspaper editorial boards that the idea was at least worth trying. We traveled to *The New York Times*'s new offices on Eighth Avenue, across the street from the Port Authority bus terminal, to pitch the plan. The editorial board was initially very skeptical. We showed them our data and street layouts, explaining how the plan would better balance the street and enhance mobility for most users. While the resulting editorial didn't endorse the proposal, it wasn't dismissive, even calling the plan "intriguing."

"Robert Moses at one point proposed a major highway just south of 34th Street, part of which would go through an office building," the editorial said. "The Bloomberg/Sadik-Khan proposal is far more sensible. The question is still whether it will really make it easier to maneuver in Manhattan."

The editorial was a victory, but it reflected both a lack of enthusiasm and the absence of any natural constituency for the project. And it came just weeks after we had installed the bike lane on Prospect Park West, around the same time as the emerging bike backlash. Newspaper columnists who had opposed all the projects that came before seized on the transitway proposal as another example of overreach. We defended the merits of the plan—that the transitway and reconfiguration could solve a lot of the traffic problems the street already had—while also fighting

Anatomy of a transit-priority street: Bus lanes and sidewalk extensions so buses don't have to pull over mean easier boarding and more room for waiting passengers.   URS, now AECOM, for NYC DOT

back on claims that the proposal would create new problems. At packed public meetings, we made clear that the transitway was only one option for the street. There were multiple design alternatives that included loading zones for businesses. Taxis and other transport services could stop to make drop-offs along the bus lane under city parking rules, but they couldn't park. And while SBS stops would be spaced farther apart, local buses would continue to make all in-between stops. The new design of the corridor could address the majority of the concerns being expressed, but could never overcome all of their fears.

Thirty-fourth Street Select Bus Service helped transform a corridor's mobility, economic vitality, and connectivity through transit without major construction or years of planning. NYC DOT—Kyle Gebhart

On a Saturday afternoon in March 2011, I convened a meeting at DOT headquarters with my brain trust. It was an intense time. Amid the bike backlash, we were trying to keep our momentum going, our political posture upright, and the press managed. We discussed the merits of the project and were convinced it would work. My deputy for planning and sustainability talked about the transitway as if it were, despite the controversies, still the best idea for 34th Street. My intergovernmental liaison reported the sad news that despite our assurances, Midtown elected officials either opposed the transitway outright or quietly admitted that they couldn't publicly support it. I often asked for a gut check from Seth Solomonow, my press director, about how different scenarios would

Transit, pedestrians, and bikes come together. Dedicated lanes and safety islands made for a more efficient street. Buses moved up to 18 percent faster alongside a 9 percent increase in ridership, there was a 21 percent reduction

play with the public. This time—and this was an excruciatingly pain-ful moment—we looked at each other and, with an almost Vulcan-like mind meld, understood that the transitway at that moment would be political suicide without local support. Merely continuing to consider it would be a bus lane too far. We were hyperaware that we had thirty-three months to go until the end of Bloomberg's term, with much of our attention still focused on getting bike share in the ground. We had too much to do and too little political capital remaining to risk it on any one project. We scrapped the transitway plan.

Reporters, columnists, and editorial boards gloated when we reversed course. The loss stung, even more than the still-fresh headlines from the

in traffic injuries in areas where safety treatments were used, vehicle travel time and volumes were maintained, and cycling ridership increased as high as 177 percent in some areas.   NYC DOT

bike backlash. But once we made that decision and focused only on the alternatives, the going immediately got easier. Reinstated parking zones and bus lanes painted in the middle of the street instead of alongside the curb looked far more appealing to residents, who eventually endorsed one of the two alternative plans, with dedicated lanes in both directions, delivery zones on one side of the street, plus sidewalk extensions at bus stations that allow buses to pick up passengers without leaving a travel lane (see pages 244–245). Had we originally proposed what we eventually built along 34th Street, we would no doubt have had to fight for it. Instead, the project was welcomed as a compromise.

The new design was installed eight months after the transitway plan was withdrawn. SBS offered faster service in just weeks and months, not years and decades. While New Yorkers were 80 years into their wait for the Second Avenue Subway, we launched or set in motion seven SBS routes in as many years in all five boroughs. By the end of the fifth year of implementation, we had updated one of the oldest forms of city transportation and saved the nearly 60 million annual bus passengers along these streets more than 550 years of cumulative travel time.

Passenger satisfaction surveys found that 98 percent of riders were satisfied with Select Bus Service along Fordham Road. Farther downtown, along 34th Street in Manhattan, SBS ran 23 percent faster than the regular local buses that the service replaced. Along the one-way pair of First and Second avenues, the number of people riding the M15 Select Bus Service increased 10 percent, and speeds increased up to 18 percent with the addition of dedicated lanes and fewer stops. The increase in ridership on SBS routes came even as there was an overall decrease in bus riders citywide, a sign that reliability, not route coverage or capacity, was the missing link.

The rebalancing of the street to favor the most efficient means of travel along it—in this case, buses—is the greatest form of transit equity. By providing designated lanes for buses, the street places transit riders at the center and puts cars into their place, streamlining the rest of the network. And it was cheap: the combined cost of these lines was just $85 million, equivalent to the cost of five and a half subway trains. Cities around the world are now reaping the benefits that come with streets that give buses priority.

The extraordinary success of the program led local city council members who were previously skeptical to demand SBS service in their districts, something almost unimaginable before the program began. Mayor Bloomberg's successor now supports the planned expansion of the program to a total of twenty routes. Success has a thousand mothers. . . .

12

Measuring the Street

In God we trust. Everyone else, bring data.

These eight words sum up the management philosophy of Michael Bloomberg, a philosophy that bound me throughout the years I ran the transportation department. Data were the lens through which Bloomberg judged ideas and projects. If you're not measuring, then you're not managing. He wanted to know what people wanted, to be sure, but first he wanted to know what the numbers said about proposed actions—and what the results were from projects implemented under his watch.

That's not how the rest of the world tends to work. City residents, elected officials, and community and interest groups do not discuss the higher purpose of streets as much as they fight over their own turf. As you've likely surmised by now, everyone who drives, walks, or swipes a transit card in a city views herself as a transportation expert from the moment she walks out the front door. And how she views the street tracks pretty closely with how she gets around. That's why we find so many well-intentioned and civic-minded citizens arguing past one another.

At neighborhood meetings in school auditoriums, and in back rooms at libraries and churches, local residents across the nation gather for often-contentious discussions about transportation proposals that would change a city's streets. And like all politics, all transportation is local and intensely personal. A transit project that could speed travel for tens of thousands of people can be halted by objections to the loss of a few parking spaces or by the simple fear that the project won't work. It's not a challenge of the data or the traffic engineering or the planning. Public debates about streets are typically rooted in emotional assumptions about how a change will affect a person's commute, ability to park, belief about what is safe and what isn't, or the bottom line of a local business.

In almost every city that I visit, people ask me how to make a convincing case for changes in the public realm. Next to safety and mobility, which should be the first considerations, the economic power of sustainable streets is probably the strongest argument for implementing dramatic change. Economic messaging and data are powerful tools against claims from what I call the Misleading Anecdotes Complex—that group of opponents who materialize around any proposed change to the street with claims that it will kill businesses by creating traffic congestion, hampering delivery trucks, and making it impossible for customers to park. These anecdotes are repeated in news stories that accompany proposals to change the streets, yet the underlying claims are based on, well, not very much.

We saw this firsthand in the fall of 2010, when a small group of protesters gathered at 14th Street on Manhattan's East Side to oppose the redesign of First and Second avenues, a redesign that included bus lanes, bike lanes, and safer pedestrian crossings. "Bloomberg did these bike lanes not for [the] environment or for people, but to get back at drivers," the protest organizer told the *Gothamist* blog, adding, "Someone at the Department of Transportation told me that." The protester claimed this revenge traffic plot removed parking spaces and caused unnamed local businesses to lose "tons and tons" of money. Another protester said that more cyclists on New York City's streets looked "ridiculous." She gave the reporter the tired refrain "This is not Amsterdam."

DOT has no Amsterdam-ometer in its traffic analysis toolbox to measure changes in the street on a scale of one to ten windmills. Analyzing economic impacts is a challenge. Traffic engineers can't walk into every store along every street and demand that every business owner open his books, or stand on the sidewalk with hand counters, clicking every time someone enters a store and then checking customers' receipts as they leave. But knowing something as simple as whether a project helped or hurt the local economy isn't a navel-gazing exercise. Analyzing how projects affect business sales is as important to the projects' survival as the projects themselves, and a key link to their expansion elsewhere. As we saw on 14th Street, everybody has an opinion about a change, and with or without data to back up the opinion, extreme claims are the ones that make the news.

Have you ever seen a car stop into a café for a sandwich, or window-shop at the boutiques in SoHo? Me neither. Cars don't shop. People do. A growing body of evidence shows that better streets mean better business. Changes that make it easier to take transit, walk, or bike also make for more interesting and walkable streets, which are much better for businesses' bottom line. This isn't an either-or proposition. But you have to know what you're measuring.

The evaluation report for Green Light for Midtown in 2009 was at the time the most elaborate traffic analysis we had ever conducted. In addition to supplying data about how the closure of Broadway to motor vehicles would likely affect traffic in the area, the study also evaluated the transit, retail, and pedestrian impacts. The study was one of the first to look at the street from the view of everyone who actually uses it, quite different from the perspective of an engineer obsessed with moving the same number of cars at any cost. While the data were extremely effective in closing the book on the controversies around Times Square, it was just one project, albeit the largest we had attempted, and the results didn't provide a get-out-of-jail-free card for future projects.

After the installation of hundreds of miles of bus and bike lanes and dozens of acres of reclaimed street space for pedestrians, the impact on New York's retail communities would have been evident all over the city by 2012. But while we heard protests from local businesses that every parking space lost to a bike lane or plaza was like a nail in the coffin of their livelihood, there were no data to confirm or contradict that premise. Transportation departments don't traditionally measure these economic data.

To be successful over the long term, we knew we had to be smart about measuring the street, but getting data isn't easy. It required that we first create an economic methodology. Working with our sister agency, the Department of Finance, which collects taxes and revenue for New York City, we obtained detailed, aggregated retail sales data for the dozens of locally owned storefronts, restaurants, and markets on streets where we introduced bike lanes, bus lanes, and plazas across the city. We compared the results on these streets with boroughwide and citywide retail sales trends as a control group. What we found was astonishing: stores along streets where changes had been made reported increased sales, far outperforming overall businesses across the boroughs.

We combined our economic data in a report called "Measuring the Street." It was the most in-depth look at the economic impact of livable street projects undertaken by any city. At Brooklyn's Pearl Street, the site of our first place-making project in 2007 in the parking lot below the Manhattan Bridge, we saw a 172 percent increase in retail sales in five years. That explosive growth would seem obvious if you visit the spot today; the triangle was a parking lot then and today bustles with workers and residents who drink coffee or eat lunch in the plaza, often having made their purchases from a café or retail shop nearby.

On Ninth Avenue in Manhattan, where we installed the first parking-protected bike path, injuries for all street users dropped by 58 percent while retail sales increased by 49 percent on the avenue between 23rd and 31st streets. Borough-wide, the retail economy grew by only 3 percent. Bronx business owners protested in 2008 that new bus-only lanes would be a store killer along Fordham Road. The sales data in 2012 told a different, opposite story. Looking at all small businesses, retail sales for the street increased by 71 percent, almost three times the 23 percent growth rate for the entire borough. Is it possible that some stores did better than others? Naturally. But on balance, businesses were clearly able to thrive with the new design, regardless of whether the store owners liked it. For years, and likely even today, it isn't hard to find a restaurant owner or shopkeeper claiming that bike lanes, bus lanes, and plazas cause local recessions. Data say otherwise.

Sales receipts alone don't tell the story. Real estate data helped us determine that there were 49 percent fewer commercial vacancies in Union Square where the transformation of Broadway eventually extended in 2011. Meanwhile, back on 14th Street, where protesters in 2010 claimed that unnamed businesses on First and Second avenues were losing "tons and tons" of money, there were 47 percent fewer commercial vacancies. That was in addition to the fact that buses moved up to 18 percent faster, ridership increased 12 percent (despite bus ridership dropping citywide at the time), 177 percent more people biked, car travel times even improved, and there were 37 percent fewer traffic crashes involving injury.

By 2012, after the bike backlash had subsided and hundreds of projects matured from new kids on the block to village elders, data produced by the once-controversial projects took on a political and rhetorical life of their own. Data showed that interventions that resolved street problems improved safety and had neutral or even positive effects on overall traffic and business. The public discussion slowly graduated from anecdote to analysis.

We published the underlying methodology for our economic analysis so that other cities could replicate our research methods. In the coming years, data on the economics of transportation will be as important as travel speeds and vehicle counts. If cities don't keep data, they will remain susceptible to spurious claims that changing streets hurts businesses.

Beyond measuring the direct impact on retail sales, data helped us uncover unfounded assumptions about who was using the street. Business owners believe they are dependent upon drivers and that bike lanes or plazas cut into their clientele. Most projects didn't significantly decrease road capacity, and road design could retain parking spaces, but as it turns out, businesses are far more reliant on nondriving customers.

Known as the City of Cars, Auckland has taken steps to revive its downtown with pedestrian-friendly streets like this one on O'Connell Street, increasing foot traffic and improving retail sales. Auckland Design Office, Auckland Council

In numerous retail districts, including on Staten Island, one of New York City's most car-dependent boroughs, the majority of people surveyed by the transportation department said that they arrived by walking, taking public transportation, or riding a bike. In seven of the nine neighborhoods surveyed, 85 to 93 percent of people arrived without a car, the highest in Jackson Heights, Queens. Even in the New Dorp district on car-loving Staten Island, only 39 percent of shoppers said they drove or took a taxi. These figures upended the presumption that small retail businesses live and die by the parking space.

What we found is not unique to New York. New evidence worldwide shows that pedestrians are the predominant customers for ground-floor retail stores. In many cities, those who drive to shops spend *less* than others. Merchants consistently overestimate their value and undervalue

those who walk, bike, or take public transportation. In a 2011 study by Transport for London, researchers conducted face-to-face interviews with shoppers in fifteen London commercial districts. They found that while people who drove cars to shop spent more on each individual visit, people who arrived on foot or by bus or the tube shopped more frequently and collectively spent almost five times more than those who drove over the course of a week or month. Similarly, in Portland, Oregon, a 2011 survey in commercial districts across the city found that "customers who arrive by automobile spend the most per visit across all of the establishments, but cyclists spend the most per month." In particular, cyclists spent $75.66 versus $61.03 for people who drove. In San Francisco, two thirds of merchants along Valencia Street in the city's Mission District reported increased sales after bike lanes and wider sidewalks were added in 1999.

In Dublin, Ireland, shop owners on Henry Street estimated that 19 percent of their customers drove while the actual figure was 9 percent, or less than half the estimate. On Grafton Street, another commercial strip in Dublin, retailers guessed that 13 percent of customers arrived by car. The actual figure, researchers found, was 10 percent, or a quarter less.

In Auckland, New Zealand, city officials removed parking and created downtown streets for pedestrians, allowing for greater concentrations of foot traffic—a 140 percent increase. This helped spur a 430 percent increase in retail on O'Connell Street, a narrow downtown road that became a lively, pedestrian-friendly street, as shown on the previous page.

Data like these help drive important traffic decisions to reorganize city streets by limiting private vehicles and expanding access to those arriving by public transportation, on foot, and by bike.

While some business owners object to every lost parking space, others more readily find that their clientele depends more on walkability than on parking. Businesses even requested the removal of parking and conversion of spaces for platform seating, enabling customers to sit down and stay awhile. A café and a restaurant in Lower Manhattan were the first to request "street seats," an idea inspired by San Francisco. Public seating where people can sip coffee and enjoy the street scene far outweighs the economic value of a couple of parking spaces. The businesses fronting the repurposed parking spaces reported a 14 percent increase in sales after the seating was installed.

Small businesses in New York are increasingly taking advantage of our bike rack program, which gives them the ability to request bike racks (what we call "corrals") that replace curbside parking spaces outside their establishments. Instead of one car monopolizing a parking space all day, a corral can house a dozen or more bikes at any moment, with turnover throughout the day. Many shops have stopped using van and car services to shuttle goods through the streets, investing in cargo

Room for eight bikes occupies the same space as a single car. Local businesses signed up to have bike-rack clusters installed in front of their storefronts, encouraging riders and improving sight lines to the street. NYC DOT

Restaurants and cafés also requested street seats, turning a few parking spaces into public table seating for everybody. Local shops reported increases in sales. NYC DOT

bikes that can more quickly haul loads across town without being stuck in bumper-to-bumper traffic.

New York real estate agents have recognized the economic benefits of our Citi Bike stations, which are a selling point for potential tenants, just as the proximity of subway stations is included in property listings. And they are not alone. Real estate speculators recognize the impact that bike lane expansions have on local development. In Minneapolis, a 5.5-mile former rail right-of-way converted into a bike and recreational path spurred $200 million in investment over the last decade, resulting in 1,200 new residential units.

A big public concern with our projects, especially larger-scale interventions like Times Square, was that they would slow traffic and bring down the economy. For all of the work across all five boroughs, there was no denser concentration of changes than in Midtown Manhattan. In 2011 we implemented a massive traffic technology project to modernize Midtown's traffic signals, installing traffic-detecting sensors on the area's utility poles, traffic signals, and street lights. The 110-square-block heart of Midtown from 42nd Street to 57th and from Second to Sixth avenues required one hundred microwave sensors and thirty-two traffic video cameras, plus twenty-three intersections equipped with E-ZPass readers that collect anonymous traffic data. We wirelessly linked this entire network of sensors and signals to identify traffic jams as they occurred, which then allowed engineers in our Traffic Management Center in Queens to instantaneously modify traffic signal patterns. Real-time traffic signal patterns to match real-time traffic conditions.

As a result of modernizing the city's traffic technology, traffic moved 10 percent faster in 2012, one year after the instrumentation of Midtown, than in 2008. Once again, the taxi GPS produced the facts. Looking at tens of millions of taxi trips in central Manhattan, we had the highest level of confidence that traffic was actually moving faster, no matter how many cabbies swore it had gotten worse.

While data on well-designed street interventions helped overcome opposition, data on public attitudes revealed that we had *underestimated* the public's appetite for changes. After years of relentless political attacks and media stories brimming with tales of traffic doom, economic and safety catastrophe, and heavy-handed official deceit, the data proved the Cassandras wrong on both the traffic and the economy. Supermajorities of New Yorkers said they supported the changes. In a *New York Times* poll in August 2013, during the waning months of the Bloomberg administration, 73 percent of New Yorkers said they supported bike share, 72 percent said they supported the plazas, and 64 percent said they supported bike lanes. If these projects were elections, they would be landslides. The *Times* poll was the final of several over the years with near-identical verdicts on plazas and bikes. New Yorkers were way ahead of the press, and far more sophisticated than a lot of politicians gave them credit for.

It was a resounding affirmation that the years-long campaign was worth it. We had successfully won over many of the most skeptical and hardened cadre of city dwellers. The increased expectations for sustainable streets underpinned the political will for the next mayor to retain or expand even our most controversial policies.

Data change the scope of how we understand the street. They change the question from whether people like or want redesigned roads to whether these redesigns make the street work better. They change how we assess the health of a street, letting us advance beyond counting how many cars a street moves to how well it works for all users. They let us move from streets designed by default and then neglected out of fear of change to streets designed for meeting social, economic, and safety necessities. And instead of leaving unchallenged the baseless claim that lost lanes or parking spaces equal lost jobs, data can provide a realistic basis for how to improve a street's operation for the critical mass of customers who take transit, walk, or ride bikes.

Had we not worked fast and attempted short-term changes, we would have had nothing for New Yorkers to experience, to react to, and, critically, to measure how our projects performed. The lessons from one project led to the next and showed us that a handful of short-term bad headlines meant little in the life cycle of a successful street-changing project.

13

Nuts and Bolts

Our road infrastructure is like an invisible thread that goes unnoticed until it fails. One of DOT's least visible but most important accomplishments was sustaining and revitalizing the city's hardware of roads, bridges, sidewalks, streetlights, and traffic lights. For all the tabloid stories focusing on the transportation department's promotion of bikes and plazas, it was our mastery of the concrete, asphalt, and steel that kept the city moving forward. Regardless of our differences over the Prospect Park West bike lane, my predecessor, Iris Weinshall, left an extremely efficient department run by experienced professionals. Our success in diversifying street life rests on the work of the more than 4,500 men and women who pave 6,300 miles of streets, fill more than 250,000 potholes a year, maintain and rehabilitate our 789 bridges, many more than a century old, and keep our ferry fleet moving, carrying 22 million passengers every year. But no one wants to hear about infrastructure. It's even less sexy than buses.

Lack of interest in infrastructure has created a nationwide crisis.

National, state, and local investment in the United States' four million miles of roads, six hundred thousand bridges, and three thousand public transportation providers has plummeted in recent decades even as population and traffic volumes have increased. The result is creaky infrastructure built mostly in the twentieth century that contributes to the five and a half billion hours Americans spend in traffic annually, costing $120 billion in extra fuel and unproductive time plus $27 billion a year in increased shipping costs.

Chinese investment in infrastructure reached 9 percent of its GDP and Europe 5 percent in 2011, compared with the United States' paltry 2.4 percent. Most Americans fail to grasp the impending infrastructure crisis and its importance for their lives and the functionality of their cities. They see road workers as an inconvenience and care only about when a road will reopen. Every pothole or canceled train somehow proves that the government can't even manage the basics of transportation infrastructure. Sixty-five percent of the nation's roads are rated as in less than good condition. Forty-five percent of Americans lack access to public transportation. But the reaction to this crisis seems to be, "Crisis? What crisis? It's either the government's problem or the government is the problem." As we saw in Vancouver, where voters rejected a referendum to improve the area's public transit system, the message is: Infrastructure, heal thyself. The reality? Buckle up, it's going to be a bumpy ride.

Deteriorating infrastructure isn't an invisible problem but an imminent threat to our cities. As transportation commissioner, I've climbed above and below bridges, scaled ladders and walked catwalks within tunnels, and seen how suspension bridge cables unwrap within bridge anchorages and bolt to the bedrock. The ironwork, sign manufacturing, and engineering that go into traffic signals and parking meters—I love it all. I love the engineering of embankments and anchorages and thrill in walking the cables to the top of the Brooklyn Bridge and other spans.

The view from the top of the Manhattan Bridge. We committed $6 billion to rehabilitate the 788 city-owned bridges, marking the first time on record that all city spans were in a state of good repair or had repair projects under way.   NYC DOT

I love the smell of asphalt, its acrid odor, its superheated shimmer and sticky texture as it tumbles from shovels and is flattened by screeds. Most of all, I love watching a crew transform a street in a few hours from a lunar landscape to a flawless mat as black as squid ink. In this regard, the tabloids got it right. I am wacko, although my partiality to heavy infrastructure helped me as commissioner.

Maybe this love of the inner workings of cities comes from my great grandfathers, who helped build the viaduct over the rail tracks on Manhattan's Park Avenue and laid the tracks for the Denver & Rio Grande Western Railroad. Their passions are the creosote in my bones, and probably why I love the scent of the subway's railroad ties.

Some of my favorite memories from this period were of filling potholes with Staten Island borough president James Molinaro. Staten Island is the least dense and most car-dependent borough in the city, and transportation is one of the most sensitive issues for its 472,000 residents. The ferry aside, Staten Island has the least developed public transportation system and no subway or train connection with other boroughs. Its streets were built in a hurry after Robert Moses oversaw the Verrazano-Narrows Bridge opening in 1964, but most of its roads lack a concrete base. Its few main roads and lack of grid road network were never expected to carry the volumes of traffic that now strafe it daily, making the system painfully vulnerable to disruption by a single breakdown.

While we made headlines in other boroughs by building bike lanes and plazas, and were accused of social engineering by the Brooklyn borough president, across the Narrows on Staten Island we were all-infrastructure-all-the-time. Staten Island was the target of some of the city's largest infrastructure investments, including a $175 million rehabilitation of the ferry terminal, whose ramps had not been updated in more than fifty years. Molinaro was legendary for importing transportation ideas he saw on vacation in Sarasota, Florida. Overhead street-name signs that can be seen from hundreds of yards away, stop signs outlined with flashing red lights to make them more visible, smart traffic signals equipped with sensors that turn green only when they detect traffic, crosswalks paved with brick-style materials. Being responsive to Molinaro's requests helped create goodwill and paved the way when we came back with big asks, like Select Bus Service with dedicated lanes along Staten Island's main street, Hylan Boulevard.

Our infrastructure summits with Molinaro sometimes lasted hours and often included a stop at the local pizza parlor or deli for a real Staten Island lunch, then decamping for handmade pastas and fresh mozzarella at Pastosa Ravioli to bring home. I enjoyed the trip to Staten Island, boarding the ferry five minutes from my office at the southern tip of Manhattan, often greeting deckhands, and ferry captains, a commissioner perk. The ferry is an extraordinary form of public transportation for seventy thousand people every weekday. It's also a workplace for some four hundred transportation department employees. Some grew up working on fishing vessels out of Brooklyn's Sheepshead Bay. A growing number were professional mariners who came through Kings Point or the State University of New York's maritime school. The latter school's former commandant of cadets, Captain Jim DeSimone, ran the ferry during my tenure. He commanded the respect of the deckhands, mates, and marine engineers as well as that of budget eggheads and administrators. Captain DeSimone took over the ferry system following the 2003 ferry tragedy, years before my time, when eleven people lost their lives after a ferry pilot blacked out at the controls as his vessel bore down on St. George's ferry terminal. DeSimone helped reorganize and professionalize the ferry operations into the most efficient system of its kind in the world.

The Staten Island infrastructure love didn't get much play outside of the borough. If transportation were covered in media proportionally to the actual dollar investment, building bridges and paving streets would be daily front-page headlines. We knew that we could not get the political leeway to reorder the streetscape unless we had mastered the basic stuff of city care. Throughout my time as commissioner, New York City witnessed numerous spectacular infrastructure failures—a steam pipe explosion on Lexington Avenue in Midtown, numerous water main breaks, and city-altering floods from storms like Sandy—that were constant reminders of the cost of disinvestment and potential price of replacement. And that's where most city investment goes: into its guts. Virtually all of city transportation departments' budgets go straight into repaving streets, producing asphalt, and maintaining and rebuilding roads and bridges.

Paving New York is a dirty, expensive business, at $1 billion over six years. One thousand lane miles are paved each year. Paving asphalt in

New York City is produced from stone mined in quarries up the Hudson River—massive boulders and outcroppings of solid stone cracked, crushed, refined, and smoothed into minute, round pebbles called aggregate. Heated up to more than 200 degrees and combined with a tar-like asphaltic cement, the mixture becomes a sticky, almost culinary mélange of material that is laid on top of the city's concrete base, like an asphalt mat. Many miles of asphalt weren't made from scratch but remade, literally, from other streets. New York City greatly expanded the use of asphalt recycling, which involves replacing some of the virgin asphalt material with old pavement that has been scraped off the street before laying new asphalt. Thanks to many experienced and innovative leaders at DOT, New York City now produces asphalt with 50 percent recycled content, recycling more than 1 million tons of materials in the last seven years. We could rip up a street in Manhattan, reconstitute some of the old asphalt into fresh blacktop, and lay it out in Brooklyn. Reducing the amount of new asphalt required to pave streets saved 174,000 tons of milled asphalt from winding up in landfills each year and eliminated the need for 840,000 barrels of oil, also saving money on landfill fees. Trucks full of crushed asphalt drive 321,000 miles every year en route to landfills, producing needless emissions and damaging the region's roads. The recycling program saved $60 million over six years.

The success of this approach led us to propose the purchase of a second asphalt-making plant to augment our sole facility in Red Hook, Brooklyn, instead of buying extra asphalt from private companies at much greater expense. Our head of roadway repair and maintenance, Galileo Orlando (the Sultan of Rock as we called him), led the lengthy negotiation and years of research, modeling, and approvals to acquire the second municipal asphalt plant near La Guardia Airport in Queens, which increased city asphalt production by 50 percent. We also experimented with asphalt that could be applied at lower temperatures, reducing the energy needed to keep it warm, and we used no-emission electric screeds to spread the asphalt evenly.

Taking over this asphalt plant and changing the formula for what we laid on our streets would never have happened without aggressive advocacy and detailed economic analysis.

Reporters started to figure out the counterintuitive fact that bike lanes and plazas were the budgetary equivalent of change found between the sofa cushions compared with our road infrastructure investment. A headline in *The New York Observer* asked, "Janette Sadik-Khan Is the Best Mechanic the City Streets Have Had in a Generation—So Why Do Motorists Hate Her So Much?"

"'She has done more for drivers than anyone since Robert Moses,' one anonymous transportation professional told *The Observer*. Rarely is that comparison a complimentary one—Janette Sadik-Khan has long been dubbed Mrs. Moses, but it is by those who disagree with her programs and (often very successful) tactics."

My hero in that story? James Molinaro. "I have 5 percent of the city's population, but 18 percent of its registered motor vehicles," Molinaro told the reporter. "She has been an asset to Staten Island, as far as I'm concerned."

In addition to being a city of asphalt roads, New York is a city of bridges and islands, and we invested $6 billion on the repair and rehabilitation of our bridge inventory alone, for the first time either restoring each of the 788 city-owned spans to a state of good repair or launching multiyear rehabilitation projects. Until you've seen the bridges, cables, anchorages, viaducts, and tunnel water mains along with their production facilities, metalworking, and sign shops, you cannot fully appreciate the complexity of a city's infrastructure and the considerable expense of maintaining it at all times and in all weather.

After I helped secure federal funding for bridge inspection and maintenance, Dr. Bojidar Yanev, DOT's top bridge engineer, agreed to take me to the top of the Brooklyn Bridge towers. One late-spring morning we walked up one of the long necklace cables, starting at six a.m., shortly after first light. I'm an adrenaline junkie and love to bungee jump, zip-line, and climb glaciers. But I was about halfway up the first cable when my heart seized in my throat. Something about the exposure and the sight of barges in the East River hundreds of feet below stopped me in my tracks. I felt a quick panic, as if I were drifting away. Yanev knew exactly what to do to pull me back into the moment. He brought his face within a foot of mine. I heard the words "Look into my eyes," in Yanev's resonant Bulgarian accent. His eyes pierced deep into me, drawing me back. He walked backward step by step, talking to me directly while we ascended. Eventually I regained my breath and composure. My strength rose with every step and with the sun. When we arrived at the top of the tower, relieved, Yanev reached into his bag and pulled out a beverage and a couple of bagels. We toasted the morning, one of the most spectacular I've ever known. That episode was the first of many visits that took me to the top of all of DOT's East River bridges, including the Verrazano-Narrows and George Washington bridges, experiences that have only made me more passionate about infrastructure.

We tried to bring a greater level of innovation, sustainability, and practical thinking to the basic materials used in building and maintaining city streets. We installed energy-efficient and long-lasting LED lights on the FDR Drive and on the "necklace" lights on the Brooklyn and Manhattan bridges. By 2017, all of New York City's streetlights will be LEDs, reducing energy use and associated costs for decades. Even this change can be controversial as residents adjust to the LEDs, which have a different color profile and appear brighter than the sepia-toned sodium lights they replaced. Different contexts require different treatments and cities are exploring new light filters to soften their glow on the street.

But the opportunities with lighting go beyond the energy efficiency of fixtures like LEDs. Lighting has long been used for arts, entertainment, and interior design to draw the eye and to create appealing environments. Using these same lighting techniques outdoors can illuminate the dusk-to-dawn city both literally and metaphorically, turning its streets into their own stages. There is a place-making and economic case for turning the street into a place that looks like somewhere where people want to be at night and not somewhere that feels unsafe or uninviting.

One of the least visible, least innovative, and most passive uses for infrastructure in cities can be seen in the curbside lanes on our streets. An alien landing in any American city would be mystified by the four-thousand-pound steel boxes that line the curbs along almost every street. A millennium from now, archaeologists examining pictures of parked cars will be convinced that vehicles were sacred cultural totems based on the way we lined our public spaces with them, like so many statues, and built structures to house them.

Many people see their private vehicles as a means of liberation, but the less romantic counterpart to our Jack Kerouac fantasy is that cars sit idle upwards of 95 percent of the time and don't disappear when not actively used. They require real estate. And whether totally free or metered at far below market rates, city parking consumes as much real estate in many cities as sidewalks or parkland. "Parking covers more acres of urban America than any other one thing," Jeff Speck writes in *Walkable City*, referring to a study that found 500 million parking spaces are empty in the nation at any given moment. Huge swaths of city centers in places like Buffalo, Detroit, Hartford, Tulsa, and St. Louis have as much, if not more, acreage turned over to parking lots than to human activity. In many cities, private parking itself is a countervailing force to development, with parking "craters"—massive tracts of open-air parking lots in downtown areas—sucking away density, eroding the streetscape, and making urban centers feel as lifeless as, well, an empty parking lot.

But the chronic inability to find parking even in metered spaces is proof that parking is a giveaway with its true cost carefully hidden. Free or cheap parking is an embossed invitation to drive into dense urban areas instead of taking transit. Futz with the parking rate and city officials risk being accused of fleecing taxpayers. Free parking is viewed as a right, a privilege bought and paid for by tax dollars. Yet pedestrians and transit riders who pay the same taxes would be arrested for "parking" their nonautomotive personal property along the curb. If, instead of parking a car, I erected a Bedouin tent at the curb, fed the meter, and arranged inside the tent a living-room furniture suite, I'd be hauled off before my sweet tea had time to cool. That space is clearly valuable, or at least too valuable to share with anything but cars. Parking spaces that came with new apartments in New York have topped one million dollars in the most extreme example. An hour of parking in many private garages starts above twenty dollars while the cost of street parking elsewhere runs from Absolutely Free to one dollar an hour in most of the city. The highest rate for the first hour of parking is four dollars in Manhattan below 96th Street. Street space is valuable, yet the curbside is treated like the rain that drains along it into the sewers.

New efforts to recalibrate the cost of parking are taking shape nationwide as cities experiment with what's known as "dynamic pricing," changing the cost of parking either by increasing it when demand is highest and available spaces are scarcest, or by setting lower rates in less congested parts of the city and at less busy times of the day. The first attempt at dynamic pricing in New York City, the Park Smart program developed by Bruce Schaller, DOT's traffic and planning commissioner, was intended to have two effects. First, it would encourage people to adjust their behavior and drive to commercial areas when the rate was cheapest—and the street the least busy. Then, during the busy period, when the streets outside stores fill up with cars circling for parking, and trucks double-parked to make or pick up deliveries, the price would rise significantly. Not so high as to deter parking altogether, but high enough so that people would park only as long as necessary to complete their errands before scurrying back to their cars.

We instituted the Park Smart program in conjunction with local merchants in areas where they specifically requested it. Many store owners looked at the spots in front of their establishments and saw them filled with the same cars all day long; they weren't getting a whole lot of transactions from those few spaces. What would make those spaces more valuable to store owners? Turnover. If the parking rate lets vehicle owners occupy the same spot all day by feeding chump change into the meter, the entire commercial strip is deprived of new customers arriving by car and plagued by the ensuing congestion and double parking on the street. In the Jackson Heights and Park Slope neighborhoods, where we increased the parking rate during the busiest hours, the duration that people parked at these spots decreased and the number of vehicles able to park increased by 20 percent, thus helping businesses by making it easier for new customers and delivery trucks to find parking.

The world's Potentate of Parking Policy, Donald Shoup, now retired from UCLA, called for a parking strategy that would set rates high enough to keep a space or two available on streets at any given moment—what he called the 85 percent solution, the ideal maximum occupancy of parking spaces on a given street. While motorists reflexively balk at paying more to park and are enticed into "free parking" lots behind stores and restaurants, hidden costs are involved there as well. Shoup notes that non–vehicle owners are forced to subsidize the cut-rate or nonexistent parking rates in private lots, which are hidden in the development costs of new real estate. We do not see this cost, but we all pay it off through higher rents, retail prices, or in the taxes that subsidize many development projects. When people who drive must pay for the true cost of their parking spaces, whether public or private, they are forced to consider if it is truly worth driving on this particular occasion.

Raising meter fees for street parking can spell political suicide if done incorrectly, but cities can't afford not to bring their meter rates into the twenty-first century and set new expectations. Any board of directors that similarly lets prices stagnate—imagine an eternal five-cent Coke—would be rightly fired by shareholders. But cities must go beyond parking's potential financial return and reexamine how parking policy can be utilized as a tool for development and livability. Instead of diverting all the revenues to their general funds, cities could reduce the sting of increased fees by investing some of those resources in ways that would incentivize smarter parking—using sensors that indicate where parking spaces are available, apps that allow drivers to pay by cell phone, and other driver-friendly strategies. And some of these funds should go to encourage would-be motorists to take other modes—improving transit, biking, and walking.

But in many cases, the city government isn't a hapless victim watching as parked cars slowly take over its streets. Some cities' own rules dictate building new parking spaces alongside new construction, which, even if the spaces are in garages and not in the street, enable greater congestion and car dependence while taking valuable real estate away from other uses. Mexico City's planning rules require that new buildings provide indoor parking, a rule taken so seriously that some new high-rise towers require the construction of ten-story mascot structures to house all the cars expected to arrive with each new office or residential development. A 2014 study by the Institute of Transportation Development Policy (ITDP) analyzed 251 new real estate developments built in Mexico City between 2009 and 2013. It found that of the 172 million square feet of new floor area developed in the federal district, 42 percent of that space was required simply to store cars driven by people using the other 58 percent of the space. That's 250,000 spaces, a virtual off-street city built just for cars—and this on top of the street space already built to keep cars moving. This parking rule robs Mexico City of the opportunity to build more residential properties and greater residential density where it's most needed—near the city's metro stations and bus, bike, and walking network. The added parking within the city center assures commuters a parking space, inducing more people to drive to work instead of taking public transit. In a sense, city regulations *require* private builders to promote more traffic. Similar parking mania is found in the regulations of cities around the world, posing significant obstacles to denser cities and more people-oriented streets.

One of the hypervisible features of city streets is the profusion of large trucks. On one level, massive, eighteen-wheel trucks are the model of efficiency, able to deliver to dozens of stores within a few miles of one another in a single day. On another level, their mere size is out of scale with most city streets, and their unusual turning radii do not mix well with people on foot in dense areas. And for all their efficiency, why is it necessary for these massive delivery trucks to arrive at midday, when city traffic is at its worst?

We worked to address this with a pilot program to incentivize trucking companies and retailers to make deliveries during nonpeak hours—not the middle of the night, when people are sleeping, but in the pre- and post–rush hour when the network has yet to fully waken and after the evening crush has passed. Companies and retailers alike—shoe stores, grocery stores—liked the program because their employees are usually slammed with rush-hour customers and don't have the time or staff to take large deliveries. Delivery companies like Sysco liked the program because they avoided traffic, got fewer parking tickets for illegal parking, made far more deliveries in far less time, and saved on gas. Of course, many businesses can't accept deliveries when they are not staffed to be open. But the cost for this shouldn't be passed along to neighborhoods, which today have to live with massive trucks plying the same streets as schoolchildren—sometimes with deadly consequences, as we saw with Amar Diarrassouba in chapter 10. Cities and businesses are experimenting with drop-off depots in congested areas, where trucks can make a single drop-off during off hours and businesses can pick up the merchandise for the final few blocks during regular business hours. It's notable that the off-hour delivery program expanded without incentives after the pilot, pointing the way to a bigger citywide shift.

And then there is the ever-present threat of climate change and severe weather, which can cause the invisible thread of any city's road infrastructure to snap. Hurricane Sandy underscored this when it swept ashore overnight on October 29, 2012. The storm's winds turned out to be a lesser problem than the surge of water into this city of low-lying islands. New Yorkers took for granted that the harbor ends just south of Battery Park and on the coast of the Rockaways in Queens and Staten Island. But with the waterline raised just a few feet, entire neighborhoods were suddenly flooded. Neighborhoods on Staten Island, at or around sea level, became bathtubs for seawater and storm runoff that had nowhere else to go.

This water inundated our premier transportation assets—the tunnels below the East and Hudson rivers. Trains could still run within parts of the boroughs, but not through any tunnels beneath or near the East River. The bridges over the river, already a mess even on a regular workday, were almost impassable the morning after the storm, not from damage but from the collective traffic of people trying to find an alternative to taking subways. During emergency meetings with the MTA, we immediately moved to create a "bus bridge," staging hundreds of shuttle buses at Brooklyn's Barclays Center arena to shuttle passengers to Manhattan, where there was limited subway service. This was a phenomenally efficient maneuver, moving almost as many people over the Manhattan Bridge just days after the storm as normally move over it on an average day, when trains run over it. The Staten Island Ferry resumed passenger service after just seventy-two hours, and the MTA reopened its tunnels quickly, but it would take years of closures and rehabilitation to restore them.

A massive contingent of the transportation department itself was shut out of its headquarters for nearly two months, the downside of being at Manhattan's southern tip. Immediately after the storm, I committed the entire DOT staff and me to the recovery effort. I spent most of that time in the drowned neighborhoods of Staten Island and Queens with Steve Lombardi, my navigator and driver, who knew almost every recess of the city and was one of my closest friends throughout my tenure. DOT employees lived in some of the most devastated areas or were close to someone who had suffered considerable destruction. Yet they still showed up with front-end loaders, dump trucks, and their

DOT's dump trucks, typically used to haul asphalt, were deployed to haul debris from homes damaged and destroyed by Sandy in 2012. NYC DOT

tools to fix traffic signals and streetlights, and haul off the remnants of people's homes so they could at least have a chance to start again.

While Sandy might seem like a localized environmental cataclysm, the storm effectively shut down 40 percent of all American transit service. U.S. transportation secretary Anthony Foxx in 2014 announced $3.59 billion in disaster relief funds for transportation projects, including funds to protect the Staten Island Ferry terminals from floods and for sealing sidewalk grates and underground facilities for the South Ferry subway station. Sandy also ushered in a new way of looking at the fragility of our transportation infrastructure. The federal government estimates that a mere two-foot rise in sea level along the East Coast could submerge six hundred miles of rail, dozens of ports, and many airports, including all three in the New York City area. Building on the promise of PlaNYC, we tried to build this resilience into the design of the city with new codes for designing buildings, waterfronts, and roads and bridges.

The near-term, change-based strategies that cities can embark on at little cost and with readily available materials are no substitute for the long-term, invisible infrastructure investment needed to sustain cities that can be swallowed up by one storm, flushed away by one water main break, or carbonized by a single vehicle fire. Infrastructure investment is an ongoing race to keep up with the erosion of our roads and bridges, a race that we are badly losing right now.

14

The Fight Continues

What is a city, if not its people and its streets? The two are inextricable, one meaningless without the other. Ancient Athenians filtered through the agora, the heart of the city-state's political, civic, social, and commercial life, and where Socrates was said to have questioned passersby on life's essential issues. I wonder if Socrates in the agora was much like any number of my eccentric neighbors in Manhattan's West Village, talking among the booksellers and fruit and hot dog stands, struggling to be heard over the police sirens, the rumble of the subway, and the whine of garbage trucks. Maybe we wouldn't recognize a modern Socrates among the thousands of Washington Square Park denizens on a sunny spring day in Manhattan. Regardless, I recognize our neighborhood and the ancient Athenian open spaces as similar. The Internet may provide a new forum for the spread of ideas, but place still matters. In Rome, the center of the ancient world and epicenter of some of the Western world's most magnificent monuments and public spaces, the living history of its public streets still fascinates

In cities like Rome and Athens, public space is as likely to be filled with parked cars as with people. A piazza in the Garbatella neighborhood in Rome.
Seth Solomonow

millions of people today. The Romans brought people together for sport at the Colosseum and established a forum in every city. Ancient Athens and Rome built monuments to represent power and please the gods, but the results ennobled the people who served and worshipped them, and still enchant us today. These two cradles of democracy and republicanism were united in the democratizing design of their public space. Streets are part of our sense of belonging, and we need them to accomplish both simple tasks and higher purposes.

Today, the streets of Athens are crammed with a toxic mix of cars, motorcycles, and tour buses as the local government attempts to claw back the central city's pedestrian streets from the hundreds of cars and scooters that illegally drive and park in the district. Two millennia ago, Julius Caesar barred carts and chariots from Rome from the morning until the afternoon, one of the first recorded examples of municipal traffic management. These days, public space in Rome is as likely to be occupied by parked cars as by people, a reality that leaders are trying to reverse. The Colosseum is surrounded by a cyclone of traffic, prompting Rome's mayor in 2013 to take the extraordinary step of closing a road adjacent to it to the city's infamous swarms of vehicle traffic, with mixed results so far as the network and ordinary Romans adjust to the new road order.

Pope Francis in 2015 issued an encyclical emphasizing people-focused development and announced that the 2016 Jubilee would be extended to all of Rome's communities. "The Vatican has asked specifically for the creation of bicycle and pedestrian routes," the mayor told the local press. "The Holy Father would be pleased if many of the people arriving in Rome could complete the last part of their journey on foot like real pilgrims." A large blessing, indeed.

When I think of what streets will look like in the next two decades, I hope that the differences will be visible in the way that space is used, with more people walking on more attractive sidewalks landscaped with trees and greenery, riding bikes in safe, well-designed lanes, or riding on state-of-the-art bus rapid transit lines that crisscross the city. And there will be cars. Nothing I've said denies the importance of the automobile. It is a question of rebalance, equity, and fairness. Even the future isn't what it used to be. It won't be a *Jetsons* world of private spaceships cruising around a stratospheric dome. It may look a lot more like a city street from the early twentieth century, with kids playing on the sidewalks, people hanging out, meeting friends in plazas, walking to and from the store, and living life at street level.

A major difference underpinning that future will depend on how we leverage technology, and it's going to be one of the biggest streetfights going forward. While we adapt our cities to a new age and update the legacy hardware of our streets to serve more varied purposes, the software also needs updating to help us use our streets more efficiently. If this book does nothing else but remind planners to follow the people, then they should also be able to see how new technologies are driving a new, shared economy in transportation that holds the key to creating safer, more accessible, and softer streets. With a couple of clicks we can get a ride with Uber or Lyft, grab a shared bike or car, or navigate a city we've never been in before. New smartphone apps are making it possible to avoid traffic jams, locate bus and subway services, and walk to points of interest. These software bits are much less expensive than the atoms of hard infrastructure and are dramatically increasing the rate of innovation on our streets, giving way to a bigger vision with mobility on demand and changing the way we travel in our cities. Ideally, these technologies will make it possible to get around without owning a car at all.

Big data, digital networks, and artificial intelligence are an increasing part of how we plan, operate, and build infrastructure. We see it in road pricing, new traffic system management technology, and new bus planning apps to optimize transit routes and buses. A future with autonomous vehicles, delivery drones, and unified payment systems is on the near-term horizon. This wave of change has landed on our streets, and these changes will advance how we get around cities and use our streets. A smartphone can eliminate the anxiety of getting around, whether you're in Boston, Bangalore, or Buenos Aires.

But these new apps also pose big questions. While new transportation services like Uber and Lyft (called transportation network companies or TNCs in transport-speak), or shared-vehicle services like Car2Go, Zipcar, and Bridj, are using technology to dramatically lower the operating and entry costs for taxi and car services, they raise questions about social equity, safety, and the true costs of these popular services. Without a regulatory framework, cities could see outcomes that run counter to goals of mobility, sustainability, accessibility, and social equity. Cities have embarked on varied paths, resulting in patchwork regulation. Taxi industries and their allies in city halls have engaged companies like Uber in pitched battles, leading to at-times violent taxi strikes in Paris, a high-stakes political battle in New York City, and legislative tugs-of-war in Seattle, Toronto, and Rio. Officials are attempting to regulate or even bar the nascent industry while Uber claims that current decades-old regulations don't apply to its business model.

The outcome of this streetfight will be different in different cities. No two cities are alike. They have different geographic, social, political, economic, and cultural realities, in addition to size and experience that will factor into their attempts to get the role of these operators right. The lines between older, more traditional taxi and car services and new TNCs are blurring and will be shaped by these new regulations, modes of enforcement, and market conditions. But it's clear to me that the future of for-hire car services will be a lot more on-demand-in-your-hand and a lot less like the 1930s model of taxis. How to deal with this new "genie" of mobility is playing out all over the world, and it's not going back into the lamp.

Fully self-driving vehicles will have even more widespread impacts on safety, mobility, land use, and the built environment. By eliminating human emotions and opportunism from the act of driving, a disinterested technology system can keep vehicles away from one another, operating at a speed appropriate for safety, optimizing road capacity, and closing the divide between those who have access to mobility and those who don't. The promise is that these vehicles can also eliminate the human errors responsible for the overwhelming number of collisions that result from speeding, drunk driving, failing to yield, and simple inattention. But the road to a driver-free road network is likely to take many years, and it's not yet clear how driverless and conventional cars will interact with one another, particularly in extreme weather or poor road conditions.

The regulatory framework is not yet in place to ensure that these new services or autonomous vehicles under development don't exacerbate or mask the very problems we're just beginning to solve. If shared rides and driverless vehicles give suburban residents all the benefits of private vehicle ownership with fewer of the costs or disadvantages, it could encourage further sprawl. Meanwhile, within cities, shared rides run the risk of shifting millions of commuters not only from private to shared cars, but also from public transportation into the backseat of one of the growing menu of TNC options. Critically, these technologies depend on smooth and free-flowing roads the same way that private cars today do. We need to think comprehensively to expand access to shared rides while similarly increasing transit and reducing the footprint of those shared vehicles on the street. New technologies must be integrated into an urban plan that seeks to increase the use of transit, riding bikes, and walking while reducing the number and danger of vehicles on the road.

So how do we prevent the mistakes we made with the car-focused hardware on our streets in the twentieth century from being repeated with car-focused software on our streets in the twenty-first century? Some promising work has been started by the National Association of City Transportation Officials (NACTO). A short list of the policy and regulatory needs includes access to anonymous traffic data to provide the granular information necessary for effective traffic management; access to "black boxes" that record vehicle operation prior to any crash, just like a plane, to comprehensively grasp safety issues for the first time; and a system to keep track of the number of miles traveled of particular vehicles for use in future programs to establish a fee structure so that people pay for the miles they drive.

Thoughtful city and federal policies must be developed to ensure that self-driving vehicles are part of a safe, integrated transportation system and don't entrench car dependence and abandonment of the street. The major near-term goal is establishing licensing and liability requirements that promote safe street operation (obeying speed limits, yielding to pedestrians) on test vehicles and the early prototypes that will be on the market. The new street code for cities must also address parking policies, such as dedicated on- and off-street spaces for shared vehicles. And with the advent of self-driving cars, cities must be prepared for an increase in the demand for curb space for pickup and drop-offs. Finally, as self-driving fleets evolve, cities will need to invest in updated signs, infrastructure, and mapping technology to accommodate the new way of getting around and dedicate funding to adapt cities' roadways. Given the shrinking federal and state infrastructure funding, this is no small task.

Cities should be on the leading edge of integrating this technology and not bury their heads by trying to bar it, limit its influence, or regulate it into obscurity. The Finnish capital of Helsinki has recognized in digital platforms not merely an opportunity to create market-based transportation convenience, but a means to eliminate the need for private car ownership by 2025. The idea is embedded in the proposal's name: "Mobility as a Service." The organizing principle is based on the view that how you get around is something that is provided for you—a service—instead of something you have to own, like a car. If all channels of public transportation—buses, trains, taxis, car pools, and car share—are integrated, citizens could pick a bundled package of these services, starting with, say, a €95 ($106) monthly transportation subscription for unlimited public transport in the city and also up to 100 kilometers (62 miles) of on-demand car services such as Uber or Hailo or Lyft. If subscribers need to visit relatives in the country or go camping for the weekend, they are entitled to up to 500 kilometers (310 miles) of shared-car use.

If subscribers stay within these usage levels, they pay only that flat fee. More expensive options would let users get door-to-door shared taxi service plus public transport plus domestic transportation anywhere in the country via public transportation.

The Helsinki model's strength is that it's not dependent upon one way of getting around. City officials have been changing the makeup of Helsinki's streets and altering the scale and scope of residential and commercial development, embarking on rails-to-trails projects, known as *baana*, where there are now bike lanes in former railroad rights-of-way, and helping with the dense residential development at the Kamppi Center and its massive transit and retail node. It's part of an explicit plan to make the city center more dense by expanding opportunities for housing and employment while increasing transit options.

"We should be talking about urban capacity instead of just car capacity," Reetta Putkonen, the director of Helsinki's Planning Department, told me. Their plan includes waterfront residential developments similar to those found in Oslo and Vancouver, and "boulevardizations" that accommodate everybody who uses the street, along with increased streetcar and light rail—components that act as counterweights to private car ownership.

If the Helsinki model, which is being phased in, works and people can get reliable transportation to wherever they are going—to work, visit a friend in the suburbs, or get away for the weekend—then private car ownership, particularly in cities, could eventually become obsolete.

But it's not all a march to victory. A stubborn, residual opposing trend in many cities has people driving away from sustainability as fast as their cars can take them. Beijing was the bike capital of the world in the 1970s, when seas of bicyclists poured through the streets. Yet Beijing residents ultimately turned their back on the bikes that global cities today are espousing. For many urbanizing Chinese, cars mean upward mobility, status, and symbols of success. Today, the streets that once were filled with bikes are choked with cars, often shrouding cities like Beijing in a thick haze of exhaust. Chinese officials beat a hasty retreat back to Beijing's republic-of-bikes days, this time armed with a bike-share system.

In equal measure to imagination and initiative, changing streets requires eternal vigilance, and hard-won gains must be defended. In New York City, just six years after we rolled construction barrels into the street and shut Broadway to cars, Mayor Bill de Blasio said he would consider ripping out the Times Square plazas. Why? Although the plazas are a hugely popular destination—increasing daily pedestrian traffic from 350,000 to 480,000 people—they are also a magnet for hucksters dressed in Elmo, Spider-Man, or SpongeBob SquarePants costumes, vying for tips and sometimes being overly aggressive with tourists. A cottage industry emerged in which women removed their tops, painted their breasts with American flags, and seduced passersby into giving tips in exchange for risqué selfies.

"You could argue that those plazas have had some very positive impact," de Blasio said to reporters after a week of tabloid coverage of the scantily clad *desnudas* (Spanish for naked women; why don't we have a word for that in English?). "You could also argue that they've come with a lot of problems. . . . Now that's a very big endeavor and like every other option comes with pros and cons," he said. "So we're going to look at what those pros and cons would be."

Police Commissioner Bill Bratton was more direct about what he wanted: "I'd prefer to just dig the whole damn thing up and put it back the way it was," he told a radio reporter. "It would eliminate this area where people just hang out," Bratton added. "The activity is not occurring anywhere else in the area."

When I first heard the comments, I was shocked, but also perplexed. Now, I don't like being hounded by Hello Kittys every few steps. No one does. But is it necessary to rip out the plaza and dislocate nearly a half million daily pedestrians just to deal with the few dozen shysters and the sight of women's breasts? Is it necessary to dismantle the Eiffel Tower just because hustlers sell selfie sticks in its shadows? New York's police department has a long history of dealing with quality-of-life issues and can figure out how to deal with the Muppets.

The implementation of the proposal would have dramatic consequences beyond the public space itself. Ripping out a $55 million project at the first sign of trouble would forfeit the money spent and might even require that the funding—including federal cash—be repaid. Then the city would have to rebuild the street at an equivalent cost. This would escalate a public nuisance into a $100 million, multiyear construction site. That's $100 million that could be used to build million-dollar plazas in one hundred less affluent neighborhoods or a decade's worth of bike lanes.

Within moments of de Blasio's comments, my iPhone erupted with messages from reporters looking for comment on the prospect of eliminating one of our signature projects. Instinctively, we brainstormed quotes, tweets, letters to the editor, joint statements, and coalitions to beat back the proposal. Within about thirty minutes, reading the rapid-response stories and tweets posting online, I realized that we didn't have to do a single thing. The rebukes from New Yorkers came fast, and they were furious. Hundreds of tweets fire hosed the mayor with criticism. A spokeswoman for the speaker of the city council quickly declared that New York City had bigger problems to deal with. Manhattan's borough president, Gale Brewer, a longtime friend and a true champion of public space, said the idea of removing the plazas was "preposterous."

"Putting back the honking, angry, fumy Broadway parking lot at the so-called center of the world would be no accomplishment," she wrote in a statement. "Surely we cannot go back to destroying the city in order to make it safe for more cars."

Brewer's bluntness echoed that of those who would be most affected

by the change: the businesses, entertainment, and hospitality industries built around Times Square. "Sure, let's tear up Broadway—we can't
govern, manage or police our public spaces," said an exasperated Tim
Tompkins, the head of the Times Square Alliance. "That's not a solution.
It's a surrender."

"It's hard to grasp [de Blasio's] calculus," a *New York Times* columnist added to the growing chorus of criticism. "One of Mr. de Blasio's
big initiatives, Vision Zero, aims to improve pedestrian safety. Ripping
up the pedestrian plazas in Times Square, restoring cars and forcing
millions of people to dodge traffic again, runs headlong into his own
policy," he wrote.

A critic at *New York* magazine observed, "Eradicating a pedestrian
plaza because you don't like who's walking there is like blasting away a
beach because you object to bikinis or paving a park because you hate
squirrels. It represents such a profound misunderstanding of public
space that it makes me question the mayor's perception of what counts
as progressive."

In a sign of how untethered the idea really was, two of the mayor's
allies for removing the plazas were two former Republican mayoral
candidates—not exactly the comrades-in-arms that a self-described progressive mayor wants on his side. Even the most strident *New York Post*
critic conceded that the plazas were there to stay: "As awful as they remain, they're an ineradicable part of Midtown."

It was difficult not to respond in the public debate as others rushed
to defend the plazas. But I recognized the signs: This was an out-and-
out backlash. Not against bikes or plazas or taking space *from* cars, but
against the idea of giving space *to* cars. And the backlash wasn't mine;
it was the new mayor's fight. An important observation that I share
from my years as commissioner is that when you push the status quo,
the status quo pushes back—hard. Six years after we rolled the first barrels into place, closing Broadway to cars, the plazas at Times Square

became the new status quo. The pushback came from New Yorkers, who passionately defended their new streets, not from the former city officials who had fought the battles to build them. Within weeks, the city relented. Officials eventually decided that establishing clear zones for different kinds of activities in Times Square—and clearing swaths of the plazas of hucksters—was preferable to destroying the public space and reopening Broadway to cars.

The Times Square saga is a reminder that in New York and other cities, changing the streets is a blood sport at all levels. Projects that alter streetscapes upset people who naturally cling to stability, even if that stability is unsafe or inefficient. The flip side is that once change is in place, it becomes the new norm and frames expectations of citizens.

The most important lesson is that safer streets work, and that they can be executed quickly and cheaply. Proof is on the streets of New York City. What works here may not work out of the box everywhere, but most ideas are scalable for cities big and small. Sustainable streets make sense for safety, traffic, and long-term planning, and they make sense for the economy.

In my current work with Bloomberg Associates, I have the privilege of working with mayors and transportation officials from the world over to tailor the ideas that worked in New York to streets in Los Angeles, Oakland, Detroit, Mexico City, Rome, and Rio, among others. Staffed by former senior officials from Bloomberg's administration, the group is managed by George Fertitta, the marketing mastermind who nearly doubled the city's already intense tourism numbers. Many cities are looking to replicate protected bike paths and pocket parks and plazas, adapting infrastructure to reproduce what the High Line has done or how Citi Bike has fundamentally transformed the basic metabolism of New York's streets.

New York City has proved that a new road order is possible. New York today is a renewed and renewing city, one changed in ways that even a decade ago would never have been predicted. Young people to-

A renewed Crossroads of the World. A 2015 proposal to remove these plazas just as long-term construction wrapped up met with a fierce backlash. In this case, the new status quo won and the plazas remain. Nick Mosquera

day grow up knowing New York as a bikeable big city, where bright blue bikes line the streets and where they can marvel at the city from the High Line, Governors Island, and other creatively adapted spaces. Millions walk annually in Times Square unaware of the former roadway. Waterfronts that once were glimpsed only from cars on highways or solely by longshoremen are reborn as public parks from Brooklyn and Long Island City to the Hudson River, and increasingly on Manhattan's East Side.

Even when streetfights are won, we must undertake a campaign of eternal vigilance. We require constant reminders that the hard-won gains to wrest back the street and create a safer public realm can fade and disappear like lines on the pavement. New York City and its fight—which continues today—show there are no guarantees preventing the next generation of leaders from reversing the course of a city and reverting the operating code back to its default position.

The headlines routinely challenge urban transformation, even in cities accustomed to change. The same tired arguments and assumptions about how streets work that led to congestion and paralysis in cities for most of the last half century are still being used to block and reverse change today. The difference is that today, there are global examples of successful cities and data showing how people-focused streets work. There is a new vocabulary for street designs that serve the needs of the people who live in cities. There are new expectations for streets. And there is New York.

If you can remake it here, you can remake it anywhere.

Acknowledgments

This book is based on a very true story, one as rich, complex, and incredible as the city in which it took place. None of this would have come to pass—certainly not as quickly or spectacularly—without the strong leadership of Michael Bloomberg and the support of Patti Harris. Bloomberg's leadership shows the power of individuals to change the world by changing their cities.

The urban transformation in New York City would not have been possible without the real-world dedication, skill, and creativity of the professionals at the New York City Department of Transportation. They made the impossible possible, the difficult easy, and the easy inspiring, stirring New Yorkers and city residents around the world. It's impossible to name everyone who had a role in the city's transformation, but any list would start with DOT's past and present leaders: Lori Ardito, Margaret Newman, Jon Orcutt, Bruce Schaller, Joe Cannisi, Galileo Orlando, Jim DeSimone, Leon Heyward, Joe Jarrin, Cordell Schachter, Michael Primeggia, Gerard Soffian; Henry Perahia, Phil Damashek, David Woloch, Margaret Forgione, Joe Palmieri, Connie Moran; Maura McCarthy, Tom Cocola, Luis Sanchez, Dalila Hall, Ryan Russo, Josh Benson, Wendy Feuer, Steve Galgano, Marlene Hochstadt, Tom Maguire, Eric Beaton, Joe Barr, Kate Slevin,

Kim Wiley-Schwartz, Nina Haiman, Susan Rogerson-Pondish, Bojidar Yanev, Brenda Rivera, and Dani Simons. And of course my daily confidant, Steve Lombardi.

I am grateful to my mom, Jane McCarthy, whose love, encouragement, and passion for the city helped make this book happen, and offered many contributions that found their way into the book. And to my wildly talented colleagues Jon Orcutt, Bruce Schaller and husband, Mark, who gave our drafts an unflinching read.

Nick Mosquera provided invaluable research assistance throughout the writing of this book, and Andy Wiley-Schwartz contributed many helpful suggestions along the way.

Thanks to our friends at city hall and at other agencies who supported our work through the years—or who just gave us enough rope to hang ourselves: Dan Doctoroff, Ed Skyler, Howard Wolfson, Kevin Sheekey, Frank Berry, Jim Anderson, Marc La Vorgna, John Gallagher, Cas Holloway, Marc Ricks, Ray Kelly, Adrian Benepe, John Doherty, Nicholas Scoppetta, Sal Cassano, David Burney, Rit Aggarwala, Carter Strickland, Michael Dardia, Jeff Kay, Nanette Smith, Stephen Goldsmith, Michael Best, Mark Muschenheim, Stu Loeser, Farrell Sklerov, Jason Post, Andrew Brent, and Evelyn Erskine.

We and all New Yorkers were lucky to have leaders like MTA/NYC Transit and its leaders, Tom Prendergast, Jay Walder, Howard Roberts, and Lee Sander.

We took great counsel from Sam Schwartz, Jeff Speck, Brent Toderian, Sir Peter Hendy, Enrique and Gil Peñalosa, Dhyana Quintanar, Seleta Reynolds, Ludo-Campbell Reid, Jennifer Keesmat, Ray LaHood, Walter Hook, Robin Chase, Gordon Price, Roberta Gratz, Joyce Purnick, Gabe Klein, Jay Kriegel, Joe DePlasco, Tom Kempner, Steve Hindy, and Eben Shapiro.

At Bloomberg Associates, thanks to George Fertitta, Rose Gill-Hearn, Kate Levin, Katherine Oliver, Linda Gibbs, Amanda Burden, Adam Freed, Jay Carson, Kelly Larson, and Kelly Henning at the Bloomberg Initiative on Global Road Safety.

We owe gratitude to advocates and the documentarians for New Yorkers who walk, bike, and take public transportation: Paul Steely

White, Caroline Samponaro, Gene Russianoff, Joan Byron, Dan Cantor, Eric McClure, Doug Gordon, Mark Gorton, Ben Fried, Stephen Miller, Brad Aaron, and the irrepressible Clarence Eckerson.

Thanks to my inspirational friends who provided wisdom and encouragement when things were tough: Gary Ginsberg, Don Hazen, Bruce Katz, John Morse, Deb Schrag, Sonya Kuo, Barbara Harnick, and Roger Boesche.

Thanks to my personal rock, my brother John Sadik-Khan, and the Sadik-Khan crew for its love and support.

Also thanks to our family at NACTO: Linda Bailey, Skye Duncan, Kate Fillin-Yeh, Corinne Kisner, and Matt Roe.

In the writing of this book we are indebted to Paul Elie, who believed in the proposal from the first read and introduced us to PJ Mark, our savvy agent. Melanie Tortoroli at Viking was an extraordinary editor who helped us each step of the way.

My deepest thanks and love go to Mark and Max Geistfeld for their love, encouragement, and good humor every night of this six-year streetfight. Their counsel and unwavering support during even the darkest hours ("Nobody really reads the papers, Mom") makes everything possible.

Seth would like to thank: My coconspirator and muse, Kate Lindquist, who introduced us to the publishing world. Thanks also to the teachers and editors who stimulated my curiosity and marked up my copy: Scott McElwain, Brian Weiner, Darrell Schramm, Gabrielle Glaser, Wendell Jamieson, Karin Roberts, Michael Pollak, Cassi Feldman, Gabriel Roth, Paul McPolin, Dean Balsamini, and Eileen AJ Connelly. My gratitude for the support of the best press office in New York City: Scott Gastel, Nicole Garcia, Nick Mosquera, and Monty Dean. Thanks for the love and support of my friends and my family, Allan and Greg Solomonow, Ofelia and Elena Alayeto, and Kathleen Haley.

Notes

PREFACE

XIII **reducing carbon emissions by 30 percent:** City of New York, *PlaNYC: A Greener, Greater New York* (New York, 2007), 133.

XIII **live in the city by 2030:** Ibid., 4.

XIV **6,300 miles of streets . . . 22 million:** "About DOT," New York City Department of Transportation, accessed August 4, 2015, www.nyc.gov/html/dot/html/about/about.shtml.

XIV **25 percent of the city's landmass:** New York City Department of Transportation, *Street Design Manual* (New York, 2009), 21.5

XIV **around 4,500 employees:** "About DOT."

XVI **"to implement, divine":** Jerold S. Kayden, "What's the Mission of Harvard's Urban Planning Program?," *Harvard Design Magazine* 22 (2005), accessed August 5, 2015, www.gsd.harvard.edu/images/content/5/3/538187/Kayden-Mission-Urban-Planning.pdf.

INTRODUCTION: A NEW STREET CODE

2 **1.24 million traffic deaths:** World Health Organization, *Global Status Report on Road Safety 2013: Supporting a Decade of Action* (Geneva, Switzerland, 2013), v.

2 **22 million miles of road worldwide:** Central Intelligence Agency, "Country Comparison: Roadways," *World Factbook*, accessed August 5, 2015, www.cia.gov/library/publications/the-world-factbook/rankorder/2085rank.html.

4 **healthy, or "vaguely French":** Dan Amira, "Why Conservatives Hate Citi Bike So Much, in One Venn Diagram," *New York*, June 5, 2013, accessed August 5, 2015, http://nymag.com/daily/intelligencer/2013/06/venn-diagram-why-conservatives-hate-citi-bike.html.

CHAPTER 1: THE FIGHT

7 **two hundred counterprotesters:** J. David Goodman, "Dueling Protests over a Brooklyn Bike Lane," *The New York Times City Room*, October 21, 2010, accessed August 10, 2015, http://cityroom.blogs.nytimes.com/2010/10/21/dueling-protests-over-a-brooklyn-bike-lane/.

8 **"outside of the Gaza Strip":** Natalie O'Neill, "The Prospect Park West Bike Lane Had Our Presses Rolling All Year Long," *The Brooklyn Paper*, December 30, 2011, accessed August 10, 2015, www.brooklynpaper.com/stories/34/52/all_year_bikelane_2011_12_30_bk.html.

9 **"Ballet of Hudson Street":** Jane Jacobs, *The Death and Life of Great American Cities* (New York: Random House, 2009), 52.

9 **"eyes on the street":** Ibid., 35.

10 **"public life may grow":** Ibid., 72.

10 **"that we must fit our plans":** Jane Jacobs, "Downtown Is for People," *Fortune*, 1958, accessed August 5, 2015, http://fortune.com/2011/09/18/downtown-is-for-people-fortune-classic-1958/.

11 **exclusively on NIMBY:** These ad hoc groups are also known, variously, as NOPE (Not on Planet Earth) or CAVEmen (Citizens Against Virtually Everything) or BANANA (Build Absolutely Nothing Anywhere Near Anything). But I digress.

13 **to bail out the city:** Sam Roberts, "Infamous 'Drop Dead' Was Never Said by Ford," *New York Times*, December 28, 2006, accessed August 5, 2015, www.nytimes.com/2006/12/28/nyregion/28veto.html.

14 **Twenty of them were cyclists:** New York City Department of Transportation, "New York City Traffic Fatalities by Mode."

15 **vital public works agencies:** Paul Goldberger, "Robert Moses, Master Builder, Is Dead at 92," *New York Times*, July 30, 1981, accessed May 21, 2015, www.nytimes.com/learning/general/onthisday/bday/1218.html.

15 **seventeen parkways and fourteen expressways:** Kenneth T. Jackson, ed, *The Encyclopedia of New York City* (New York: Yale University Press, 1995), 1131.

15 **doubled the acreage of city parks:** Anthony Flint, *Wrestling with Moses: How Jane Jacobs Took on New York's Master Builder and Transformed the American City* (New York: Random House, 2009), Kindle Location 1738.

16 **41,000 miles of modern highways:** Richard F. Weingroff, "The Greatest Decade 1956–1966: Celebrating the 50th Anniversary of the Eisenhower Interstate System," Federal Highway Administration, updated October 15, 2013, accessed August 5, 2015, www.fhwa.dot.gov/infrastructure/50interstate.cfm.

NOTES

18 **"capital of the world"**: Kenneth T. Jackson, "Robert Moses and the Rise of New York: The Power Broker in Perspective," in *Robert Moses and the Modern City: The Transformation of New York* (New York: W. W. Norton, 2007), 68.

18 **"not have been possible without Robert Moses"**: Ibid.

CHAPTER 2: DENSITY IS DESTINY

23 **a carbon footprint**: City of New York, *PlaNYC*, 9.

24 **twelve times the national rate**: United States Census Bureau, "Census Bureau Reports 1.6 Million Workers Commute into Manhattan Each Day," March 5, 2013, accessed August 5, 2015, www.census.gov/newsroom/press-releases/2013/cb13-r17.html, http://www.census.gov/newsroom/press-releases/2014/cb14-r06.html

24 **lower per capita energy use**: David Owen, "Greenest Place in the U.S.? It's Not Where You Think," Yale Environment 360, October 2009, accessed August 5, 2015.

24 **three quarters of the nation's economic**: Bruce Katz and Jennifer Bradley, *The Metropolitan Revolution: How Cities and Metros Are Fixing Our Broken Politics and Fragile Economy* (Washington, DC: Brookings Institution Press, 2013), 1.

24 **1 million people in New York City**: City of New York, PlaNYC, 4.

24 **nationwide by 2050**: United Nations, *World Urbanization Prospects*, 24.

25 **"they become more expensive"**: Edward Glaeser, *Triumph of the City: How Our Greatest Invention Makes Us Richer, Smarter, Greener, Healthier, and Happier* (New York: Penguin Group, 2011), Kindle Edition, Locations 238–41.

26 **fewer miles on average than a decade ago**: Doug Short, "Vehicle Miles Traveled: The Latest Look at Our Evolving Behavior," *Advisor Perspectives*, July 21, 2015, accessed August 5, 2015, www.advisorperspectives.com/dshort/updates/DOT-Miles-Traveled.php.

26 **below 70 percent**: Michael Sivaka and Brandon Schoettlea, "Update: Percentage of Young Persons with a Driver's License Continues to Drop," *Traffic Injury Prevention* 3(4) (2012): 341, www.tandfonline.com/doi/abs/10.1080/1538958 8.2012.696755#.VcKR6_ljtBE.

26 **dropped 30 percent**: Cliff Weathers, "4 Ways Young Americans Are Saying No to Car Ownership," AlterNet, March 10, 2014, accessed August 12, 2015, http://www.alternet.org/environment/4-ways-young-americans-are-saying-no-car-ownership.

27 **the car boom in 1956**: American Public Transportation Association, "Record 10.8 Billion Trips Taken on U.S. Public Transportation in 2014," March 9, 2015,

accessed August 5, 2015, www.apta.com/mediacenter/pressreleases/2015/Pages/150309_Ridership.aspx.

27 **decreased over the last decade:** U.S. Public Interest Research Group, "U.S. Dept. of Transportation Forecasts of Future Driving vs. Reality," January 7, 2015, accessed August 5, 2015, www.uspirg.org/resources/usp/us-dept-transportation-forecasts-future-driving-vs-reality.

27 **to just 11 cents:** *USA Today* Editorial Board, "Raise the Gas Tax: Our View," *USA Today,* June 17, 2014, accessed August 5, 2015, www.usatoday.com/story/opinion/2014/06/17/highway-trust-fund-gas-tax-editorials-debates/10708791/.

27 **paid $1 trillion more:** Tony Dutzik, Gideon Weissman, and Phineas Baxandall, Ph.D., *Who Pays for Roads? How the "Users Pay" Myth Gets in the Way of Solving America's Transportation Problems* (Frontier Group, U.S. PIRG Education Fund, 2015), 11, accessed August 5, 2015, http://www.uspirg.org/sites/pirg/files/reports/Who%20Pays%20for%20Roads%20vUS.pdf.

27 **$69 billion in highway spending:** Ibid., 17.

27 **only about half:** Ibid., 6.

27 **10 percent from municipal bonds:** Ibid., 8.

28 **pays more than $1,100:** Ibid., 2.

28 **transit, walking, and biking** *combined*: Ibid.

28 **$1 trillion a year drag:** Todd Litman, *An Analysis of Public Policies That Unintentionally Encourage and Subsidize Urban Sprawl* (Victoria, BC, Canada: Victoria Transport Policy Institute, LSE Cities, 2015), 40, accessed August 5, 2014, http://static.newclimateeconomy.report/wp-content/uploads/2015/03/public-policies-encourage-sprawl-nce-report.pdf.

29 **nearly 33,000 people can lose their lives:** National Highway Traffic Safety Administration, "U.S. Department of Transportation Announces Decline in Traffic Fatalities in 2013," December 19, 2014, accessed August 5, 2015, http://www.nhtsa.gov/About+NHTSA/Press+Releases/2014/traffic-deaths-decline-in-2013.

29 **2.6 million miles of paved roads:** U.S. Department of Transportation Federal Highway Administration, "Highway Statistics Series: Public Road Length," updated June 2013, accessed August 5, 2015, www.fhwa.dot.gov/policyinformation/statistics/2011/hm12.cfm.

30 **two hundred of these new treatments:** Green Lane Project, "Inventory of Protected Bike Lanes," accessed August 5, 2015, www.peopleforbikes.org/green-lane-project/pages/inventory-of-protected-bike-lanes.

30 **forty miles of protected paths:** New York City Department of Transportation,

"Bicycle Network Expansion, Fiscal Years 2007–2014," 2014, accessed August 12, 2015, www.nyc.gov/html/dot/downloads/pdf/bikeroutedetailsfy07-fy14.pdf.

30 **dramatic decreases in traffic injuries:** New York City Department of Transportation, "Protected Bicycle Lanes in NYC," 2014, www.nyc.gov/html/dot/downloads/pdf/2014-09-03-bicycle-path-data-analysis.pdf.

30 *Designing Walkable Urban Thoroughfares: A Context Sensitive Approach,* available at http://library.ite.org/pub/e1cff43c-2354-d714-51d9-d82b39d4dbad.

30 *Urban Street Design Guide* . . . NACTO: available at http://nacto.org/publication/urban-street-design-guide/.

31 **nine states and forty-five cities:** National Association of City Transportation Officials, "Member Cities," accessed December 10, 2015, http://nacto.org/publication/urban-bikeway-design-guide/endorsement-campaign/.

31 **secetary Ray LaHood:** Despite widespread acceptance and acclaim for the guide, it wasn't until spring 2015, as this book was written, that the Federal Highway Administration issued its own guide on protected bike paths. AASHTO is also reportedly working to update its library with a similar guide.

CHAPTER 3: SETTING THE AGENDA

33 **fiberglass blue whale:** American Museum of Natural History, "The Blue Whale," accessed August 6, 2015, www.amnh.org/exhibitions/permanent-exhibitions/biodiversity-and-environmental-halls/milstein-hall-of-ocean-life/the-blue-whale.

33 **grew by 200,000 people:** City of New York, *New York City Population Projections by Age/Sex & Borough, 2000–2030* (2006), 4, accessed August 6, 2015, www.nyc.gov/html/dcp/pdf/census/projections_briefing_booklet.pdf.

34 **"nine million people in New York City":** Dan Doctoroff in discussion with the author, February 2015.

34 **stock of 265,000 units:** City of New York, *PlaNYC*, 12.

34 **plant a million trees:** Ibid., 128.

35 **ten-minute walk of open space:** Ibid.

36 **bike commuting rate of around 6 percent:** Michael Anderson, "Census Shows Big Leaps for Biking in a Few Cities, but Portland Inches Backward," *Bike Portland,* September 18, 2014, accessed August 6, 2015, http://bikeportland.org/2014/09/18/census-shows-big-leaps-biking-cities-portland-inches-backward-111088.

36 **more than half a million people:** League of American Bicyclists, Bicycle Commuting Data, accessed August 12, 2015, http://bikeleague.org/commutingdata.

36 **from 2000 to 2012:** Ken McLeod, *Where We Ride: Analysis of Bicycle Commuting in American Cities* (League of American Bicyclists, 2014), accessed August 6, 2015, http://bikeleague.org/sites/default/files/ACS_report_2014_forweb.pdf.

36 **in forty years:** Lizzy Duffy, "Portland's Tilikum Crossing Bridge Is Open for Business," September 12, 2015, accessed October 2, 2015, http://www.opb.org/news/article/portlands-1st-bridge-in-over-40-years-opens/.

37 **said Rit Aggarwala:** Rit Aggarwala in discussion with the author, January 21, 2015.

37 **4,500-person agency:** "About DOT," New York City Department of Transportation, accessed August 4, 2015, www.nyc.gov/html/dot/html/about/about.shtml.

38 **bus rapid transit lines:** City of New York, *PlaNYC*, 82.

38 **strategic plan, Sustainable Streets:** New York City Department of Transportation, "Sustainable Streets," 2008, www.nyc.gov/html/dot/html/about/stratplan.shtml.

41 **doubles every weekday:** United States Census Bureau, "Census Bureau Reports 1.6 Million Workers Commute into Manhattan Each Day," March 5, 2013, accessed August 5, 2015, www.census.gov/newsroom/press-releases/2013/cb13-r17.html.

41 **6.6 percent . . . 5 percent of commuters taking transit:** Ibid.

41 **30 million miles daily:** Data analysis by Bruce Schaller, former deputy commissioner for traffic management and planning, New York City Department of Transportation.

41 **$13 billion each year:** Partnership for New York City, *Growth or Gridlock? The Economic Case for Traffic Relief and Transit Improvement for a Greater New York*, December 2006, 2, accessed August 6, 2015, http://www.pfnyc.org/reports/Growth%20or%20Gridlock.pdf.

42 **"improving air quality":** City of New York, press release, "Mayor Bloomberg Delivers PlaNYC: A Greener, Greater New York," April 22, 2007, accessed August 6, 2015, www.nyc.gov/portal/site/nycgov/menuitem.c0935b9a57bb4ef-3daf2f1c701c789a0/index.jsp?pageID=mayor_press_release&catID=1194&doc_name=http%3A%2F%2Fwww.nyc.gov%2Fhtml%2Fom%2Fhtml%2F2007a%2Fpr120-07.html&cc=unused1978&rc=1194&ndi=1.

42 **estimated 30 percent:** Transport for London, *Central London Congestion Charging: Impacts Monitoring, Fourth Annual Report*, June 2006, 2, accessed August 6, 2015, https://tfl.gov.uk/cdn/static/cms/documents/fourthannualreportfinal.pdf.

42 **decreased greenhouse gases:** C40, "London's Congestion Charge Cuts CO2 Emissions by 16%," November 3, 2011, accessed August 6, 2015, www.c40.org/case_studies/londons-congestion-charge-cuts-co2-emissions-by-16.

42 **in increasing numbers:** Todd Litman, Victoria Policy Institute, *London Conges-tion Pricing: Implications for Other Cities,* November 24, 2011, 5, accessed August 12, 2015, www.vtpi.org/london.pdf.

43 **Again, traffic decreased:** Association for European Transport, "The Stockholm Congestion Charging System: An Overview of the Effects After Six Months," 2006, 6, accessed August 6, 2015, http://web.mit.edu/11.951/oldstuff/albacete/Other_Documents/Europe%20Transport%20Conference/traffic_engineering_an/the_stockholm_cong1720.pdf.

43 **south of 86th Street:** City of New York, *PlaNYC,* 89.

43 **$380 million a year:** Ibid., 96.

44 **$124 for a seven-axle truck:** Metropolitan Transportation Authority, "Approved Bridges and Tunnels Tolls," accessed August 15, 2015, http://web.mta.info/mta/news/hearings/2015FareTolls/FaresBT.html.

44 **five wealthiest counties:** New York counties ranked by per capita income, Wikipedia, accessed August 12, 2015, https://en.wikipedia.org/wiki/New_York_locations_by_per_capita_income.

45 **57 percent of households:** Tri-State Transportation Campaign, "NYC Metropolitan Area Fact Sheets on Congestion Pricing: Brooklyn," accessed August 7, 2015, http://www.tstc.org/reports/cpfactsheets.php.

45 **100 percent higher:** Ibid.

45 **two thirds of Brooklyn workers:** Ibid.

45 **97.5 percent of Brooklyn:** Ibid.

45 **27 percent in a poll:** Quinnipiac University, "State Voters Back NYC Traffic Fee 2–1, If Funds Go to Transit, Quinnipiac University Poll Finds; Voters Back Millionaire's Tax 4–1," March 24, 2008, accessed August 7, 2014, www.google.com/url?sa=t&rct=j&q=&esrc=s&source=web&cd=3&ved=0CC8QFjAC&url=http%3A%2F%2Fwww.quinnipiac.edu%2Fimages%2Fpolling%2Fny%2Fny03242008.doc%2F&ei=iG1fVZrHPIKtyAS86IOICA&usg=AFQjCNHsNR41DMlS-d-dAhEoTEWQ-TRtaA&sig2=F4W2GpU0k4r81uqk4ZlYJA&bvm=bv.93990622,d.aWw.

45 **by spring 2008:** Sewell Chan, "U.S. Offers New York $354 Million for Congestion Pricing," *New York Times City Room,* August 14, 2007, accessed August 7, 2015, http://cityroom.blogs.nytimes.com/2007/08/14/us-will-give-new-york-354-million-for-congestion-pricing/?_r=0.

45 **March 31, 2008:** Sewall Chan, "Council Votes 30–20 for Traffic Fees," *New York Times City Room,* March 31, 2008, accessed August 7, 2015, http://cityroom.blogs.nytimes.com/2008/03/31/council-panel-approves-congestion-pricing-measure/.

45 **without even taking a vote:** Nicholas Confessore, "Congestion Pricing Plan Dies in Albany," *New York Times City Room*, April 7, 2008, accessed August 7, 2015, http://cityroom.blogs.nytimes.com/2008/04/07/congestion-pricing-plan-is-dead-assembly-speaker-says/.

46 **"biggest cop-outs in New York's history":** Elizabeth Flood Morrow and Joan Gralla, "New York Anti-traffic Fees Wither Without a Vote," Reuters, April 7, 2008, accessed August 7, 2015, www.reuters.com/article/2008/04/07/us-new yorkcity-traffic-idUSN0758003520080407.

CHAPTER 4: HOW TO READ THE STREET

47 **"This looks like Carvana":** Martha Groves, "405 Freeway Carpool Lane, Eric Garcetti Calls Smooth Opening 'Carvana,'" *Los Angeles Times*, May 23, 2014, accessed August 7, 2015, www.latimes.com/local/lanow/la-me-ln-405carpool-lane-opens-20140523story.html.

48 **seventy-mile continuous lane:** Martha Groves and Matt Stevens, "New Carpool Lane on Northbound 405 Finally Opens," *Los Angeles Times*, May 22, 2014, accessed August 7, 2015, www.latimes.com/local/la-me-0523-405 20140524-story.html.

48 **in the previous year:** Brian Watt, "405 Traffic: A Little Slower After $1 Billion Upgrade," 89.3 KPCC, October 10, 2014, accessed August 7, 2015, www.scpr.org/blogs/economy/2014/10/10/17413/405-traffic-a-little-slower-after-1-billion-upgrad/.

50 **eight and a half feet across:** U.S. Department of Transportation Federal Highway Administration, "Federal Size Regulations for Commercial Motor Vehicles," modified December 3, 2013, accessed August 7, 2015, http://ops.fhwa .dot.gov/FREIGHT/publications/size_regs_final_rpt/index.htm.

54 **safer than the twelve-footers:** Jeff Speck, "Why 12-Foot Traffic Lanes Are Disastrous for Safety and Must Be Replaced Now," *The Atlantic Citylab*, October 6, 2014, accessed August 7, 2015, www.citylab.com/design/2014/10/why-12-foot-traffic-lanes-are-disastrous-for-safety-and-must-be-replaced-now/381117/.

55 **"what are the sight lines":** Jeff Speck in discussion with the author, April 30, 2015.

55 **severity of crashes on city streets:** National Association of City Transportation Officials, *Urban Street Design Guide* (New York: Island Press: 2013), 24–27.

56 **less is more:** New York City Department of Transportation, *Making Safer Streets*, November 2013, 20–23, www.nyc.gov/html/dot/downloads/pdf/dot making-safer-streets.pdf.

59 **fell by 30 to 60 percent:** New York City Department of Transportation, "4th Ave: Atlantic Av-15th St Project Evaluation and Next Phases," April 16, 2015, accessed August 7, 2015, http://a841-tfpweb.nyc.gov/4thave/files/2015/05/4th-Ave_ Park-Slope_CB6-project-evaluation-and-next-phases-April-2015_final.pdf.

62 **'fundamental law of road congestion':** Gilles Duranton and Matthew A. Turner, "The Fundamental Law of Road Congestion: Evidence from US Cities," University of Toronto Department of Economics, 42, (September 8, 2009), accessed August 7, 2015, https://www.economics.utoronto.ca/public/ workingPapers/tecipa-370.pdf.

63 **"environment influences behavior":** Speck, conversation with author.

63 **"that lane will cause traffic":** Ibid.

63 **loosening one's belt:** Carlton Reid, *Roads Were Not Built for Cars: How Cyclists Were the First to Push for Good Roads & Became the Pioneers of Motoring* (New York: Island Press, 2015), 109, Google Books edition, accessed August 7, 2015, https:// books.google.com/books?id=tHGeBwAAQBAJ&dq=Building+more+roads+to +prevent+congestion+is+like+a+fat+man+loosening+his+belt+to+prevent+obesity +mumford&source=gbs_navlinks_s.

64 **result of a concerted effort:** Peter D. Norton, *Fighting Traffic: The Dawn of the Motor Age in the American City* (Cambridge, MA: MIT Press, 2011), Kindle edition.

65 **hundred thousand cars . . . Embarcadero Freeway:** San Francisco | Embarcadero Freeway, Congress for New Urbanism, accessed August 19, 2015, http://cnu.org/highways-boulevards/model-cities/embarcadero.

66 **110,000 cars daily:** Washington State Department of Transportation, "Viaduct History," accessed August 7, 2015, www.wsdot.wa.gov/Projects/Viaduct/About/ History.

66 **cost estimate: $3.1 billion:** Tim Newcomb, "America's Biggest Tunnel-Boring Machine Is Stuck Beneath Seattle," *Popular Mechanics,* February 20, 2014, accessed August 7, 2015, www.popularmechanics.com/technology/infrastrucure /a10044americas-biggest-tunnel-boring-machine-is-stuck-beneath-seattle-16514815/.

66 **9,270-foot path:** Mike Lindblom, "Bertha Repair Will Take Longer—There Are Lots of Broken Parts," *Seattle Times,* May 18, 2015, accessed August 7, 2015, www.seattletimes.com/seattle-news/transportation/bertha-repair-will-take-longer-theres-more-damage/.

66 **2000-ton mass:** Mike Lindblom, "Giant Crane to Lift 4 Million Pounds of Tunnel Drill Bertha," *Seattle Times,* January 16, 2015, accessed August 7, 2015, www.seattletimes.com/seattle-news/giant-crane-to-lift-4-million-pounds-of-tunnel-drill-bertha/.

67 Georgia and Dunsmuir viaducts: Frances Bula, "City Engineers to Recommend Removal of Vancouver's Two Viaducts," *The Globe and Mail*, July 22, 2015, accessed August 7, 2015, www.theglobeandmail.com/news/british-columbia/city-engineers-to-recommend-removal-of-vancouvers-two-viaducts/article25620997/.

67 foremost public realm thinkers: Brent Toderian in discussion with the author, May 5, 2015.

67 $7.5 billion of investments: Lisa Johnson and Tamara Baluja, "Transit Rreferendum: Voters Say No to New Metro Vancouver Tax, Transit Improvements," *CBC News*, July 2, 2015, accessed August 7, 2015, http://www.cbc.ca/news/canada/british-columbia/transit-referendum-voters-say-no-to-new-metro-vancouver-tax-transit-improvements-1.3134857.

68 "an intelligent conversation": Toderian, in discussion with the author, May 5, 2015.

68 "Welcome to our existential crisis": Gordon Price in discussion with the author, April 17, 2015.

69 87 miles of subways: Metro, "Facts at a Glance," accessed August 7, 2015, http://www.metro.net/news/facts-glance/.

69 regional connector system: Noah Bierman and W. J. Hennigan, "Obama's Budget Includes Windfall for L.A. Transportation," *Los Angeles Times*, February 2, 2015, accessed August 7, 2015, www.latimes.com/local/california/la-me-obama-budget-california-20150203-story.html.

69 to Los Angeles International Airport: Los Angeles Metro, press release, "Crenshaw/LAX Transit Project," January 21, 2014, accessed August 12, 2015, www.metro.net/projects/crenshaw_corridor/.

69 threw out the case in 2014: Laura J. Nelson, "Judge Backs Subway Route," *Los Angeles Times*, April 3, 2014, accessed August 13, 2015, http://articles.latimes.com/2014/apr/03/local/la-me-subway-lawsuit-ruling-20140403.

70 "it will be gone forever": Adam Nagourney, "Facelift Project for Hollywood Stirs Divisions," *New York Times*, March 28, 2012, accessed August 7, 2015, www.nytimes.com/2012/03/29/us/far-reaching-rezoning-plan-for-hollywood-gains-key-support.html.

70 "Seattle will get moving": Mike Lindblom, "Voters Saying Yes to Seattle's Big Ask for Transportation," *Seattle Times*, November 2, 2015, accessed November 11, 2015, http://www.seattletimes.com/seattle-news/transportation/move-seattle/.

70 ride bikes, or take transit: Tim O'Brien, "Radical Plan Seeks to Take Cars Out of Dublin City Centre," *The Irish Times*, June 10, 2015, accessed August 7, 2015, www.irishtimes.com/news/ireland/irish-news/radical-plan-seeks-to-take-cars-out-of-dublin-city-centre-1.2244222.

70 **($1.4 billion) over ten years:** London.gov.uk, "Mayor's Vision for Cycling," accessed August 7, 2015, www.london.gov.uk/priorities/transport/cycling-revolution.

70 **double the city's network of bike lanes:** Feargus O'Sullivan, "Now Paris Wants to Become the 'World Capital of Cycling,'" *The Atlantic CityLab,* April 6, 2015, accessed August 10, 2015, www.citylab.com/commute/2015/04/now-paris-wants-to-become-the-world-capital-of-cycling/389724/?utm_content=buffer92443&utm_medium=social&utm_source=twitter.com&utm_campaign=buffer.

71 **seventy-five miles of protected bike paths:** Peter Walker, "How Seville Transformed Itself into the Cycling Capital of Southern Europe," *The Guardian,* January 28, 2015, accessed August 7, 2015, http://www.theguardian.com/cities/2015/jan/28/seville-cycling-capital-southern-europe-bike-lanes.

71 **$5.6 billion tunnel:** Laura J. Nelson, "Report: Closing the 710 Freeway Gap Would Take Years and Cost Billions," *Los Angeles Times,* March 6, 2015, accessed August 7, 2015, http://www.latimes.com/local/lanow/la-me-ln-710-freeway-report-20150306-story.html.

CHAPTER 5: FOLLOW THE FOOTSTEPS

77 **twelve feet wide in downtown or commercial areas:** National Association of City Transportation Officials, *Urban Street Design Guide* (New York: Island Press: 2013), 38.

78 **twelve people per minute per yard:** New York City Department of Transportation, *World Class Streets: Remaking New York City's Public Realm* (2008), 20.

78 **less than one third of the street space:** Ibid., 22.

79 **30 percent of the city's population:** Ibid., 30.

84 **"If DOT's new plazas":** Aaron Naparstek, "Meat Market Plaza Is Open for Business," *Streetsblog NYC,* September 27, 2007, accessed August 24, 2015, www.streetsblog.org/2007/09/27/gansevoort-plaza-is-open-for-business/.

86 **170-foot, seven-lane journey:** Madison Square Pedestrian Project, Presented to Community Board 5, March 3, 2008, www.nyc.gov/html/dot/downloads/pdf/madisonsqimprov.pdf.

89 **sixty-five thousand square feet of pedestrian space:** City of New York, "Mayor Bloomberg and DOT Commissioner Sadik-Khan Unveil New Public Space at Madison Square," September 5, 2008, accessed August 10, 2015, www1.nyc.gov/office-of-the-mayor/news/346-08/mayor-bloomberg-dot-commissioner-sadik-khan-new-public-space-madison-square.

89 **more safely, with better organization:** New York City Department of Transportation, *Making Safer Streets*, November 2013, 6, www.nyc.gov/html/dot/downloads/pdf/dot-making-safer-streets.pdf.

89 **Andy Wiley-Schwartz:** Andy Wiley-Schwartz in discussion with the author, April 2015.

CHAPTER 6: BATTLE FOR A NEW TIMES SQUARE

91 **belonged to cars:** New York City Department of Transportation, *World Class Streets: Remaking New York City's Public Realm* (2008), 33.

91 **did so on foot:** New York City Department of Transportation, "Broadway Pilot Program: Improving Traffic Flow & Safety in the Heart of Midtown," February 2009, 9, accessed August 10, 2015, www.nyc.gov/html/dot/downloads/pdf/broadway_0223409.pdf.

92 **137 percent more pedestrians:** New York City Department of Transportation, "Broadway Pilot Program," 10.

92 **to fifty-three seconds:** Ibid., 6.

93 **to fifty-four seconds:** William Neuman, "In New York, Broadway as Great Walk Way," *New York Times*, February 26, 2009, accessed August 12, 2015, www.nytimes.com/2009/02/27/nyregion/27broadway.html?ref=nyregion&_r=0.

93 **17 percent through Times Square:** Aaron Naparstek, "Bloomberg Puts Forward a Bold, Transformative New Vision for Broadway," *Streetsblog NYC*, February 26, 2009, accessed August 10, 2015, www.streetsblog.org/2009/02/26/a-bold-and-transformative-new-vision-for-broadway/.

93 **"Ten minutes later she had convinced me":** Michael Bloomberg and Janette Sadik-Khan, "Dynamic Duos: Michael Bloomberg and Janette Sadik-Khan on the Future of Walking, Biking, and Driving," *Fast Company Design*, September 11, 2013, accessed August 10, 2015, www.fastcodesign.com/3016252/new-york-city-bloomberg-and-janette-sadik-khan.

94 **"do the right thing, period":** Michael Bloomberg in discussion with the author, winter 2009.

94 **cost of $1.5 million:** City of New York, press release, "Mayor Bloomberg and Commissioner Sadik-Khan Announce Pilot 'Green Light for Midtown' Program to Reduce Congestion," February 26, 2009, accessed August 10, 2015, www.nyc.gov/portal/site/nycgov/menuitem.c0935b9a57bb4ef3daf2f1c701c789a0/index.jsp?pageID=mayor_press_release&catID=1194&doc_name=http%3A%2F%2Fwww.nyc.gov%2Fhtml%2Fom%2Fhtml%2F2009a%2Fpr095-09.html&cc=unused1978&rc=1194&ndi=1.

95 **"do something about it":** Nick Summers, "New York City Embraces a Bold New Traffic Theory," *Newsweek,* February 26, 2009, accessed August 10, 2015, www.newsweek.com/new-york-city-embraces-bold-new-traffic-theory-82647.

98 **"Dead End Streets":** Steve Cuozzo, "Dead End Streets," *New York Post,* March 1, 2009, accessed August 10, 2015, http://nypost.com/2009/03/01/dead-end-streets/.

98 **"The Wrong Crusade":** *New York Post* Editorial Board, "The Wrong Crusade," *New York Post,* March 2, 2009, accessed August 10, 2015, http://nypost.com /2009/03/02/the-wrong-crusade/.

98 **"meant for walking, not idling":** Cuozzo, "Dead End Streets."

98 **"will be a small hero":** New York *Daily News* Editorial Board, "Mike's Broadway Tryout: Mayor Bloomberg's Big Midtown Traffic Plan Is Worth Testing," New York *Daily News,* February 26, 2009, accessed August 10, 2015, www .nydailynews.com/opinion/mike-broadway-tryout-mayor-bloomberg-big-midtown-traffic-plan-worth-testing-article-1.391860.

99 **colors at $10.74 each:** Michael E. Grynbaum, "Tourists and New Yorkers Take a Rubber Seat in Times Square," *New York Times,* June 10, 2009, accessed August 10, 2015, www.nytimes.com/2009/06/11/nyregion/11chairs.html.

99 **"the king of trailer trash":** Grynbaum, Ibid.

99 **"a petting zoo":** Steve Cuozzo, "Killing Times Square," *New York Post,* August 24, 2009, accessed August 10, 2015, http://nypost.com/2009/08/24/killing-times-square/.

102 **data from 1.1 million:** New York City Department of Transportation, *Green Light for Midtown Evaluation Report,* January 2010, 7, accessed August 10, 2015, www.nyc.gov/html/dot/downloads/pdf/broadway_report_final2010_web2 .pdf.

102 **Uptown traffic moved better:** Ibid., 1.

102 **fewer people walking in the street:** Ibid.

102 **dropped 35 percent:** Ibid.

102 **plummeted by 63 percent:** Ibid.

102 **had improved dramatically:** Times Square Alliance, "Broadway Plaza Surveys Commissioned by the Times Square Alliance," February 2010, accessed August 10, 2015, www.timessquarenyc.org/about-the-alliance/public-space projects/times-square-bowtie/download.aspx?id=736.

102 **should be made permanent:** Ibid.

102 **doubled in a single year:** Jordan Heller, "Retail Rents Rising in Many Manhattan Neighborhoods," *DNAinfo,* November 8, 2010, accessed August 10, 2015,

www.dnainfo.com/new-york/20101108/manhattan/asking-retail-rents-rising
-across-manhattan-report-says.

102 **would eventually triple:** New York City Department of Transportation, *Sustainable Streets: 2013 and Beyond* (2013), 140, accessed August 10, 2015, www
.nyc.gov/html/dot/downloads/pdf/2013-dot-sustainable-streets-lowres.pdf.

102 **opened new stores:** Ibid.

102 **top ten retail districts on the planet:** Theresa Agovino, "Manhattan Boasts 4 of Top 10 Retail Strips," *Crain's New York Business*, September 1, 2011, accessed August 10, 2015, www.crainsnewyork.com/article/20110901/REAL_ESTATE/110839967.

103 **moved 2 percent slower:** New York City Department of Transportation, *Green Light for Midtown Evaluation Report*, 1.

106 **plazas in the five boroughs:** New York City Department of Transportation, *Sustainable Streets: 2013 and Beyond*, 121.

107 **a few years earlier:** Times Square Alliance, "Pedestrian Counts," www
.timessquarenyc.org/do-business-here/market-facts/pedestrian-counts/index
.aspx#.VcjjaPljtBE.

CHAPTER 7: STEALING GOOD IDEAS

110 **381 people for every 100,000 inhabitants:** "Medellin: A City Transformed," Inter-American Development Bank, accessed August 7, 2015, www.iadb.org/en/topics/citizen-security/impact-medellin,5687.html.

110 **26 per 100,000 inhabitants:** "Colombia's Homicide Rate Reaches 30 Year Low in 2014," *Finance Colombia*, January 5, 2015, accessed August 7, 2015, www
.financecolombia.com/colombias-homicide-rate-reaches-30-year-low-in
-2014/.

110 **rise 1,300 feet:** "Metrocable (Medellín)," Wikipedia, accessed August 7, 2015, https://en.wikipedia.org/wiki/Metrocable_%28Medell%C3%ADn%29.

110 **cut the two-hour commutes:** Numerous examples varying with origin and destinations, including Michael Kimmelman, "A City Rises, Along with Its Hopes," *New York Times*, May 18, 2012, accessed August 7, 2015, www.nytimes
.com/2012/05/20/arts/design/fighting-crime-with-architecture-in-medellin
-colombia.html.

114 **sixty thousand passengers a day:** Global BRT Data, EMBARQ, accessed August 7, 2015, http://brtdata.org/location/latin_america/colombia/medellin.

115 **15 percent a year:** Hernán López, discussion with the authors, February 26, 2015.

116 **twelve miles . . . 808 acres:** Loren Moss, "Medellín's Parques del Rio Project Seeks to Transform Urban Civic Life—1st Phase on Track for January Completion," *Finance Colombia*, July 26, 2015, accessed August 7, 2015, www.finance-colombia.com/medellins-parque-del-rio-project-seeks-to-transform-urban-civic-life-1st-phase-on-track-for-january-completion/.

116 **"just a few miles":** Gil Peñalosa in discussion with the authors, May 4, 2015.

122 **150,000 . . . doubled by 2013:** New York City Department of Transportation, press release, "DOT Commissioner Invites New Yorkers to Kick Off Summer Streets 2009," August 3, 2009, accessed August 7, 2015, www.nyc.gov/html/dot/html/pr2009/pr09_033.shtml; New York City Department of Transportation, *Sustainable Streets: 2013 and Beyond*, November 2013, 130, accessed August 7, 2015, www.nyc.gov/html/dot/downloads/pdf/2013-dot-sustainable-streets-lowres.pdf.

122 **opened in 1834:** Christopher Gray, "Putting the Park in Park Avenue," *New York Times*, July 21, 2011, accessed August 7, 2015, www.nytimes.com/2011/07/24/realestate/putting-the-park-in-park-avenue-streetscapesmidtown.html?_r=0.

122 **portal of sound and light:** New York City Department of Transportation, "Voice Tunnel," Summer 2013, accessed August 7, 2015, www.nyc.gov/html/dot/summerstreets/downloads/pdf/2013-summer-streets-voice-tunnel-factsheet.pdf.

123 **eighteen neighborhoods . . . twenty-four neighborhoods:** New York City Department of Transportation, press release, "NYC DOT Announces Summer Streets' Return, Bringing Sand Castles, Climbing Wall and Family-fun Activities to Car-free Streets for Three Saturdays in August," June 28, 2011, accessed August 7, 2015, www.nyc.gov/html/dot/html/pr2011/pr11_56.shtml; New York City Department of Transportation, press release, "NYC DOT Commissioner Sadik-Khan Invites New Yorkers to Come Out for Summer Streets 2013, Starting Sat., Aug. 3," July 29, 2013, accessed August 7, 2015, http://a841-tfp-web.nyc.gov/dotpress/2013/07/summer-streets-2013-2/#more-102.

124 **Neighborhood Plaza Partnership:** New York City Department of Transportation, press release, "NYC DOT Commissioner Sadik-Khan Announces Innovative New Neighborhood Plaza Partnership, Providing Funding and Creating Jobs for New Public Spaces Through Major Gift from Chase," November 26, 2013, accessed August 7, 2015, http://a841-tfpweb.nyc.gov/dotpress/2013/11/neighborhood-plaza-partnership/#more-134.

127 **Castro, and Seventeenth streets:** City and County of San Francisco, "Jane Warner Plaza," accessed August 11, 2015, http://pavementtoparks.sfplanning.org/castro_commons.htm.

131 **more than five hundred pedestrians:** Two Twelve Associates, AIG, New York City Department of Transportation, *I Walk New York: A Plan for Pedestrian Wayfinding in New York City*, January 2011, 16–17.

132 **your north from your south:** Ibid., 17.

134 **In a video:** Improv Everywhere, "The Tourist Lane," June 8, 2010, accessed August 7, 2015, www.youtube.com/watch?v=RKx0aek1T0w.

135 **Reasonably Polite Seattleites:** Tom Fucoloro, "Guerrilla Road Safety Group 'Politely' Installs Illegal Bike Lane Protectors on Cherry Street," *Seattle Bike Blog*, April 4, 2013, accessed August 7, 2015, www.seattlebikeblog.com/2013/04/04/guerrilla-road-safety-group-politely-installs-illegal-bike-lane-protectors-on-cherry-street/.

135 **In Dallas, neighbors:** Mike Lydon and Anthony Garcia, *Tactical Urbanism* (Washington, DC: Island Press, 2015), 103–8, 121–22.

CHAPTER 8: BIKE LANES AND THEIR DISCONTENTS

143 **"to talk about bicycles":** City Council, City of New York, "Transcript of the Minutes of the Committee on Transportation—December 9, 2010," 8, accessed August 10, 2015.

143 **"a policy our city pursues":** Ibid., 9.

144 **"simmering cultural conflict":** J. David Goodman, "Expansion of Bike Lanes in City Brings Backlash," *New York Times*, November 22, 2010, accessed August 10, 2015, www.nytimes.com/2010/11/23/nyregion/23bicycle.html?_r=0.

144 **271 New Yorkers that year:** New York City Department of Transportation, "New York City Traffic Fatalities by Mode."

144 **$8 million invested over three years:** City Council, "Transcript," 25.

144 **to paint the Brooklyn Bridge:** New York City Department of Transportation, *Bridges and Tunnels Annual Condition Report 2011*, 54, accessed August 10, 2015, www.nyc.gov/html/dot/downloads/pdf/dot_bridgereport11.pdf.

144 **Willis Avenue Bridge:** William Neuman, "A Bridge No Longer So Humble, at $600 Million," *New York Times*, March 31, 2007, accessed August 10, 2015, www.nytimes.com/2007/03/31/nyregion/31bridge.html.

145 **"My Favorite Things":** City Council, "Transcript," 156–57.

146 **cyclists in Melbourne:** Melissa Davey, "Melbourne Cycling Route Still Plagued by Tacks Despite Efforts to Catch Offender," *The Guardian*, June 22, 2015, www.theguardian.com/australia-news/2015/jun/22/melbourne-cycling-route-still-plagued-by-tacks-despite-efforts-to-catch-offender.

146 **Queensboro Bridge's bike path:** Christopher Robbins, "War on Cyclists:

Someone Scattered These Tacks on Queensboro Bridge Bike Path," *Gothamist*, October 2, 2012, http://gothamist.com/2012/10/02/photo_metal_tacks_give_cyclists_fla.php.

146 **Central Park, and one attacker:** Bill Sanderson, "Cyclists Targeted in Central Park Tack Attack," *New York Post*, June 12, 2012, http://nypost.com/2012/07/12/cyclists-targeted-in-central-park-tack-attack/.

146 **Brooklyn's Prospect Park:** Lauren Evans, "Prospect Park Rope Trap Snags Cyclist, Cops See No Crime," *Gothamist*, May 31, 2014, http://gothamist.com/2014/05/31/prospect_park_trip_wire_leaves_cycl.php#photo-1.

146 **recorded in London:** Stuart Clarke, "Drawing Pins Found Scattered on London Cycle Path," *Cycling Weekly*, February 23, 2015, www.cyclingweekly.co.uk/news/latest-news/drawing-pins-found-scattered-on-london-cycle-path-159307.

146 **Portland, Oregon, and in large:** Michael Graham, "Richard Sabotage! Tire-Busting Tack-Strip Found on Portland Bike Lane," *Treehugger*, October 21, 2011, www.treehugger.com/bikes/sabotage-tire-busting-track-strip-found-portland-bike-lane.html.

146 **"hate cyclists using the road":** Facebook, "God I Fucking Hate Cyclists Using the Road," accessed October 5, 2015, www.facebook.com/pages/God-I-fucking-hate-cyclists-using-the-road/200926809928921.

146 **"worth paying the fine":** Courtland Milloy, "Bicyclist Bullies Try to Rule the Road in D.C.," *The Washington Post*, July 8, 2014, accessed August 10, 2015, www.washingtonpost.com/local/bicyclist-bullies-try-to-rule-the-road-in-dc/2014/07/08/f7843560-06e3-11e4-bbf1-cc51275e7f8f_story.html.

147 **"swimming with the sharks":** Jason Margolis, "Cyclists Accuse Toronto Mayor Ford of 'War on Bikes,'" BBC News via PRI's *The World*, May 3, 2012, accessed August 10, 2015, www.bbc.com/news/magazine-17914504.

149 **killed around the world annually:** World Health Organization, "More than 270,000 Pedestrians Killed on Roads Each Year," May 2, 2013, accessed August 10, 2015, www.who.int/mediacentre/news/notes/2013/make_walking_safe_20130502/en/.

152 **traffic in central Amsterdam:** iAmsterdam, "Cycling Facts and Figures," accessed August 10, 2015, www.iamsterdam.com/en/media-centre/city-hall/dossier-cycling/cycling-facts-and-figures.

152 **trips in Copenhagen:** Jakob Schiøtt Stenbæk Madsen, "Copenhagen's Bicycle Account," *Cycling Embassy of Denmark*, June 3, 2013, accessed August 10, 2015, www.cycling-embassy.dk/2013/06/03/6995/.

152 **commuting trips by bike:** Michael Anderson, "Census Shows Big Leaps for

Biking in a Few Cities, but Portland Inches Backward," *Bike Portland,* September 18, 2014, http://bikeportland.org/2014/09/18/census-shows-big-leaps-biking-cities-portland-inches-backward-111088.

152-53 **ripped them out:** Transportation Alternatives, *Bicycle Blueprint: A Plan to Bring Cycling into the Mainstream in New York City,* 1998, accessed August 10, 2015, www.transalt.org/sites/default/files/resources/blueprint/chapter4/sidebar.html.

153 **doubled the number of bike commuters:** Jonathan Maus, "Census Bureau: Portland Bike Commute Mode Split Doubles in Five Years," *BikePortland.org,* January 12, 2007, accessed August 10, 2015, http://bikeportland.org/2007/01/12/census -bureau-portland-bike-commute-mode-split-doubles-in-five-years-2824.

153 **less than three miles:** New York City Department of Transportation, *Sustainable Streets: 2013 and Beyond,* 83.

153 **fifty miles a year:** City of New York, *PlaNYC,* 88.

155 **first parking-protected bike lane:** PeopleForBikes, "Inventory of Protected Bike Lanes," accessed August 12, 2015, https://docs.google.com/spreadsheets/d/ 11H0gArHxo6kMop1I18yMcq7ArbNrwaGBLmIXgqI1Gjk/edit#gid=3.

155 **ten-foot-wide protected bike lanes:** New York City Department of Transportation, "Protected Bicycle Lanes in NYC," September 2014, 20, www.nyc.gov/ html/dot/downloads/pdf/2014-09-03-bicycle-path-data-analysis.pdf.

157 **exposed to car traffic:** New York City Department of Transportation, "9th Avenue Bicycle Facility & Complete Street Redesign—W16th Street—W23rd Street," September 19, 2007, 18, accessed August 10, 2015, www.nyc.gov/ html/dot/downloads/pdf/9thavecomp.pdf.

158 **two hundred miles of bike lanes:** New York City Department of Transportation, "DOT Completes Unprecedented Three-Year, 200-Mile Installation of Bike Lanes, Making City Streets Safer for All Users," July 8, 2009, accessed August 10, 2015, www.nyc.gov/html/dot/html/pr2009/pr09_030.shtml.

158 **Gehl would later remark:** Kriston Capps, "Jan Gehl, Copenhagen, and the Trajectory of City Planning," *Architect,* February 4, 2014, accessed August 25, 2015, www.architectmagazine.com/design/urbanism-planning/jan-gehl-copenhagen -and-the-trajectory-of-city-planning_o.

159 **bike lane expenditures:** City Council, "Transcript," 2; http://www.streets-blog.org/2010/12/09/quick-hits-from-todays-city-council-hearing-on-bike-policy/.

159 **"without speaking to the community":** Ben Fried, "Bill Thompson: I'll Rip Out Bike Lanes and 'Review' Safer Streets," *Streetsblog NYC,* September 18, 2009, accessed August 10, 2015, www.streetsblog.org/2009/09/18/bill-thompson-ill-rip-out-bike-lanes-and-review-safer-streets/.

159 **project in a 33–1 vote:** Community Board No. 2, Manhattan, "Full Board Minutes (July 24, 2008)," accessed August 10, 2015, www.nyc.gov/html/mancb2/downloads/pdf/fullboard_2008/07july2008.pdf.

162 **"'Grand' FDNY Pain":** Tom Namako, "'Grand' FDNY Pain," *New York Post*, November 29, 2008, accessed August 10, 2015, http://nypost.com/2008/11/29/grand-fdny-pain/.

162 **"something we've been talking about":** Ibid.

162 **39–2 community board vote:** Colin Moynihan, "New Bike Lanes Touch Off Row in Brooklyn," *New York Times*, January 3, 2009, accessed August 10, 2015, www.nytimes.com/2009/01/04/nyregion/04lanes.html?pagewanted=all.

163 **"Brooklyn bike war":** Rich Calder, "Hasid Lust Cause," *New York Post*, September 12, 2008, accessed August 10, 2015, http://nypost.com/2008/09/12/hasid-lust-cause/.

163 **hundreds of parking spaces:** New York City Department of Transportation, "Kent Avenue Improvement Plan: Implementation Update," August 7, 2009, accessed August 10, 2015, www.nyc.gov/html/dot/downloads/pdf/kent_ave.pdf.

164 **heavily used sections:** New York City Department of Transportation, *Sustainable Streets: 2013 and Beyond*, 85.

165 **cars monitored on the street were speeding:** New York City Department of Transportation, "Prospect Park West Bicycle Path and Traffic Calming Update," January 20, 2011, 7, accessed August 10, 2015, www.nyc.gov/html/dot/downloads/pdf/20110120_ppw.pdf.

165 **illegally on the sidewalk:** Ibid., 5.

166 **petition signed by 1,300 people:** "CB6 approves Prospect Park West Bike Lane," *Brooklyn Downtown Star*, April 1, 2011, accessed August 10, 2015, www.brooklyndowntownstar.com/view/full_story/12789750/article-CB6-approves-Prospect-Park-West-Bike-Lane?instance=lead_story_left_column.

167 **"She is a zealot":** Andrea Bernstein, "The Latest Skirmish in the Bike Lane Battles," WNYC 93.9 FM, April 12, 2010, accessed August 10, 2015, www.wnyc.org/story/87730-the-latest-skirmish-in-the-bike-lane-battles/.

168 **"legitimate policy issues":** Stephen Brown, "Marty: Enough with the Bike Lanes! Brooklyn Is Not Amsterdam!," *The Brooklyn Paper*, October 20, 2010, accessed August 10, 2015, www.brooklynpaper.com/stories/33/43/ps_bikelanemarty_2010_10_22_bk.html.

168 **"own their automobiles":** Bernstein, "The Latest Skirmish in the Bike Lane Battles."

170 **"It's a Bike Lane War":** Stephen Brown, "It's a Bike Lane War on Prospect Park West!" *Brooklyn Paper*, June 23, 2010, www.brooklynpaper.com/stories/33/26/ps_ppwbikelane_2010_06_25_bk.html.

170 **"Spurs Shouting Match"**: Alejandro Lopez de Haro, "Bike Lane Controversy Spurs Shouting Match," *Brooklyn Ink*, October 22, 2010, http://thebrooklynink .com/2010/10/22/16910-bike-lane-controversy-heats-up/.

170 **"That Zippy Cyclists"**: Erica Pearson, "Pedestrians Argue That Zippy Cyclists on Prospect Park West Bike Lane Put Safety at Risk," *Daily News*, June 19, 2010, www.nydailynews.com/new-york/pedestrians-argue-zippy-cyclists-prospect -park-west-bike-lane-put-safety-risk-article-1.183339.

171 **"triple the former annual rates"**: Louise Hainline, Norman Steisel, and Iris Weinshall, "To the Editor," *New York Times*, December 22, 2010, accessed August 10, 2015, www.nytimes.com/2010/12/23/opinion/l23bike.html.

172 **just 20 percent after:** New York City Department of Transportation, "Prospect Park West Bicycle Path," 7.

172 **4 percent after:** Ibid., 5.

172 **dropped 63 percent:** Ibid., 12.

172 **time remained unchanged:** Ibid., 8, 10–11.

172 **conducted by Brad Lander:** "Community Survey Results on Prospect Park West Reconfiguration," New York City Council member Brad Lander, accessed August 10, 2015, http://bradlander.nyc/ppwsurvey.

172 **"Disputes Lane 'Success'"**: Sally Goldenberg, "Bikes 'Inflated,'" *New York Post*, January 21, 2011, accessed August 10, 2015, http://nypost.com/2011/01/21/ bikes-inflated/.

173 **"was a terrorist!"**: John Del Signore, "Local TV Reporter Blows Whistle on Bike Lane Terrorist Threat," *Gothamist,* July 8, 2011, accessed August 10, 2015, http://gothamist.com/2011/07/08/local_tv_reporter_warns_of_bike_lan.php.

174 **"or perhaps Beijing"**: John Cassidy, "Battle of the Bike Lanes," *New Yorker*, March 8, 2011, accessed August 10, 2015, www.newyorker.com/news/ john-cassidy/battle-of-the-bike-lanes.

174 **"nutso bike commissioner"**: Cindy Adams, "Jake & Taylor split?," *New York Post*, January 25, 2011, accessed August 10, 2015, http://pagesix.com/2011/ 01/25/jake-taylor-split/.

174 **"Too New York for Bike Lanes?"**: Matthew Shaer, "Not Quite Copenhagen: Is New York Too New York for Bike Lanes," *New York*, March 20, 2011, accessed August 10, 2015, http://nymag.com/news/features/bike-wars-2011-3/.

174 **Love or Hate:** Theresa Agovino, "Janette Sadik-Khan's Drive Alters City," *Crain's New York Business*, November 21, 2010, accessed August 13, 2015, www.crains newyork.com/article/20101121/FREE/311219981.

174 **"don't accept the status quo"**: Marc La Vorgna, e-mail message to the authors.

174 **"fucking bike lanes"**: Michael M. Grynbaum, "For City's Transportation

Chief, Kudos and Criticism," *New York Times*, March 4, 2011, accessed August 10, 2015, www.nytimes.com/2011/03/06/nyregion/06sadik-khan.html.

175 **"exhaust and noise pollution"**: Supreme Court of the State of New York County of Kings, Index No. 5210/2011, April 8, 2011, accessed August 10, 2015, www.streetsblog.org/wp-content/uploads/2011/07/Seniors-for-Safety -Am.-Petition-4-11-Legal-2983853.pdf.

175 **"they're saving lives"**: Shaer, "Not Quite Copenhagen."

176 *"but people are saying this"*: E-mail message to the author.

176 **with New Yorkers at large**: Howard Wolfson, "Memorandum," March 21, 2011, accessed August 10, 2015, www.nyc.gov/html/om/pdf/bike_lanes_memo.pdf.

176 **"Bike lanes have become a metaphor"**: Howard Wolfson, "Bike Lanes: A Choice, Not a Metaphor," *Huffington Post New York*, updated May, 25, 2011, accessed August 10, 2015, www.huffingtonpost.com/howard-wolfson/bike-lanes-a-choice-not-a_b_839076.html.

176 **"get the *Post* to demand that I fire you"**: *New York Post* Editorial Board, "We ♥ Janette," *New York Post*, March 7, 2011, accessed August 10, 2015, http://nypost .com/2011/03/07/we-%E2%99%A5-janette/.

177 *"Pleeeeease don't fire her"*: Ibid.

177 **1,700 thank-you letters**: Ben Fried, "Advocates Deliver 1,700 Thank Yous to Sadik-Khan and Bloomberg," *Streetsblog NYC*, March 9, 2011, accessed August 10, 2015, www.streetsblog.org/2011/03/09/advocates-deliver-1700-thank-yous-to-sadik-khan-and-bloomberg/.

177 **"a good thing"**: Michael M. Grynbaum, "New Yorkers Support Bicycle Lanes, Poll Finds," *New York Times City Room*, March 18, 2011, accessed August 10, 2015, http://cityroom.blogs.nytimes.com/2011/03/18/new-yorkers-support-bicycle-lanes-poll-finds/.

177 **as high as 66 percent**: Marist Poll, "About Two-Thirds Favor NYC Bike Lanes . . . Only One in Four Says Lanes Improve Traffic," August 9, 2011, http://marist poll.marist.edu/89-about-two-thirds-favor-nyc-bike-lanes%E2%80%A6only-one-in-four-says-lanes-improve-traffic/?utm_source=feedburner&utm_medium =feed&utm_campaign=Feed%3A+PebblesAndPundits+%28Pebbles+and+ Pundits%29; "New Yorkers' Views on Their Mayor and His Programs," *New York Times* Poll, August 16, 2013, accessed August 10, 2015, www.nytimes.com/inter active/2013/08/18/nyregion/new-yorkers-views-on-bloomberg-poll.html.

177 **"Thanks" and "Bicycle Visionary"**: Frank Bruni, "Bicycle Visionary," *New York Times*, September 10, 2011, accessed August 10, 2015, www.nytimes.com/ 2011/09/11/opinion/sunday/bruni-janette-sadik-khan-bicycle-visionary.html.

178 **fourfold increase measured over a decade**: New York City Department of

Transportation, "2014 NYC In-Season Cycling Indicator," accessed August 13, 2015, www.nyc.gov/html/dot/downloads/pdf/2014-isci.pdf.

178 **"it's not a terrible thing":** Jason Gay, "The City and Bikes: Rubber Meets Road," *Wall Street Journal*, June 22, 2011, accessed August 10, 2015, www.wsj.com/articles/SB10001424052702304070104576399972538343738.

CHAPTER 9: BIKE SHARE:
A NEW FRONTIER IN THE SHARED ECONOMY

179 **"There are a lot of important stories":** "Full Pedal Racket," *The Daily Show with Jon Stewart*, June 6, 2013, accessed August 19, 2015, http://thedailyshow.cc .com/videos/ramgwg/full-pedal-racket.

183 **1 million rides:** "Citi Bike Data 2013—Launch thru Sept. 2013," http://cf .datawrapper.de/pe6k4/2/ (accessed August 5, 2015).

183 **10 million rides:** "Citi Bike Data 2014 Q2," http://cf.datawrapper.de/dhq4m/1/ (accessed August 5, 2015).

184 **712 cities and more than 806,000 bikes:** Susan A. Shaheen, et al., "Public Bike-sharing in North America During a Period of Rapid Expansion, Understanding Business Models, Industry Trends and User Impacts," Mineta Transportation Institute, October 2014, accessed August 5, 2015, http://transweb.sjsu.edu/PDFs/research/1131-public-bikesharing-business-models-trends-impacts.pdf.

185 **A 2009 city study:** New York City Department of City Planning, "Bike-Share Opportunities in New York City," Spring 2009, www.nyc.gov/html/dcp/html/transportation/td_bike_share.shtml (accessed August 5, 2105).

185 **ten thousand bikes at 750 stations:** *The Velib Blog*, "How It Works," http://blog .velib.paris.fr/en/2014/07/24/discover-paris-by-bike-with-velib/   (Accessed August 5, 2015).

186 **A design flaw:** Steven Erlanger and Maïa de la Baume, "French Ideal of Bicy-cle-Sharing Meets Reality," *New York Times*, October 30, 2009, accessed August 5, 2015, www.nytimes.com/2009/10/31/world/europe/31bikes.html?pagewanted =al; "Thefts puncture Paris bike scheme," BBC, February 10, 2009, accessed August 5, 2015, http://news.bbc.co.uk/2/hi/europe/7881079.stm.

186 **twenty thousand bikes:** Velib Web site, accessed August 5, 2015, http://en .velib.paris.fr/How-it-works/Bikes.

189 **"software doesn't work, duh":** Tina Moore, "Bike Share Program Delayed Again: Mayor Bloomberg," *Daily News*, August 12, 2012, accessed August 5, 2015, www .nydailynews.com/new-york/bike-share-program-delayed-mayor-bloomberg-article-1.1138498.

190 **"Bike lanes . . . dinner parties"**: Andrea Bernstein, "Chris Quinn: Don't Talk About Bike Lanes at Dinner Parties," *Transportation Nation*, January 11, 2013, accessed August 5, 2015, www.wnyc.org/story/284074-chris-quinn-dont-talk-about-bike-lanes-at-dinner-parties/.

190 **"radical" . . . "incrementalist" approach**: David Seifman, "De Blasio's Bike Warpath," *New York Post*, August 19, 2012, accessed August 15, 2015, http://nypost.com/2012/08/19/de-blasios-bike-warpath/.

190 **"We don't do incrementalism"**: Dana Rubinstein, "'We Don't Do Incrementalism,'" *Capital*, May 14, 2014, accessed August 5, 2015, www.capitalnewyork.com/article/city-hall/2014/05/8545368/we-dont-do-incrementalism.

191 **In Paris . . . operation**: Nicole Gelinas, "Bike Share's Promise and Peril," *City Journal*, May 30, 2013, accessed August 5, 2015, www.city-journal.org/2013/eon0530ng.html.

191 **Barclays . . . safer than riders on private bikes**: James Woodcock, et al., "Health Effects of the London Bicycle Sharing System: Health Impact Modelling Study," *BMJ* 2014, 348:g425, February 13, 2014, accessed August 5, 2015, http://dx.doi.org/10.1136/bmj.g425.

194 **community outreach report**: New York City Department of Transportation, "NYC Bike Share Designed by New Yorkers," April 2013, accessed August 5, 2015, www.nyc.gov/html/dot/downloads/pdf/bike-share-outreach-report.pdf.

196 **"I'm all for bike sharing"**: Kevin Fasick, "Bicycles? Tough Sit!" *New York Post*, April 19, 2013, accessed August 5, 2015, http://nypost.com/2013/04/19/bicycles-tough-sit/.

196 **"serious threat to public safety"**: Edgar Sandoval and Dareh Gregorian, "City Removes a Bike Share Rack After Residents Sue," *Daily News*, April 30, 2013, accessed August 5, 2015, www.nydailynews.com/new-york/city-removes-bike-share-rack-article-1.1331475.

196 **"ambulance couldn't" . . . station**: Julia Marsh, "Bike Racks Block EMS at Victim's Co-op," *New York Post*, May 21, 2013, accessed August 5, 2015, http://nypost.com/2013/05/21/bike-racks-block-ems-at-victims-co-op/.

197 **"livid . . . not bikes"**: Andrea Swalec, "SoHo Bike Dock to Remain in Former Art Spot Despite Outcry," *DNAinfo*, May 9, 2013, accessed August 5, 2015, www.dnainfo.com/new-york/20130509/soho/soho-bike-dock-remain-former-art-spot-despite-outcry.

197 **"We feel . . . put in"**: Kathryn Cusma "Angry Tenants Trash Citi Bike Racks—Literally," *New York Post*, June 4, 2013, accessed August 5, 2015, http://nypost.com/2013/06/04/angry-tenants-trash-citi-bike-racks-literally/.

197 **Plaza Hotel . . . aesthetics**: Julia Marsh and Laura Italiano, "Plaza Wants Citi

Bikes Out," *New York Post,* October 14, 2013, accessed August 5, 2015, http://nypost.com/2013/10/14/plaza-wants-citi-bikes-out/.

197 **"bombs . . . global terrorists":** Mary Johnson, "Residents Say Bike-Share Site Near UN Creates Safety Risk," *DNAinfo,* June 18, 2012, accessed August 5, 2015, www.dnainfo.com/new-york/20120618/midtown-east/residents-say-bike-share-site-near-un-creates-safety-risk.

197 **"struggling to survive":** Julia Marsh, "Lower E. Side Bicycle Shop Owner Fears Citi Bike Share Program Will Run Him Out of Business," May 27, 2013, accessed August 5, 2015, http://nypost.com/2013/05/27/lower-e-side-bicycle-shop-owner-fears-citi-bike-share-program-will-run-him-out-of-business/.

198 **750,000 people pass:** Metropolitan Transportation Authority, press release, "Governor Cuomo Announces Completion of Energy Efficiency Project at Grand Central Terminal," April 21, 2015, accessed August 5, 2015, www.mta.info/news-grand-central-terminal-earth-week-earth-day-nypa-energy/2015/04/21/governor-cuomo-announces.

198 **171 gallons . . . crushed gravel:** New York City Department of Transportation, video, "Pershing Square East: A New Bike Share Station and Pedestrian Plaza," June 21, 2103, accessed August 5, 2015, www.youtube.com/watch?v=46N1rQFHdTI.

200 **100,000 riders successfully:** New York City Department of Transportation, press release, "NYC DOT Commissioner Sadik-Khan, NYC Bike Share Announce That Citi Bike Exceeds 100,000 Rides in Just 10 Days," June 5, 2013, accessed August 5, 2015, http://a841-tfpweb.nyc.gov/dotpress/2013/06/nyc-dot-commissioner-sadik-khan-nyc-bike-share-announce-that-citi-bike-exceeds-100000-rides-in-just-10-days/#more-78.

200 **would grow ten times:** New York City Department of Transportation, press release, "NYC DOT and NYC Bike Share Release Statistical Report Card of First Month of Citi Bike Operation: 529,000 Trips, 1.28 Million Miles Traveled," June 27, 2013, accessed August 5, 2015, http://a841-tfpweb.nyc.gov/dotpress/2013/06/citi-bike-statistical-report-card/#more-93.

201 **"Death by Bicycle":** Dorothy Rabinowitz, video, "Opinion: Death by Bicycle," May 31, 2013, accessed August 5, 2015, www.wsj.com/video/opinion-death-by-bicycle/C6D8BBCE-B405-4D3C-A381-4CA50BDD8D4D.html.

202 **"Begrimed! . . . dildo shop":** *The Colbert Report,* video, "NYC Bike Share," June 12, 2013, accessed August 5, 2015, http://thecolbertreport.cc.com/videos/2ildb8/nyc-bike-share.

202 **"There were times when I was begrimed":** *The Colbert Report,* video, "Paul McCartney," June 12, 2013, accessed August 5, 2015, http://thecolbertreport.cc.com/videos/9i45f0/paul-mccartney.

204 **66,500 bikes . . . "first mile/last mile":** "In Hangzhou, Getting Around Is More Fun on Two Wheels," Xinhua News Agency, June 1, 2009, accessed August 5, 2015, www.china.org.cn/environment/health_green_living/2009-06/01/content_17868564.htm.

204 **reporter, Matt Flegenheimer . . . Oh, No!:** Matt Flegenheimer, "As Easy as . . . Look Ahead! Turn! Oh, No!," *New York Times*, August 10, 2012, accessed August 5, 2015, www.nytimes.com/2012/08/11/nyregion/a-reporter-learns-to-ride-a-bicycle-as-an-adult.html?_r=0.

CHAPTER 10: SAFETY IN NUMBERS

207 **to tell him what he had done:** Melanie M. Canon, "In Doctor's Account of Scene, Boy's Blood Pooled in Street," *New York Times*, March 4, 2013, accessed August 10, 2015, http://cityroom.blogs.nytimes.com/author/melanie-m-canon/.

207 **177 people in New Yoyk City:** New York City Department of Transportation, New York Police Department, "New York City Traffic Fatalities by Mode, 1910–2013."

207 **issued two citations:** Matt Flegenheimer, "Fingers Are Pointed After Truck Kills Boy," *New York Times*, March 15, 2013, accessed August 10, 2015, www.nytimes.com/2013/03/06/nyregion/assigning-blame-after-boy-is-killed-by-truck.html.

208 **Nearly 17,000 American servicemen:** National Archives, "Statistical Information About Fatal Casualties of the Vietnam War," accessed August 10, 2015, www.archives.gov/research/military/vietnam-war/casualty-statistics.html#date.

208 **an estimated 32,675 American lives were snuffed out:** United States Department of Transportation Federal Highway Traffic Safety Administration, "Early Estimate of Motor Vehicle Traffic Fatalities in 2014," www-nrd.nhtsa.dot.gov/Pubs/812160.pdf.

208 **more than three times as many people killed:** Department of Defense, Operations Iraqi Freedom, New Dawn, Enduring Freedom, Inherent Resolve, Freedom's Sentinel, accessed August 10, 2015, www.defense.gov/news/casualty.pdf; "Casualties of the September 11 Attacks," Wikipedia, accessed August 10, 2015, https://en.wikipedia.org/wiki/Casualties_of_the_September_11_attacks.

209 **nearly three times the number:** Centers for Disease Control and Prevention, "Fast Stats: Assault or Homicide," accessed August 10, 2015, www.cdc.gov/nchs/fastats/homicide.htm.

209 **29 percent of traffic deaths:** United States Department of Transportation, Federal Highway Traffic Safety Administration, "Traffic Safety Facts," June 2015, 1, accessed August 10, 2015, www-nrd.nhtsa.dot.gov/Pubs/812162.pdf.

209 **alcohol (31 percent):** United States Department of Transportation, Federal Highway Traffic Safety Administration, "Alcohol Impaired Driving," December 2014, 1, accessed August 10, 2015, www-nrd.nhtsa.dot.gov/Pubs/812102.pdf.

209 **4,735 people were killed while walking . . . another 66,000:** United States Department of Transportation, Federal Highway Traffic Safety Administration, "Traffic Safety Facts, Pedestrians," February 2015, 1, accessed August 10, 2015, www-nrd.nhtsa.dot.gov/Pubs/812124.pdf.

209 **failure to yield to pedestrians:** New York City Department of Transportation, "The New York City Pedestrian Safety Study & Action Plan," August 2010, 26, accessed August 10, 2015, www.nyc.govhtml/dot/downloads/pdf/nyc_ped _safety_study_action_plan.pdf.

209 **about one person killed every day:** New York City Department of Transportation, New York Police Department, "New York City Traffic Fatalities by Mode, 1910–2013."

210 **safest big city:** New York City Department of Transportation, "The New York City Pedestrian Safety Study & Action Plan," August 2010, 7–8, accessed August 10, 2015, www.nyc.gov/html/dot/downloads/pdf/nyc_ped_safety_study_ action_plan.pdf.

211 **2008 strategic plan:** New York City Department of Transportation, *Sustainable Streets*, 2008, 8, accessed August 10, 2015, www.nyc.gov/html/dot/html/ about/stratplan.shtml, www.nyc.gov/html/dot/downloads/pdf/stratplan_ safety.pdf.

212 **seven thousand serious crashes:** New York City Department of Transportation, "The New York City Pedestrian Safety Study & Action Plan," August 2010, 7, accessed August 10, 2015, www.nyc.gov/html/dot/downloads/pdf/ nyc_ped_safety_study_action_plan.pdf.

212 **$4.2 billion in property damage:** Ibid.

213 **three to six a.m. . . . revved up with alcoholic bravado:** Ibid., 24, 27–28.

213 **most New Yorkers didn't even know:** Ibid., 26.

214 **79 percent of crashes :** Ibid., 29.

214 **40 percent less deadly for pedestrians:** Ibid., 23.

214 **injury rates plunged as much as 43 percent:** New York City Department of Transportation, *Sustainable Streets: 2013 and Beyond*, 30, November 2013, accessed August 7, 2015, www.nyc.gov/html/dot/downloads/pdf/2013-dot-sustainable -streets-lowres.pdf.

214 **the number of bike riders involved in crashes:** New York City Department of Transportation, "New York City Cycling Risk, 2014," 2, accessed August 10, 2015, www.nyc.gov/html/dot/downloads/pdf/2013-nyc-cycling-risk-indicator.pdf.

214 **12 percent . . . 38 percent of pedestrian fatalities:** New York City Department of Transportation, "The New York City Pedestrian Safety Study & Action Plan," August 2010, 11, accessed August 10, 2015, www.nyc.gov/html/dot/downloads /pdf/nyc_ped_safety_study_action_plan.pdf.

215 **"Rosetta stone" . . . the front page of *The New York Times*:** Michael M. Grynbaum, "Deadliest for Walkers: Male Drivers, Left Turns," *New York Times*, August 16, 2010, accessed August 10, 2015, http://www.nytimes.com/2010/08/17/ nyregion/17walk.html?_r=0.

215 **173 by the second year:** New York City Department of Transportation, *Sustainable Streets: 2013 and Beyond*, 41, November 2013, accessed August 7, 2015, www .nyc.gov/html/dot/downloads/pdf/2013-dot-sustainable-streets-lowres.pdf.

215 **742 people . . . fourteen locations:** New York City Department of Transportation, press release, "NYC DOT Commissioner Sadik-Khan, State Sen. Squadron, Elected and Community Officials Cut Ribbon on Delancey Street Redesign, the Latest in a Series of Street Safety Projects Citywide," September 27, 2012, accessed August 10, 2015, www.nyc.gov/html/dot/html/pr2012/pr12_51.shtml.

217 **21 percent fewer crashes:** New York City Department of Transportation, *Sustainable Streets: 2013 and Beyond*, 22, November 2013, accessed August 10, 2015, www.nyc.gov/html/dot/downloads/pdf/2013-dot-sustainable-streets-lowres.pdf.

218 **hit by a car moving 40 miles per hour . . . difference between life and death:** New York City Department of Transportation, press release, "NYC DOT, NYPD Announce New Initiatives to Improve Safety for Pedestrians, Motorists and Cyclists," October 21, 2010, accessed August 10, 2015, www.nyc.gov/html/ dot/html/pr2010/pr10_053.shtml.

218 **"Don't Be a Jerk":** New York City Department of Transportation, press release, "NYC DOT Commissioner Sadik-Khan Announces Launch of 'Don't Be a Jerk' Bike Safety Ad Campaign," May 10, 2011, accessed August 10, 2015, www .nyc.gov/html/dot/html/pr2011/pr11_43.shtml.

219 **Look on the ground:** New York City Department of Transportation, press release, "NYC DOT Commissioner Sadik-Khan, US Transportation Secretary LaHood Launch Innovative 'LOOK' Safety Campaign, Bringing Innovative Pedestrian Street Markings, Distracted Driving Ads Alerting New Yorkers to Walk Safe and Drive Smart," September 12, 2012, accessed August 10, 2015, www.nyc.gov/html/dot/html/pr2012/pr12_46.shtml.

219 **fatalities dropped 34 percent:** New York City Department of Transportation,

Sustainable Streets: 2013 and Beyond, 18, November 2013, accessed August 10, 2015, www.nyc.gov/html/dot/downloads/pdf/2013-dot-sustainable-streets-lowres.pdf.

219–20 **33rd Street and Park Avenue . . . 88 percent:** New York City Department of Transportation, *Making Safer Streets*, November 2013, 6, accessed August 10, 2015, www.nyc.gov/html/dot/downloads/pdf/dot-making-safer-streets.pdf.

220 **Jewel Avenue . . . 37 percent:** Ibid.

220 **Southern Boulevard . . . 28 percent:** Ibid.

220 **Luten Avenue . . . one third:** "Sustainable Streets Index 2011," 43–45, accessed August 10, 2015, www.nyc.gov/html/dot/downloads/pdf/sustainable_streets_index_11.pdf.

220 **top 12 percent . . . 153rd Street:** New York City Department of Transportation, "Improving Adam Clayton Powell, Jr. Blvd," presented to Community Board 10, June 13, 2012, accessed August 10, 2015, www.nyc.gov/html/dot/downloads/pdf/2012-06-13-adam-clayton-powell-cb10.pdf.

220 **more information or proof:** Laignee Barron, "City Makes Alterations to Dangerous Adam Clayton Powell Jr. Blvd., Despite Community Board Delays," *Daily News*, July 18, 2013, accessed August 10, 2015, www.nydailynews.com/new-york/uptown/city-sidesteps-roadblocks-boulevard-safer-article-1.1403048.

220 **its historical character:** Michael J. Feeney, "Community Leader Julius Tejiddin Rallies Opposition to Safety Fixes for Adam Clayton Powell Blvd," *Daily News*, July 26, 2012, accessed August 10, 2015, www.nydailynews.com/new-york/uptown/community-leader-julius-tejiddin-rallies-opposition-safety-fixes-adam-clayton-powell-blvd-article-1.1122731.

221 **"We just don't understand it yet":** Kia Gregory, "Changes Planned to Calm Flow of Traffic on Harlem's 'Boulevard of Death,'" *New York Times*, July 1, 2012, accessed August 10, 2015, www.nytimes.com/2012/07/02/nyregion/on-harlems-boulevard-of-death-changes-planned-to-calm-traffic.html.

221 **Speeding and serious crashes . . . even better during rush hour:** New York City Department of Transportation, "Adam Clayton Powell Jr. Blvd Post Implementation," presented to Community Board 10, December 12, 2012, accessed August 10. 2015, www.nyc.gov/html/dot/downloads/pdf/2012-12-adam-clayton-powell-evaluation.pdf.

222 **"doubling or even tripling of bike deaths":** Matt Flegenheimer, "No Riders Killed in First 5 Months of New York City Bike-Share Program," *New York Times*, November 4, 2013, accessed August 10, 2015, www.nytimes.com/2013/11/05/nyregion/no-riders-killed-in-first-5-months-of-new-york-city-bike-share-program.html.

222 **bike deaths plummeted:** New York City Department of Transportation, "New York City Cycling Risk, 2014," 2, accessed August 10, 2015, www.nyc.gov/ html/dot/downloads/pdf/2013-nyc-cycling-risk-indicator.pdf.

222 **one hundred thousand New Yorkers with them:** New York City Department of Transportation, *Sustainable Streets: 2013 and Beyond*, 44, November 2013, accessed August 10, 2015, www.nyc.gov/html/dot/downloads/pdf/2013-dot-sustainable -streets-lowres.pdf.

223 **growing evidence that cities:** See, for example, European Cyclists' Federation, "Safety in Numbers," 2012, accessed August 10, 2015, www.ecf.com/wp -content/uploads/ECF_FACTSHEET4_V3_cterree_SafetyNumb.pdf.

223 **European nations like Denmark and the Netherlands:** Ibid., 2.

223 **Melbourne, a city:** Clay Lucas, "Helmet Law Makes Nonsense of Bike Hire Scheme," *The Age*, July 23, 2010, accessed August 11, 2015, www.theage.com .au/victoria/helmet-law-makes-nonsense-of-bike-hire-scheme-20100722- 10my2.html; Adam Carey, "Spoke Too Soon: Melbourne Bike Share to Drag Chain Another Year," *The Age*, September 4, 2014, accessed August 11, 2015, www.theage.com.au/victoria/helmet-law-makes-nonsense-of-bike-hire- scheme-20100722-10my2.html#ixzz3iWFYwkBN.

223 **Mexico City, Tel Aviv:** Sean Patrick Farrell, "A Gentle Push for Bikers, Not a Shove," *New York Times*, October 14, 2011, accessed August 11, 2015, www .nytimes.com/2011/10/16/nyregion/bike-helmets-arent-required-for-new- york-share-program.html?_r=0.

223 **Dallas, specifically repealed:** Tom Benning, "Dallas Bike Helmet Rules Now Apply Only to Cyclists Under Age 18," *Dallas Morning News*, June 11, 2014, accessed August 11, 2015, http://cityhallblog.dallasnews.com/2014/06/dallas -bike-helmet-rules-now-apply-only-to-cyclists-under-age-18.html/.

223 **the United States as a whole . . . the number of cyclists killed remained stable:** United States Department of Transportation, "Traffic Safety Facts: Bicyclists and Other Cyclists," accessed August 10, 2015, www-nrd.nhtsa.dot.gov/ Pubs/812151.pdf.

224 **270,000 pedestrians die globally:** World Health Organization, "More than 270,000 Pedestrians Killed on Roads Each Year: WHO Calls for Action to Save Lives," May 2, 2013, accessed August 11, 2015, www.who.int/mediacentre/ news/notes/2013/make_walking_safe_20130502/en/.

224 **4,735 of them in the United States:** United States Department of Transportation, Federal Highway Traffic Safety Administration, "Traffic Safety Facts, Pedestrians," February 2015, 1, accessed August 10, 2015, www-nrd.nhtsa.dot .gov/Pubs/812124.pdf.

228 **only 7 percent . . . top risk factors:** World Health Organization, *Global Status Report on Road Safety 2013: Supporting a Decade of Action*, viii, accessed August 11, 2015, www.who.int/violence_injury_prevention/road_safety_status/2013/en/; *Global Health Estimates Summary Tables: Project of Deaths by Cause, Age and Sex: Leading Causes of Death*, July 2013, accessed August 11, 2015, www.who.int/entity/healthinfo/global_burden_disease/GHE_DthGlobal_Proj_2015_2030.xls?ua=1.

228 **World Health Organization . . . fifteen to twenty-nine:** World Health Organization, "The Top 10 Causes of Death," May 2014, accessed August 11, 2015, www.who.int/mediacentre/factsheets/fs310/en/.

228 **Decade of Action for Road Safety:** City of New York, Office of the Mayor, press release, "Mayor Bloomberg, UN Secretary-general Ban Ki-moon and Transportation Commissioner Sadik-Khan Announce New Traffic Safety Initiatives," May 12, 2011, accessed August 11, 2015, www1.nyc.gov/office-of-the-mayor/news/151-11/mayor-bloomberg-un-secretary-general-ban-ki-moon-transportation-commissioner-sadik-khan.

228 **dedicated $250 million:** Bloomberg Philanthropies, "Road Safety," accessed August 11, 2015, www.bloomberg.org/program/public-health/road-safety/#progress.

229 **at the rate they did in 2001 . . . 1,113 more New Yorkers killed:** New York City Department of Transportation, New York Police Department, "New York City Traffic Fatalities by Mode, 1910–2013."

229 **announcement of Vision Zero:** City of New York, Office of the Mayor, press release, "Mayor de Blasio Releases 'Vision Zero' Action Plan, Launching Citywide Effort to Prevent Traffic Fatalities," February 18, 2014, accessed August 11, 2015, www1.nyc.gov/office-of-the-mayor/news/054-14/mayor-de-blasio-releases-vision-zero-action-plan-launching-citywide-effort-prevent-traffic#/0.

230 **Vision Zero . . . Los Angeles, Boston, Chicago, and Seattle:** Vision Zero SF, "Vision Zero in Other Cities," accessed August 11, 2015, http://visionzerosf.org/about/vision-zero-in-other-cities/.

CHAPTER 11: SORRY TO INTERRUPT, BUT WE HAVE TO TALK ABOUT BUSES

234 **561,000 . . . 30 percent:** Global BRT Data, EMBARQ, accessed August 8, 2015, http://brtdata.org/location/latin_america/brazil/curitiba.

234 **194 cities . . . 32 million daily passengers along 3,200 miles of streets:** Ibid.

235 **"An advanced city":** "Enrique Peñalosa: 'América Latina debe mirar más a

Amsterdam que a Miami,'" *Semana*, January 13, 2011, accessed August 8, 2015, www.semana.com/vida-moderna/articulo/enrique-penalosa-america-latina-debe-mirar-mas-amsterdam-miami/234025-3.

235 **around 5 percent of a new metro system:** Lars Friberg, "Innovative Solutions for Public Transport; Curitiba, Brazil," *Sustainable Development International* 3 (2000): 154, accessed August 8, 2015, http://infohouse.p2ric.org/ref/40/39732.pdf.

235 **2.2 million daily:** Global BRT Data, EMBARQ, accessed August 8, 2015, http://brtdata.org/location/latin_america/colombia/bogota.

236 **5,667-bus fleet:** Metropolitan Transportation Authority, "The MTA Network," accessed August 23, 2015, http://web.mta.info/mta/network.htm.

236 **792 million . . . 2.5 million passengers:** Metropolitan Transportation Authority, "MTA New York City Transit Bus Ridership at a Glance," accessed August 8, 2015, http://web.mta.info/nyct/facts/ridership/#intro_b.

236 **slowest average bus speeds:** MTA New York City Transit, Presentation, "34th Street Transitway Community Advisory Committee Meeting," June 15, 2010, accessed August 8, 2015, www.nyc.gov/html/brt/downloads/pdf/20100614_34th_transitway_cac.pdf.

236 **The group's final report:** New York City Department of Transportation/MTA New York City Transit, "Introduction to Bus Rapid Transit Phase II" (2009), accessed August 8, 2015, www.nyc.gov/html/dot/downloads/pdf/intro_to_brt_phase2.pdf.

239 **travel times . . . ridership increased 10 percent:** New York City Department of Transportation/MTA New York City Transit, "Select Bus Service" (2013), 10, accessed August 8, 2015, www.nyc.gov/html/dot/downloads/pdf/nyc-dot-select-bus-service-report.pdf.

240 **First and Second avenues:** Ibid.

240 **300,000 people work within a quarter mile of 34th Street:** MTA New York City Transit, Presentation, "34th Street Transitway Community Advisory Committee Meeting," June 15, 2010, 20, accessed August 10, 2015, www.nyc.gov/html/brt/downloads/pdf/20100614_34th_transitway_cac.pdf.

240 **900,000 transit riders:** MTA New York City Transit, "Average Weekday Subway Ridership," 2014, accessed August 10, 2015, http://web.mta.info/nyct/facts/ridership/ridership_sub.htm; Eleanor Randolph, "Transplanting Madison Square Garden," *New York Times*, March 28, 2013, accessed August 10, 2015, http://takingnote.blogs.nytimes.com/2013/03/28/transplanting-madison-square-garden/.

240 **90 percent of the traffic . . . 4.5 miles per hour:** MTA New York City Transit, Presentation, "34th Street Transitway Community Advisory Committee Meet-

ing," June 15, 2010, 23–24, accessed August 10, 2015, www.nyc.gov/html/brt/downloads/pdf/20100614_34th_transitway_cac.pdf.

241 **thirty-three thousand passengers:** Ibid., 33.

249 **just $85 million:** New York City Department of Transportation/MTA New York City Transit, "Select Bus Service" (2013), 10–11, accessed August 10, 2015, www.nyc.gov/html/dot/downloads/pdf/nyc-dot-select-bus-service-report.pdf.

249 **Mayor Bloomberg's successor now supports:** Alex Davies, "Here's How Bill De Blasio Can Make Public Transit Work for a Lot More New Yorkers," *Business Insider*, December 23, 2013, accessed August 10, 2015, www.businessinsider.com/de-blasio-improve-fix-nyc-public-transportation-mta-2013-12.

CHAPTER 12: MEASURING THE STREET

252 **"Bloomberg . . . told me that":** Zoe Schlanger, "Anti-Bike Lane Protest Small, Full of Hot Air," *Gothamist*, October 16, 2010, accessed August 11, 2015, http://gothamist.com/2010/10/16/anti-bike_lane_protest_small_full_o.php#photo-1.

254 **"Measuring the Street":** New York City Department of Transportation, *Measuring the Street*, 2012, www.nyc.gov/html/dot/downloads/pdf/2012-10-measuring-the-street.pdf.

254 **below the Manhattan Bridge:** Ibid., 7.

255 **Ninth Avenue . . . 58 percent . . . 49 percent:** Ibid., 4.

255 **Fordham . . . entire borough:** Ibid., 8.

255 **49 percent fewer commercial vacancies:** Ibid., 6.

255 **47 percent fewer commercial vacancies:** Ibid., 9.

257 **In seven of the nine neighborhoods:** New York City Department of Transportation, *Sustainable Streets Index*, 2011, 20–21, accessed August 11, 2015, www.nyc.gov/html/dot/downloads/pdf/sustainable_streets_index_10.pdf.

258 **In a 2011 study:** Transport for London, *Town Centre Study*, September 2011, ii, accessed August 11, 2015, www.ctc.org.uk/sites/default/files/1111_tfl_town-centre-study_rep_0.pdf.

258 **Portland . . . $61.03:** Kelly J. Clifton, Sara Morrissey, and Chloe Ritter, "Business Cycles: Catering to the Bicycling Market," *TR News*, May–June 2012, 29, http://kellyjclifton.com/Research/EconImpactsofBicycling/TRN_280_Clifton Morrissey&Ritter_pp26-32.pdf.

258 **San Francisco, two thirds of merchants:** Emily Drennen, "Economic Effects of Traffic Calming on Urban Small Businesses," Department of Public Administration, San Francisco State University, December 2003, 46, accessed August 11, 2015, http://www.sfbike.org/download/bikeplan/bikelanes.pdf.

258 In Dublin, Ireland: D. O'Connor, J. Nix, S. Bradshaw, and E. Shield, "Shopping Travel Behaviour in Dublin City Centre," ITRN2011, University College Cork, Cork, Ireland, August 31–September 1, 2011, 2, http://arrow.dit.ie/cgi/viewcontent.cgi?article=1010&context=comlinkoth,

258 140 percent . . . 430 percent: Auckland Council, "An Evaluation of Shared Space in the Fort Street Area, Auckland, New Zealand," July 2012, www.auckland council.govt.nz/EN/planspoliciesprojects/plansstrategies/ccmp/Documents/ fortstareaevaluationfullreport.pdf.

259 14 percent increase in sales: Measuring the Street, 7.

261 included in property listings: Joseph Cutrufo, "Realtors Already Touting Citi Bike as an Amenity," Mobilizing the Region, Tri-State Transportation Campaign, July 11, 2013, http://blog.tstc.org/2013/07/11/realtors-already-touting-citi-bike -as-an-amenity/.

261 In Minneapolis . . . 1,200 new residential units: Thomas Fisher, "Streetscapes: Midtown Greenway Spurs Urban Development, Especially in Uptown," Star Tribune, May 9, 2015, http://m.startribune.com/variety/303081591.html ?section=/.

261 10 percent faster in 2012: Measuring the Street, 11.

262 New York Times poll: "New Yorkers' Views on Their Mayor and His Programs," New York Times, August 16, 2013, www.nytimes.com/interactive/2013/08/18/ nyregion/new-yorkers-views-on-bloomberg-poll.html.

CHAPTER 13: NUTS AND BOLTS

265 6,300 miles of streets: New York City Department of Transportation, Sustainable Streets: 2013 and Beyond, 156.

265 more than 250,000 potholes a year: five-year average based on 2013 Mayor's Management Report, 150, accessed August 26, 2015, www.nyc.gov/html/ ops/downloads/pdf/mmr2013/2013_mmr.pdf.

265 22 million passengers every year: New York City Department of Transportation, "Staten Island Ferry," http://www.nyc.gov/html/dot/html/ferrybus/staten-island-ferry.shtml.

266 $27 billion a year in increased shipping costs: National Economic Council and the President's Council of Economic Advisers, An Economic Analysis of Transportation Infrastructure Investment, July 2014, 2, accessed August 11, 2015, www.whitehouse.gov/ sites/default/files/docs/economic_analysis_of_transportation_investments.pdf.

266 paltry 2.4 percent: "Life in the Slow Lane," The Economist, April 28, 2011, accessed August 11, 2015, www.economist.com/node/18620944.

266 **less than good condition:** National Economic Council and the President's Council of Economic Advisers, *Economic Analysis*, 2.

266 **access to public transportation:** United States Department of Transportation, "Grow America: Building Ladders of Opportunity," accessed August 13, 2015, www.transportation.gov/policy-initiatives/grow-america-facts/grow-america-building-ladders-opportunity.

268 **$175 million rehabilitation:** New York City Department of Transportation, "St. George Ferry Terminal Ramps Rehabilitation," accessed August 11, 2015, www.nyc.gov/html/dot/downloads/pdf/stgeorge_ramps_brochure.pdf.

269 **people every weekday:** New York City Department of Transportation, "Staten Island Ferry," accessed August 11, 2015, http://www.nyc.gov/html/dot/html/ferrybus/staten-island-ferry.shtml.

269 **$1 billion over six years:** New York City Department of Transportation, *Sustainable Streets: 2013 and Beyond*, 156.

269 **One thousand lane miles:** Ibid., 156.

270 **last seven years:** Ibid., 159.

270 **840,000 barrels of oil:** Ibid.

270 **321,000 miles every year:** Ibid.

270 **$60 million over six years:** Ibid.

270 **increased city asphalt production by 50 percent:** City of New York, Office of the Mayor, press release, "Mayor Bloomberg and Transportation Commissioner Sadik-Khan Open New Asphalt Plant to Make Road and Pothole Repairs More Efficient, Less Expensive and More Environmentally Friendly," May 24, 2010, accessed August 13, 2015, www.nyc.gov/portal/site/nycgov/menuitem .c0935b9a57bb4ef3daf2f1c701c789a0/index.jsp?pageID=mayor_press_release &catID=1194&doc_name=http%3A%2F%2Fwww.nyc.gov%2Fhtml%2Fom% 2Fhtml%2F2010a%2Fpr224-10.html&cc=unused1978&rc=1194&ndi=1.

270 **spread the asphalt evenly:** New York City Department of Transportation, *Sustainable Streets: 2013 and Beyond*, 162.

271 **"Hate Her So Much":** Ibid.

271 **$6 billion on the repair:** Amy Spitalnick, "NYC Dot Commissioner Sadik-Khan and State Sen. Squadron Announce Major Expansion of Brooklyn Bridge Access Ramps, Easing Congestion," May 13, 2013, accessed August 11, 2015, http://www.nysenate.gov/press-release/nyc-dot-commissioner-sadik-khan-and-state-sen-squadron-announce-major-expansion-brookl.

272 **streetlights will be LEDs:** City of New York, press release, "Mayor Bloomberg and Transportation Commissioner Sadik-Khan Announce All 250,000 Street Lights in New York City Will Be Replaced with Energy-Efficient LEDs by 2017,

Reducing Energy Consumption and Cost," October 24, 2013, accessed August 11, 2015, www1.nyc.gov/office-of-the-mayor/news/343-13/mayor-bloomberg-transportation-commissioner-sadik-khan-all-250-000-street-lights-in#/0.

273 **95 percent of the time:** Donald Shoup, *The High Cost of Free Parking* (New York: APA Planners Press, 2011), 624.

273 **500 million parking spaces:** Jeff Speck, *Walkable City: How Downtown Can Save America, One Step at a Time* (New York: North Point Press/Farrar, Straus and Giroux, 2012), iBooks edition.

274 **most extreme example:** Amy Zimmer, "$1M Parking Spaces Among High-End Amenities for Cars at Manhattan Apts.," *DNAinfo*, May 5, 2015, accessed August 11, 2015, www.dnainfo.com/new-york/20150505/tribeca/motor-courts-valets-1m-spots-parking-as-ultimate-manhattan-amenity.

274 **below 96th Street:** New York City Department of Transportation, "Street Parking Rates," accessed August 11, 2015, www.nyc.gov/html/dot/html/motorist/parking-rates.shtml.

275 **thus helping businesses:** New York City Department of Transportation, "Park Smart 2.0," 2014, accessed August 11, 2015, www.nyc.gov/html/dot/downloads/pdf/2014-10-park-smart-road-show.pdf.

275 **85 percent solution:** Donald Shoup, "Cruising for Parking," *Access* (Spring 2007, issue 30), accessed August 11, 2015, http://shoup.bol.ucla.edu/Cruising ForParkingAccess.pdf.

276 **That's 250,000 spaces:** Institute for Transportation and Development Policy, "The Urgent Need to Improve Parking in Mexico City," September 26, 2014, accessed August 5, 2015, www.itdp.org/urgent-need-improve-parking-mexico -city/.

277 **during nonpeak hours:** New York City Department of Transportation, "NYC DOT Pilot Program Finds Economic Savings, Efficiencies for Truck Deliveries Made During Off-hours," July 1, 2010, accessed August 11, 2015, www.nyc .gov/html/dot/html/pr2010/pr10_028.shtml.

278 **create a "bus bridge":** New York City Department of Transportation, *Sustainable Streets: 2013 and Beyond,* 203.

279 **after just seventy-two hours:** Ibid., 197.

280 **American transit service:** Anthony Foxx, "DOT Awards $3.59 Billion to Add Resilience After Sandy, Mitigate Climate Change Effects," September 22, 2014, accessed August 11, 2015, www.transportation.gov/fastlane/dot-awards-post-sandy-climate-change-resilience-grants.

280 **South Ferry subway station:** U.S. Department of Transportation, "Transportation Secretary Foxx Announces Nearly $3.6 Billion to Make Transit Systems

More Resilient in New York, New Jersey, and Beyond," September 22, 2014, accessed August 11, 2015, www.transportation.gov/briefing-room/transportation-secretary-foxx-announces-nearly-36-billion-make-transit-systems-more.

280 **in the New York City area:** U.S. Department of Transportation, *Beyond Traffic 2014: Trends and Choices* (2015), 124, accessed August 11, 2015, www.transportation.gov/sites/dot.gov/files/docs/Draft_Beyond_Traffic_Framework.pdf.

CHAPTER 14: THE FIGHT CONTINUES

283 **municipal traffic management:** Romolo Augusto Staccioli, *The Roads of the Romans* (Los Angeles: Getty Trust Publications, 2004), 21.

283 **told the local press:** Agenzia Nazionale Stampa Associata, "Rome Plans 'Minimalist' Jubilee," May 12, 2015, accessed August 11, 2015, www.ansa.it/english/news/vatican/2015/05/12/rome-plans-minimalist-jubilee_7d0e681feb75-4194-b563-a5f02655b919.html.

287 **"Mobility as a Service":** Adam Greenfield, "Helsinki's Ambitious Plan to Make Car Ownership Pointless in 10 Years," *The Guardian*, July 10, 2014, accessed August 11, 2015, www.theguardian.com/cities/2014/jul/10/helsinki-shared-public-transport-plan-car-ownership-pointless.

287 **monthly transportation subscription:** Anni Sinnemäki, in discussion with the authors, May 31, 2015. Also see Sonja Heikkilä Tekes, "Mobility as a Service," The Finnish Funding Agency for Innovation, May 29, 2015, accessed August 13, 2015, www.eltis.org/sites/eltis/files/case-studies/documents/mobility_as_a_service_heikkila.pdf.

288 **Reetta Putkonen, the director:** Reetta Putkonen in conversation with the author, May 31, 2015.

288 **Beijing was the bike:** Patti Waldmeir, "Wheels Come Off China's Bike-Share Schemes," *Financial Times*, September 4, 2014, www.ft.com/intl/cms/s/0/815c5378-33e211e4-85f1-00144feabdc0.html#axzz3jwgfjjaA.

289 **"You could argue . . . pros and cons would be":** Jennifer Fermino, Rocco Parascandola, and Corky Siemaszko, "De Blasio Suggests Eliminating Times Square Pedestrian Plazas to Kick Out Topless Women, Costumed Characters," *Daily News*, August 21, 2105, www.nydailynews.com/new-york/de-blasio-suggests-eliminating-times-square-pedestrian-plaza-article-1.2332127.

289 **"dig the whole damn thing up":** Juliet Papa, "Bratton Suggests Tearing Up Times Square Pedestrian Plaza," 1010 WINS, August 20, 2015, http://newyork.cbslocal.com/2015/08/20/bill-bratton-times-square/.

290 **plaza was "preposterous":** Gale Brewer, "Manhattan Borough President Gale

A. Brewer Statement on the Times Square Plazas and Their Future," Facebook, August 24, 2015, www.facebook.com/galeabrewer/posts/484455241714718.

291 **"Sure, let's tear up":** Michael Kimmelman, "Challenging Mayor de Blasio over Times Square Plazas," *New York Times*, August 21, 2015, www.nytimes.com/ 2015/08/22/arts/design/challenging-mayor-de-blasio-over-times-square-plazas .html?smprod=nytcore-ipad&smid=nytcore-ipad-share.

291 **"Eradicating . . . progressive":** Justin Davidson, "De Blasio's Proposal to Destroy Pedestrian Times Square Is the Opposite of Progressive," *New York*, August 20, 2015, http://nymag.com/daily/intelligencer/2015/08/de-blasio-times -square-progressive.html.

291 **"ineradicable part of Midtown":** Steve Cuozzo, "The Business Fears Behind the Sudden Times Square Furor," *New York Post*, August 21, 2015, http://nypost .com/2015/08/21/the-business-fears-behind-the-sudden-times-square-furor/.

Index

Note: *Italic page references* indicate photographs.